Response Effects
in Surveys

norc

NATIONAL OPINION RESEARCH CENTER
MONOGRAPHS IN SOCIAL RESEARCH

Response Effects in Surveys

———

A Review and Synthesis

———

by

SEYMOUR SUDMAN
and
NORMAN M. BRADBURN

ALDINE PUBLISHING COMPANY
Chicago

First published 1974 by
ALDINE Publishing Company
529 South Wabash Avenue
Chicago, Illinois 60605

Second printing, 1977

Library of Congress Catalog Card Number 73-89510
ISBN 0-202-30270-9
Designed by Greer Allen
Printed in the United States of America

Preface

Since surveys are the most common method of data collection in the social sciences, there is great interest in response effects that may distort survey results. In addition, because an interview is a controlled social interaction between two people, response effects may be intrinsically interesting and not merely nuisances to be eliminated. Such interest in response effects is demonstrated by the large number of studies that have been conducted and that are analyzed in this monograph.

Initially we had planned to conduct experiments to measure response effects in threatening situations. Peter Rossi in particular, and our colleagues at NORC, however, strongly urged us to wait until we did a comprehensive review of the literature and could better see the gaps that needed filling. We agreed, and as is often the case in research, the project snowballed as we uncovered new sources and refined our analysis. We do not claim that the bibliography that resulted from this review is complete. We believe that few U.S. sources have been overlooked, but we suspect that there are many foreign studies of which we were unaware, beyond the number of studies from Britain, France, Germany, and Sweden that are included.

Our analysis differs from the usual review of literature that describes the results of different studies. Drawing on our survey research backgrounds, we coded each study and treated the separate results as individual respondents would be treated in a survey. That is, we show distributions and statistics for combined studies rather than for individual studies. Obviously, this procedure depends heavily on the very careful coding of individual studies. We are grateful to Neil Shover, Said Atamna, and Dan Waung for their conscientious efforts, both in coding and in tracking down the references used in the analysis.

The final preparation of the bibliography and subject index was done with great skill by Mary Spaeth, who also edited parts of the initial draft of the manuscript. The final manuscript was edited by Paige Wickland and proofread by Susan Campbell. The final typing of the manuscript was capably handled by Nella Siefert.

We owe special thanks to Charles Cannell at the Survey Research Center, University of Michigan, not only for his helpful suggestions throughout the project, but especially for making available to us an unpublished bibliography on survey methodology that was the nucleus for our bibliography.

Other colleagues who read the manuscript and made very helpful suggestions were Barbara Bailer of the Bureau of the Census; James A. Davis, Eve Weinberg, and James Murray of the National Opinion Research Center; Barbara Dohrenwend of the City University of New York; Robert Ferber of the University of Illinois, Urbana-Champaign; and Peter Rossi of Johns Hopkins University.

We also wish to express our deep gratitude to the Alexander von Humboldt Stiftung, Bad Godesberg, West Germany, whose generous support of the junior author during the academic year 1970–71 enabled him to collect data from German sources as well as work on the manuscript; to Professor Dr. E. K. Scheuch, Herr H. Stegemann, and the staff of the Zentral Archiv für Empirische Forschung, Universität Köln, who provided excellent facilities and congenial colleagueship which enriched our study; to Professor Dr. Elizabeth Noelle-Neumann, Institut für Demoskopie Allensbach, both for the data made available to us and for her warm support of our efforts; to Professor Dr. K. C. Behrens and Dipl.-Kfm. A. Grommann of the Freie Universität Berlin and Dr. K. Schreiber, Berlin-Test, Berlin, for allowing us to analyze unpublished data on response effects.

Several tables in this monograph originally appeared in other publications. We acknowledge with thanks permission to reprint granted by the American Sociological Association, the Columbia University Press, the Journal Press, and the University of Chicago Press.

This project was funded under National Science Foundation Grant GS-2008. We acknowledge with gratitude the financial and moral support from the staff of the National Science Foundation, without whose help this and other NORC studies in research methodology would not have been possible.

SEYMOUR SUDMAN
Survey Research Laboratory
University of Illinois, Urbana–Champaign

NORMAN M. BRADBURN
National Opinion Research Center
University of Chicago

Contents

List
of
Tables

1

Introduction

It is a wise experimenter who knows his artifact from his main effect; and wiser still is the researcher who realizes that today's artifact may be tomorrow's independent variable.[1]

The importance of response factors as artifacts in survey results is now widely recognized by survey users and practitioners. There are literally hundreds of methodological studies that demonstrate various response effects or non-effects. Interest in the problem has been heightened by the work of Orne,[2] Rosenthal (670–689),[3] and others in psychology who have demonstrated the presence of experimenter effects and other artifacts affecting responses even in experimental studies previously believed immune from such effects.

As McGuire points out, there are three stages in the life of an artifact: the ignorance stage, the stage of coping, and the exploitation stage. Regarding the last step, he notes:

It is rather heartwarming to observe that in the final stage in the career of an artifact, the variable comes into its own. The ugly duckling becoming the Prince Charming which gives rise to a new line of research.[4]

We are now well past the ignorance stage and into the stage of coping. Although there have been some examples of exploiting response factors, such as the notion of acquiescence· or yeasay-

---

[1] William J. McGuire, "Suspiciousness of Experimenter's Intent," in *Artifact in Behavioral Research,* ed. by R. Rosenthal and R. L. Rosnow (New York: Academic Press, 1969), p. 13.

[2] Martin T. Orne, "Demand Characteristics and the Concept of Quasi-Controls," in *Artifact in Behavioral Research,* ed. by R. Rosenthal and R. L. Rosnow (New York: Academic Press, 1969), pp. 143–79.

[3] Numbers in parentheses correspond to items in the Bibliography.

[4] McGuire, "Suspiciousness of Experimenter's Intent," p. 20.

ing, survey research is still quite far from the exploitation stage. The lack of a general theoretical structure within which to study response factors has limited our ability to cope with or exploit such effects. Most studies have demonstrated response effects in highly specific situations from which it is difficult to generalize.

In this monograph, we present a general framework for studying response effects and use that framework to examine what we know empirically from methodological studies about the causes and magnitudes of various types of responses. It would be presumptuous to claim that we have developed a general theory of response, but that is the direction of this research. The results presented here will hopefully provide the first stage in the development of such a theory.

DEVELOPMENT OF THE CONCEPTUAL FRAMEWORK

Let us begin by examining the concept of "response effect" more closely. If, for example, we ask someone (a respondent), "What was the total income you received from all sources in 1973?" we can conceive that there is a true answer. We can also imagine that it is extremely difficult to determine what that number really is because factors intervening between the asking of the question and the giving of the answer may result in the respondent's answer differing from the true answer. (We ignore here problems related to the possibility that the respondent may give us no answer at all.) We speak of a response error when the respondent's answer differs from the true answer; the direction and magnitude of a response error is measured by the direction and distance of the obtained answer from the true answer.

There are a multitude of factors that might affect the size and direction of the response error. In response to the question cited above, the respondent may not wish to count money he received from illegal sources such as gambling or the sale of stolen goods, or money received from sources that might be embarrassing if someone else in his family found out about them, such as money won at the race track. The respondent may simply forget some sources of income such as dividends from stocks; he may exclude some sources of income because they are not thought of as income, such as gifts from relatives. On the other hand, the respondent may include income that was actually received in another year; he may estimate some sources of income, such as that from tips, and the estimation may be too high or too low. The respondent may also decide that he would like the interviewer to think that he made more money than he actually did and inflate his income by some arbitrary percentage. Anyone who is at all familiar with the problems of measuring income or with surveys in general can present a long list of hypothetical factors that could result in overestimation or underestimation of real income.

We shall call the amount of the error in the response to a question that is associated with a particular factor the *response effect* associated with that factor. Thus, for example, we may speak of the response effect associated with the respondent's misunderstanding of the question, that associated with faulty memory, or that associated with attempts to enhance one's self-presentation.

Our principal task in this section is the development of a conceptual framework that will allow us to speak more meaningfully about the sources of response effects. If it is a fruitful framework, it will direct us to relevant research questions that will enable us not only to measure the size and direction of the effects, but also to develop methods either to control or correct for the effects in our theoretical data analysis.

Let us borrow some concepts for thinking about response errors from psychometrics, a field of psychology that has devoted more thought to the conceptualization and measurement of response errors than any other field in the social sciences. The answer we obtain to our question about total income may be conceptualized as a function of the true answer plus the average of all the response effects (Observed Response $[OR]$ = True Response $[TR]$ + $\overline{X}_e$). In psychometric applications, errors of measurement are ordinarily assumed to be variables with a mean of zero and independent of the true score. If this assumption is true, repeated measurements on the same individual will produce a distribution of responses; the measurement error associated with each measurement will have an average of zero over all the repetitions, so that the mean of the repeated measurements will tend toward the true score.

Researchers engaged in survey work tend to assume that the same process is at work in their field. It is assumed that there is some sort of error attached to a particular measurement of each individual, but that over a sample of homogeneous individuals (for example, respondents homogeneous on some particular analytic variable such as education or age), the mean of the measurement errors will tend toward zero and the group mean will thus approximate the true score for the group.

If the mean of the measurement errors does in fact approximate zero, this assumption would not present serious problems, particularly if one were not interested in making statements about individuals. Since survey researchers are rarely interested in the single individual, the comfortable assumption of measurement error as a variable with a mean of zero can lead to a rather cavalier attitude toward problems of measurement error and response effects.

Even if such an assumption did not seem so obviously contrary to common sense, there is ample empirical evidence indicating that errors of measurement are *biased;* that is, that their mean does not tend toward zero but toward some positive or negative value. Furthermore, it is probable that measurement errors are correlated with the true values they are affecting. This last assumption is a very complex assumption to deal with. For the purposes of this monograph, we shall continue to assume that the errors of measurement are independent of the variable being measured and shall confine our investigations to the problems of direction and size of the bias due to various response effects.

MODEL OF THE INTERVIEW

In order to improve measurement in social survey research, we must develop a model of the interview process that will specify a comprehensive but limited number of variables that allow us to investigate the principal sources of response effects in interviews. The model that we shall develop here will be framed in terms of a personal interview, but with the alteration of a few variables, it can be applied to more impersonal forms of data collection such as the mail questionnaire. In the empirical testing of the model, we shall be concerned with the differences between various forms of data collection such as self-administered questionnaires and personal interviews.

Bingham and Moore (85) defined the interview as a "conversation with a purpose." While this definition focuses on one of the most important features of the interview—that it is task-oriented and differs sharply from the non–task-oriented social conversation—it is not sufficiently precise to serve as a starting point for model building, nor does it differentiate the research interview from other types of interviews, such as therapeutic or employment interviews.

Hyman (389), Kahn and Cannell (408), Noelle (594), Scheuch (714), and others have further specified the defining attributes of the research interview as a particular form of data collection instrument. The common threads that run through these discussions stress the following characteristics:

1. The purpose of a research interview is to collect information to be used in the answering of a research question. The research interview is general in nature and does not directly affect the respondent's needs or interests.

2. The interview is a special type of social relationship involving two people, a respondent and an interviewer. The relationship has special characteristics: it takes place between two strangers, it is task-oriented, it exists under conditions of approximate anonymity, and it lasts for a relatively short period of time.

3. The social relationship is initiated by the researcher through his agent, the interviewer. The purposes, the rules of behavior, and the limits of the relationship are determined primarily by the interviewer. Thus, the interviewer initiates the conversation, "teaches" the respondent his proper role, and in most instances is the person who terminates the relationship.

4. The task in which the respondent and interviewer engage is organized and structured in order to accomplish the research goals. While the interviewer exercises considerable control over the interview, she herself acts within a set of behavioral rules that limit her freedom of action.

5. Although the interview has special characteristics that differentiate it from ordinary social encounters, it is nonetheless subject to and influenced by many of the general norms of social behavior. Indeed, it is this mixture of the special task-oriented character of the relationship and the general characteristics of a social encounter, such as the problems of presentation of self and social desira-

bility, that is one of the primary areas of interest to those studying response effects.

In summary, we might quote Scheuch's definition (714):

Unter Interview als Forschungsinstrument sei hier verstanden ein planmässiges Vorgehen mit wissenschaftlicher Zielsetzung, bei dem die Versuchsperson durch eine Reihe gezielter Fragen oder mitgeteilter Stimuli zu verbalen Informationen veranlasst werden soll. (p. 138.)

Let the concept "interview as a research instrument" be understood as referring to a structured procedure with a scientific purpose, by means of which the respondent, through a series of questions or presented stimuli, is induced to give verbal information.

Building on these common elements, let us conceptualize the interview as a microsocial system in which there are two roles, that of respondent and that of interviewer, joined by the common task of giving and obtaining information. By the analysis of these three elements—the two roles and the task—we shall build our model of the interview and outline the variables that appear to be the main sources of response effects.

While most of the empirical research reviewed in later chapters concerns itself with the role behavior of the actors in the interview situation, we feel that this emphasis is misplaced. The characteristics of the task itself are the proper focus of a model of the research interview because it is the task that gives rise to what Orne has called "the demand characteristics of the situation."[5] The demand characteristics, in turn, play a large role in determining the behavior of the actors. Thus, we shall give a central place in our model to the interviewing task.

We start with a distinction between the two main types of information sought in an interview: information about behavior and information about attitudes or "psychological states." By behavioral reports we mean the answers to such questions as: "For whom did you vote in the last Presidential election?" "How many pounds of coffee did you purchase during the last two weeks?" "What is the highest grade you completed in school?" "In what state (country) were you born?" The distinguishing characteristic

[5] Orne, "Demand Characteristics and the Concept of Quasi-Controls."

of behavioral information is that, *in principle,* it can be verified by appeal to outside sources (although frequently it is not verified). Indeed, the reason for gathering such information through an interview is typically because it would be too time-consuming or too expensive to obtain the information from other sources, even though one might suspect that getting the information from records would be more accurate.

All other information that we collect from respondents we shall call attitudinal information. Under this term we include data on attitudes, intentions, expectations, personality attributes, self-judgments, and any other matter about which there is, in principle, no objective external evidence against which to verify the response.

While one frequently speaks of "accuracy" with respect to both types of data, it is, strictly speaking, possible to call only behavioral reports accurate or inaccurate, and this only in comparison with the external sources of information. For attitudinal reports, we can speak only loosely about accuracy, and indeed, it would be better if we eliminated the term altogether. We can speak of the variability of the responses as obtained by different methods or by the same method at different points in time. We can talk about the relation between stated expectations or attitudes and behavior, which might be measured independently. We can talk about the consistency of responses to different questions that are designed to measure the same attitude, or among related attitudes that we believe have some consistent logical relationship. But we cannot speak about accuracy in the strict sense without some external criterion to which everyone is willing to compare the response. Since self-reporting is involved in some way in all the measures of psychological states or attitudes, it is difficult to obtain a consensus about which type of self-report will be taken as the criterion for the true response against which others could be measured. Thus, we shall refer to the *accuracy* of behavioral reports and to the *variability* of attitudinal reports.

Task Variables

Let us now examine the principal variables that affect the accuracy of behavioral information and the variability of attitudinal information. We distinguish three types of variables under which may be subsumed many discrete aspects of the interviewing task that have been investigated as potential sources of response effects. The three types of variables are: (1) task structure, (2) the degree to which the task engages problems of self-presentation for the respondent, and (3) the salience of the required information.

1. *Task structure.*—Perhaps the best-known and most debated aspect of interview structure is the use of open-ended versus closed-ended questions. While there are various degrees to which a question may be open or closed, the essential variable is the degree to which the respondent is encouraged to provide the desired information in his own language with minimal guidance from the interviewer, as contrasted with the tendency to provide structured alternatives from which the respondent chooses. Under the concept of task structure we would also include the use of any supplementary devices, such as aided-recall techniques, provision for the use of records, the use of cards, pictures, or other stimuli, that serve to standardize the questions and to reduce variation arising from the vagaries of individual interviewer or respondent interpretation or from temporary sources of variation peculiar to that specific interview.

The method of administration might also be included under the rubric of task structure, since different methods tend to offer the respondent opportunities for differing degrees of freedom to vary his interpretation of the task requirements. It is not immediately obvious that different methods of administration can be unequivocally arrayed along a dimension of the degrees of structure. Thus, for example, a self-administered questionnaire would appear to be more structured than an interview schedule that allows the interviewer to explain some things to the respondent. But the self-administered questionnaire might lead the respondent to respond haphazardly because he does not fully understand the questions. Having an interviewer use the same questionnaire might eliminate haphazard responses because the interviewer could answer questions or clarify points for the respondent during the interview.

While conditions of low structure provide for maximal adaptation of the interview task to the uniqueness of the individual respondent, conditions of high structure tend toward the maximal adaptation of the task to the commonalities among respondents and to reduce sources of variation. Hence:

Hypothesis 1: The greater the degree of structure in the task, the lower the relative response effects will be.

2. *Problems of self-presentation.*—It is generally assumed that, other things being equal, people will act in such a way as to reduce personal or social discomfort or to make as good an impression on other people as possible. Within the interview situation, part of making a good impression on the interviewer is behaving like a "good" respondent by conforming to the demand characteristics of the situation. While such behavior generally would be conducive to the administration of valid interviews, there are four widely-noted situations in which the forces that motivate the respondent toward presenting himself favorably or toward reducing anxiety might produce significant response effects.

The first situation involves questions that pose a threat to the respondent and tend to arouse anxiety in him. Questions that require the respondent to think about aspects of his life which arouse anxiety, such as the consideration of health problems, the death of loved ones, debt problems, illegal behavior, or sexual behavior, may cause the respondent to bias his answers. Threatening questions may introduce an element of tension into the interview which alters the relation between interviewer and respondent and may interrupt the easy flow of information. Obviously, good interviewers are trained to minimize such tension, but the potentiality for bias is always there and, we hypothesize, may be one of the more important sources of response effects.

The second situation is closely related to the first. It is usually referred to as the problem of the socially desirable response. Some questions call for the respondent to provide information on topics that have highly desirable answers, that is, answers that involve attributes considered desirable to have, activities considered desirable to engage in, or objects considered desirable to possess. If a respondent has a socially undesirable attitude or if he has engaged in socially undesirable behavior, he may face a conflict between a desire to conform to the definition of good respondent behavior, which says that one should tell the truth, and a desire to appear to the interviewer to be in the socially desirable category. It is frequently assumed that most respondents resolve this conflict in favor of biasing their answer in the direction of social desirability.

The third situation involves the respondent giving answers to questions when he does not know the answer. One assumes here that the respondent often faces a conflict between his desire to tell the truth (by admitting that he does not know the answer to a question or that he has no opinion about a subject) and his desire to be a good respondent by answering the question he is asked. Again, it is assumed that respondents resolve the conflict in favor of providing information by guessing or by choosing an answer haphazardly in order to avoid the embarrassment of not having an answer for the question.

The fourth situation involves acquiescence. The norms of politeness that govern ordinary social encounters make us tend to avoid conflicts that might disrupt the social relationship. Since disagreements, particularly about attitudes, may lead to conflict, there is some pressure in the interview situation toward agreeing with the interviewer insofar as one can determine her opinion. If there are no clues about the interviewer's views on a particular question, a respondent might decide that it would be polite to tend to agree with all statements in which one has the opportunity to agree. Clearly, there are individual differences in the degree to which respondents believe that disagreeing with the interviewer will have unpleasant consequences for the social situation. Since the interviewer's role demands that she present a neutral or supportive front to the respondent, her behavior to some extent sets a model for the respondent to follow. If the respondent discovers that he can disagree with a question or statement without disagreeing with the interviewer, he is then free to answer in any way he chooses without fear of being impolite to the interviewer. If, however, the interviewer is not able to establish a relationship in which the respondent realizes at least in some vague sense that the interviewer will not disagree with him no matter what he says, then problems of acquiescence may become very serious. Controversial questions, such as those which the respondent has found frequently lead to disagreements and uncomfortable social situations, may also bring acquiescence problems to the fore.

It is important to note a paradoxical effect resulting from problems of self-presentation. The types of variables we are considering here have the general effect of reducing the observed variance in responses. We hypothesize that the reaction of respondents to cues that are tension producing or that tend toward making a favorable self-presentation important will be to bend answers toward socially conventional or stereotypic responses. Thus, the net effect will be to produce response distributions with a lower variance than would be obtained without such cues. On the other hand, we hypothesize that changes in task structure, such as method of administration, structure of question, position of question in the questionnaire, or interviewer characteristics, might have a greater effect on questions that pose problems of self-presentation than on questions that do not. If this is true, we expect that the magnitude of response effect will vary when questions that are similar in terms of posing problems of self-presentation are given under different conditions. When we hypothesize greater variability for attitudinal questions that are high in problems of self-presentation, we are referring to a high "method" variance rather than a high observed variance in the responses to the particular questions.

We can summarize the effects of problems of self-presentation in the following hypothesis:

Hypothesis 2: The greater the problems of self-presentation evoked by a question (that is, the more socially desirable some of the answers are), the greater the pressure on the respondent to answer a question; or the more controversial a question, the higher the relative response effects will be.

3. *Saliency of the requested information.*—The problem of saliency is somewhat different for the two types of data. For behavioral data, the problem is primarily one of memory. Those factors known to be associated with differential remembering will be important to consider as sources of response effects. The four most important variables relevant to memory appear to be (a) recency, (b) importance, (c) complexity, and (d) affect or "repression."

There are, of course, other factors, such as general intellectual ability, special mnemonic devices, and age, that are outside of the influence of the task definition but that also affect the respondent's memory. The requirements that the task itself places on the respondent's memory, however, are mostly determined by the length of time involved in the report, the importance of the subject matter to the respondent, the number of different details required, and the degree of affect surrounding the event.

The problem of saliency with regard to attitudinal information is somewhat more complicated. While it seems likely that recency, the importance of the issue to the respondent, its complexity, and the degree of affect present will influence the stability of the response, there is also another important variable to be considered: the clarity of the respondent's state relevant to the issue. By "clarity" we mean the extent to which the respondent has a well-formulated attitude or idea about the question he is asked, or conversely, the extent to which the subject matter of the question exists for the respondent only when the question is asked. It is likely that clarity is correlated with the importance of the issue to the respondent, for example, his attitude toward language reform in Outer Mongolia. Clarity and importance of the issue are not, however, exactly the same concepts. For example, the task may concern questions about health or emotional relationships with other people; these may be issues that are quite important to the respondent, but the question may be phrased in a way he had not thought about before, or it may ask about an aspect of the issue that he had never reflected upon. We might expect such questions to arise frequently when the questions stem from a particular social-scientific, theoretical framework that is not shared by the respondent. Thus, we might find that the subject matter is important but that the question is low on clarity because the respondent has no clear formulation of his ideas or attitudes on the matter.

We can formulate a general hypothesis for saliency with two sub-hypotheses:

Hypothesis 3: The greater the saliency of the information required, the lower the relative response effects will be.

Hypothesis 3a: The more recent the event, the more important it is to the respondent, the less complex, and the more positive affect toward the event, the lower the relative response effects will be.

Hypothesis 3b: The more recent the event, the less complex, the more positive affect, and the clearer the subject of a question about an attitude, the lower the relative response effects will be.

The task variables are primarily determined by the interview schedule or questionnaire. The questionnaire content, independent of the formulation of the questions, will have some influence, particularly on the variables of saliency and self-presentation. The formulation of the questions, however, plays an important role because it determines the degree of structure in the questionnaire, can radically affect the perceived saliency of the requested information, and can exacerbate or modify problems of self-presentation. Thus, we believe that questionnaire construction and question formulation lie at the heart of the problem of response effects.

Role of the Interviewer

It has long been recognized that the interviewer is in a strategic position to bias responses. Since interviewer effects are such an obvious potential source of bias, they have received the lion's share of research on effect and control. But this research has been done for the most part without any theoretical framework, and the results have not advanced us very far in our understanding of the ways in which interviewers do in fact bias results nor in estimating the extent to which different types of effects actually occur. In this section, we will outline a simple conceptual framework which we will then use in later chapters to systematically review the empirical studies of interviewer effects.

Studies of interviewer effects appear to be concerned with three types of variables: (1) the interviewer's role demands, or the rules of behavior which the interviewer is expected to follow; (2) the interviewer's role behavior, or the degree of competence with which she carries out these role demands; and (3) the interviewer's extra-role characteristics, such as social background characteristics, which "type" the interviewer for the respondent and cause the respondent to respond to the interviewer in ways that are irrelevant for the task at hand.

1. *Interviewer role demands.*—Different types of interview situations allow interviewers different degrees of freedom to vary their behavior. At one end of the continuum is a model of interviewer behavior in which the interviewer's behavior approximates that of an automaton. In this model, the interviewer's behavior is exactly prescribed in order to reduce inter-interviewer variability. At the other end of the continuum is a model of interviewer behavior in which the interviewer is viewed as a sensitive, information-gathering individual. In this model, it is the interviewer's job to obtain certain information, but she is allowed, even encouraged, to go about the task in whatever manner seems to work best with that particular respondent. The degree of freedom allowed the interviewer may vary over all parts of the interviewer's task, from the selection of the respondent to such things as variation in the wording of questions or the order in which questions are asked, to the kinds of things that the interviewer may do or say beyond the narrowly-defined task of asking questions and recording answers. For example, the interviewer's role may allow supplementary explanations to questions in some instances and prohibit it in others; it may allow or prohibit the use of verbal encouragements to the respondent; it may allow or prohibit the interviewer from engaging in extra-task social behavior, such as accepting coffee or food from the respondent or engaging in friendly conversation, that is not related to the interviewing task.

The role demands are defined by the researcher and must be transmitted to the interviewer during her training. The interviewer must, in turn, convey during the course of the interview the limits that have been placed on her behavior and "teach" the respondent how to behave in relation to the interviewer. The teaching of the nature of the respondent-interviewer relationship defines for the respondent the way in which the interview situation differs from ordinary social conversations between strangers.

We recognize that the full automatization of the interview process is likely to be counter-productive and that some discretion on the part of the interviewer is desirable to adapt to the innumerable differences among respondents. We shall, however, frame our hypothesis in linear terms because we do not know at this point how to specify the point at which too much structure becomes dysfunctional.

Hypothesis 4: The greater the degree of structure in the interviewer's role, the lower the relative response effects will be.

2. *Interviewer role behavior.*—There is inevitably some discrepancy between the defined role demands and the actual role performance of the interviewer. Even when an interviewer knows what she ought to do, she may at times forget to do it or she may judge that a particular case is so different from what was envisaged when the specifications were written that it justifies deviating from her instructions. If the interviewer training and selection procedures are not adequate, however, the interviewer may not follow the specifications, either because she did not understand them fully or because she is temperamentally or intellectually incapable of fulfilling them. Factors of the quality and scope of selection and training techniques, interviewer experience, and overall competence would seem to be important here. We would thus hypothesize:

Hypothesis 5: The greater the degree to which the interviewer actually carries out the role demands, the lower the relative response effects will be.

3. *Extra-role characteristics of the interviewer.*—Ideally, the respondent-interviewer interaction is carried on strictly in terms of role behavior of the two individuals. It is inevitable, however, that the respondent will perceive the interviewer not only as an interviewer, but also in terms of other role characteristics, such as her race, educational level or social class, age, and, perhaps, religious, ethnic, political, or other affiliation. We should stress here that just because the respondent perceives that the interviewer possesses certain social role characteristics does not mean that this perception will necessarily cause him to behave any differently toward the interviewer. The potentiality, however, always exists. We expect that the degree to which the potentiality is realized depends to a great extent upon the degree to which the interviewer can teach the

respondent to interact with her only in her role as interviewer. Thus, one aspect of this variable is subsumed under the previous variable, since it deals with the interviewer's competence in carrying out her role.

There are times, however, when extra-role characteristics may become so salient that they produce a response effect independent of the interviewer's actual behavior. Probably the most notable example of this phenomenon in the United States is that of a white interviewer asking a black respondent (or vice versa) about race relations. We would thus formulate our hypothesis:

Hypothesis 6: The greater the saliency of an interviewer's extra-role characteristics for the questions being asked, the greater the relative response effects will be.

Respondent Role Behavior

It might seem strange to consider respondent behavior as an important source of response effects, since presumably it is the respondent's behavior (his responses) that is in fact the dependent variable. There is, however, one variable involving the respondent that can be conceptualized as a source of important response effects. This variable is the respondent's motivation to perform the role of respondent. The primary demand of the respondent's role is that he answer the interviewer's questions. Answering certain questions will require considerable effort on his part. If the respondent is not sufficiently motivated to perform his role, the whole enterprise falls apart. While one might argue that this variable is strongly influenced by the behavior of the interviewer, it can also be seen that there may be other factors that serve to undermine the respondent's motivation to take the time or make the effort to be a "good" respondent. Such factors would include persistent personality traits, events that happened to the respondent before the interview began, environmental factors such as the presence of others, and outside pressures not to cooperate with any strangers. The fact that many of these factors are beyond the control of the researcher and his co-workers does not minimize the need to recognize them as potential sources of response effects and to estimate their relative size. While it may be a truism, we would formulate our final leading hypothesis as follows:

Hypothesis 7: The better motivated the respondent to perform his task of providing information, the less the relative response effects will be.

Summary

We have attempted to outline a simple model of the research interview that identifies seven variables of primary interest as sources of response effects. Perhaps the model can best be summarized by putting it in diagrammatic form:

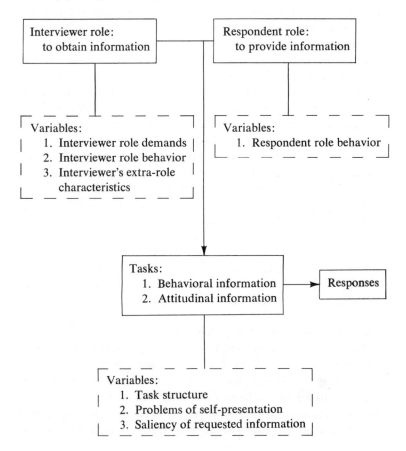

We consider the task to be the central concept and the task variables to be the most important sources of response effects. We anticipate that there may be an interaction between the importance of the task variables and the type of task; that is, we expect that the task variables will have different effects or be differentially important according to whether the respondent is asked for behavioral or attitudinal information. Except for our earlier conclusion that the concept of saliency has a somewhat different meaning for attitudinal and behavior reports, we do not know enough at this point to hypothesize exactly the nature of these interactions.

This model abstracts from the interviewing process only those aspects that appear to play a major role in influencing response bias and, of course, does not try to do justice to all the subtleties of interaction that occur in interviewing. This relatively simple scheme has enabled us to organize the empirical studies that have been done on response effects, to test out our leading hypotheses, and to develop and test more refined hypotheses. It further enabled us to chart the areas that need research in order to put our knowledge of the relative importance and magnitudes of the different sources of response effects on a firmer foundation.

The first stage of the project consisted of the preparation of a bibliography of books and articles related to the topic of response effect. This bibliographic research was greatly aided by a more general bibliographic file on survey methods that had been compiled under Charles Cannell's direction at the Survey Research Center, University of Michigan. The bibliographic file for this project consists of 935 items, and is included in this report in its entirety. About one-half of the items could not be coded using our coding system. An index of the coded items in the bibliography has been included to make it more usable for readers.

THE DEPENDENT VARIABLE: RESPONSE EFFECT

Throughout this study, the dependent variable remains the relative response effect. Many studies gave information that demonstrated response effects, but did not give enough information to enable us to determine the relative magnitude of these effects. Since we are attempting to measure the response effects of a large number of independent variables, we needed sufficient data both on the actual figures reported and on some validation measure in order to establish a reasonably accurate estimate of the magnitude of the relative response effect.

The field work for this project consisted of obtaining copies of the studies and coding them in a uniform format (described in detail below). The sample consists of the information coded from these studies. The number of items of information obtained from a single survey varied from one to several hundred. Thus, when we use unsummarized results, these results are weighted toward the studies that provided more items of information. In some of the analyses, all results from a given study are combined so that the studies are given equal weight.

Since many different types of studies were included, absolute size of effects became meaningless without a way of combining studies. We therefore adopted measures of relative effect, which we define as:

$$RE = \frac{(\text{Actual} - \text{Validating})}{s}$$

where s is the standard deviation of the population, obtained from the validation information if possible. Where no data were given on the size of s, an estimate of RE was made using (Actual − Validating) / Validating. This estimate is satisfactory for populations where the coefficient of variation approaches one, but becomes quite poor as the validating mean approaches zero. In the latter cases, the results were omitted.

Where studies reported information about attitudes, the weighted mean of all observations was used for validation. Thus, for example, in a study that contrasted the responses of black respondents to black and white interviewers, the grand mean was found by combining the responses to black interviewers and the responses to white interviewers and weighting by the sample sizes. The relative effect was found by computing the difference between the response given to black (or white) interviewers and the grand mean, with s being computed from the grand mean.

Readers may have some difficulty in interpreting this statistic for relative effect for attitudinal questions because it is an unfamiliar one. Basically, the relative effect is an index of how much difference a particular variable (e.g., race of interviewer) makes to a particular response category relative to the standard deviation of the responses for the sample as a whole. The larger the number, the greater the differences between the responses of groups that differ on values of the independent variable, relative to the overall variability of all groups combined. If the relative effect is zero, it means that changes in the independent variable, such as race of interviewer or method of administration, are not related to the responses to that answer category for that question. A large number means that changes on the independent variable are related to differences in responses. Unfortunately, differences in magnitude of relative effect cannot be interpreted except as differences in order; we can say that one is larger than the other, but not how much larger than the other it is.

While this method of computing relative response effects for attitudinal questions has the virtue of enabling us to compute a measure that can then be compared across a large number of studies and used to analyze variables that were only an incidental part of the original study, it has a serious drawback. Since we use deviations from the grand mean for the sample as a whole as the numerator, the size of the deviation for a particular group may be affected by the size of the subsample for that group, as well as by the raw difference between groups. For example, if two groups, *A* and *B,* differ in the proportion of "yes" responses to a question by 15 percentage points, their deviation scores will be the same if they are of equal size; their deviation scores will be different if one group is much larger than the other and contributes more heavily toward the grand mean. In such cases there is an asymmetry between the relative response effects for the two groups that would not have occurred if they had been equally represented in the sample. Such differences in weighting do occur, as indicated in our hypothetical example below, and are a potential source of spurious results for the response effects on attitudinal questions.

The reader will have to decide for himself how serious he finds this fault in the measure. It is clear that the results reported in this monograph for attitudinal questions will need to be treated much more cautiously than those for behavioral data. But we feel that there are several mitigating factors that make the presentation of the response effects for attitudinal data worthwhile. First, we can compare results between response effects for behavioral and attitudinal data. Where findings are consistent, we have reason to believe that we can have confidence in the measures. Where findings are inconsistent, we need to reserve judgment, to perform further analyses if possible, and, ultimately, to administer better studies. Second, the data present average responses over a large number of studies that vary in many ways, including the relative weights given to subsamples. We hope, but we do not know, that differing group sizes will tend to cancel one another out, or at least greatly reduce differences due to this factor. Of course, if there is a systematic tendency in the subsamples to weight one value of an independent variable greater than another, the reported average values may be seriously biased. Thus, while we are aware of the problem, we do not see any way we can correct for it, and feel that the results will be of sufficient interest and importance to report. At the very least, the results can start a controversy that can be resolved by conducting further systematic research.

CODING THE INDEPENDENT VARIABLES

The coding scheme used in this study is included in Appendix A. The 46 independent variables coded were placed into three major groups, as follows:

1. Task variables

    Effects of question, questionnaire design, and interviewing situation:
    Length of interview
    Location of interview, presence of others
    Subject of report
    Threat
    Saliency
    Method of administration
    Structured or unstructured questions
    Position of question in questionnaire
    Position of question relative to related questions
    Deliberate bias in questionnaire wording or deception in experiment

Number of words in question
Difficulty of words in question
Social desirability of answer

Time and memory factors:
Time period
Records available
Aided recall

Type of data:
Behavior
Financial (including employment)
Ownership, debts, savings
Medical (including mental health care)
Large household expenditures
Small household expenditures
Media usage (including movies)
Social behavior
Voting
Knowledge
Demographic (age, education)
Attitudes or expectations about
Foreign policy
Local policy
Race relations or prejudice
Sexual behavior, child rearing, family
Other attitudes
Personality measures (including mood, anxiety)
Ability and self-judgment ratings

2. Interviewer role

Characteristics of interviewers:
Age
Sex
Education
Occupation of household head in interviewer's household
Race
Religion
Social class

Interviewer role performance:
Experience

Training
Expectations
Hostility
Anxiety
Proportion of refusals or no answers

3. Respondent role

Characteristics of respondent:
Age
Sex
Occupation
Income
Education
Race
Religion
Political preference
Mobility
Yeasayer
Personal effectiveness

Respondent's motivation:
Anxiety
Hostility
Evaluation of respondent's interests

EXAMPLE OF THE TREATMENT OF DATA

In order to give the reader a better understanding of the manner in which the data are treated, let us take a hypothetical example of the type of result that forms the raw data for our study. In a typical study of response effects, the hypothetical table shown on the next page might be found.

First, descriptive information about the study from which the data were taken is coded (see Appendix A for exact description). This information remains the same for all entries from the table. A separate IBM card is coded for each of the cell entries in the table (except for the total, which is the same for each column). Percentages that include "no answers" (NAs) are recomputed to exclude NAs. If there are a significant number of NAs, these might be coded separately as an indication of the effect of the independent

Hypothetical Table   Question: In general, do you expect prices to rise, fall, or remain the same during the next twelve months?

Categories	Site of Interview		Total for All R's (N = 600)
	Per Cent at Home (N = 500)	Per Cent Away from Home (N = 100)	
Rise	36	29	35
Remain the same	50	56	51
Fall	14	15	14
Total	100	100	100

variable on respondent cooperation or on interviewer performance, depending on the independent variable under study.

Next, the task, interviewer, and respondent variables are coded with as much information as was given in the study. For most studies, of course, information relative to many of the independent variables was missing. In our hypothetical example, the content of the question would be coded as having to do with "expectations," the subject of the report would be coded "self," the expectations would be coded as applying to the "future," the time period involved would be coded "52 weeks," and the subject matter would be coded "non-threatening" and "salient." These codes remain the same for each of the four relative effects computed from this table.

To compute the relative effect for the percentage of respondents interviewed at home who said that they expected prices to rise, we would take the difference between that percentage and the marginal percentage for all respondents $(36 - 35 = + 1)$ and divide by an estimate of the standard deviation. We have used consistently $S = \sqrt{PQ}$ as the estimate of the standard deviation for percentages, even though in almost all cases the samples are not simple random samples. We have adopted this convention because of its simplicity and, in most cases, in the absence of any viable alternative. Since this estimate is probably smaller than the actual standard deviation, our results tend to overestimate the average size of response effects.

In our hypothetical case, we compute the relative error of the first cell of the table, with $S = .477$, as $1/.477 = .02$, or a relative effect of .02 standard deviation units. This figure is entered in Columns 71–73 as "002," and "35" is entered in Columns 78–79 as the percentage on which the relative effect was computed. For this cell, the number of cases is entered in Column 15 and the fact that it was conducted in the home is coded in Column 66.

Similarly, the relative effect for the percentage of respondents interviewed away from home who expected prices to rise is computed $(29 - 35/.477 = .13)$ and entered in the appropriate columns on another IBM card, together with the appropriate changes in the number of respondents and the conditions of interview codes, but with all the other information about the study remaining the same. Two additional relative effects are computed from this table—those for the percentage of respondents who expect prices to remain the same under the two conditions of conducting the interview. Thus, a table such as our hypothetical table with six cells yields four relative effects, one for each response category and condition of administration (excepting the final two redundant cells).

Once data from a number of studies dealing with conditions of interview administration have been coded, we can look across studies and see the direction and average magnitude of response effects by computing the average relative error produced in each type of administration.

ANALYSIS

The basic approach in analyzing the results is to treat the several thousand items of information as one would treat responses in a typical survey. One observes differences in the dependent variable (here response effects) and proceeds to search for the combination of independent variables that best explains the results. One never finds complete consistency in the real world. Thus, in studies of prejudice, it is generally the case that prejudice by whites against blacks declines with increasing education, but regional factors are also critical. College graduates in the South have higher prejudice scores than do northern respondents with only an elementary school education; nevertheless, there are some southerners with little education who show no prejudice.

Similarly, in this analysis of response effects, we are unable to find absolute truths. We may make generalizations, but there will be counter-examples reported so that we deal with probabilities less than one.

There are two chief differences between our analysis and that of a typical survey. For a typical survey, one could have the complete range of information on independent variables for all respondents. That is not the case for the studies we have reported. Most of these studies have been concerned only with the relation between one or a few independent variables and response effects. In some instances it is possible through careful reading to determine the characteristics of other variables that are not analyzed in the study. For most studies, however, there are a large number of independent variables for which no information is available. Thus, our large sample size of items and studies is misleading, since much of the information is missing. Most of the generalizations made are based on samples much smaller than the total. Unfortunately, this limits our ability to discuss interaction effects in great detail. As the reader will observe, some of these interaction effects appear to be of great importance. These results point to the gaps in information about response effects that may be fruitfully explored in future research.

The other difference between a typical survey and this meta-study is that on a survey, respondents are considered to be equally reliable. In this study, a cursory reading of a few articles is enough to persuade anyone that there are large differences in the quality of the research. We have attempted to quantify the quality of the research by considering the following factors:

1. Researcher's reputation
2. Type of sample
3. Methodological details given in report
4. Type of validating information

In preliminary analyses, we weighted studies according to their estimated quality. In these analyses, however, we did not find that the weighted results differed from the unweighted ones, so we report the unweighted results. We also coded the journal in which the report was found, the year of the study, the researcher's professional background, and the size of the sample. Our analyses did not indicate that these are important variables in explaining differences in response results and thus are not reported here.

While the data analyzed in this study come from several different countries as well as the United States, the overwhelming proportion of the data are based on samples of American respondents. Therefore, any generalizations that we are able to make, even with limited confidence, may not be valid in other cultural contexts. Much more specifically comparative methodological research will need to be done before we will be in a position to say which of the generalizations that we think are true for the United States will be valid for other countries.

ORGANIZATION OF THE REPORT

We have tried to organize our analysis around the principal variables we described in the development of our conceptual framework. Since these variables do not act in isolation, they may be treated in several sections of a chapter. Thus, there is some discussion of interviewer and respondent characteristics in each chapter. In general, Chapters 2–3 deal primarily with the task variables. The discussion of interviewer effects for attitudinal data is found in Chapter 4, and the reader who is particularly interested in these effects should turn there first.

In addition to the statistics on response effects given in each chapter, several studies are discussed to illustrate the results. It should be kept in mind that these case studies are selected to illustrate the statistical results and that the generalizations are based on the statistics and not on the case studies.

Since we are looking at many variables in many contexts, it is highly likely that, initially, we would call some of the relations important that are in fact due to chance. For this reason, the initial search procedure used only one-third of the coded results to develop hypotheses. The remainder of the data were used to test these hypotheses.

Chapter 5 summarizes the data, both present and missing, and suggests areas that need more study. The bibliography is indexed so that readers interested in specific independent variables may find the studies relating to those variables.

2

Task Variables

In our conceptual framework, we took the common task upon which respondent and interviewer are engaged—that of giving and obtaining information—as the focal point for analysis. We distinguished three types of task variables which, on theoretical grounds, appeared to be important in influencing the accuracy or the variance of responses: (1) task structure, (2) problems of self-presentation, and (3) the saliency to the respondent of the requested information. In this chapter, we shall present the results of our secondary analysis of studies of response effects that deal with these variables. Since the research under consideration was not designed using our framework, there is no neat or easy way to organize the discussion so that it exactly parallels our framework. We have tried, in the following discussion, to interpret the research in terms of our variables, and to argue that much of the apparent diversity among studies can be subsumed under a few, relatively simple, general variables.

Among the many studies of response effects, surprisingly little attention has been given to the effects of the task (including the conditions under which the task is performed) on response. Apparently, there is a tacit assumption among researchers that it is not very important: if the interview is conducted in the home or in the classroom, if the topic of the interview appears threatening or nonthreatening to the self-esteem of the respondent, or if the topic is of great concern to the respondent or remote from his stage in life. The results of this chapter, however, indicate that the nature of the task and the conditions under which it is performed are among the variables that have the strongest effects on response. These effects are typically far larger than the effects due to interviewer characteristics. This result is not surprising when one considers the interview as a social encounter within the framework discussed in the previous chapter.

Careful experiments to measure response effects caused by the task or the conditions under which it is performed would require deliberate variation of the task or the conditions of the interview when other variables are controlled. Our data are not usually of this type. Thus, for example, our comparisons of responses to interviews administered inside and outside the home are based on different studies with different tasks and different respondents and interviewers. While we attempt to control for these differences in the analysis, the available data do not always permit this. Although some confounding is unavoidable, the major conclusion of this chapter is inescapable: the task of the interview and the interview conditions do influence responses.

Among the task variables about which we have evidence, the following seem to have the largest effect on response, and will be discussed in this chapter:

1. The location of the interview
2. The method of administration of the questionnaire
3. The level of threat and the possibility of a socially desirable answer
4. The saliency of the questions to the respondent

We shall also give some attention to the following variables that seem to have a lesser, but still noticeable, influence:

5. The position and structure of questions
6. The subject matter of the study
7. The referent person about whom the questions are asked (e.g., self, household, other household member)

In the tables that summarize the data and in discussions of them, a distinction is made between behavioral and attitudinal data. For behavioral results, outside validating information is available, and it is appropriate to speak of overreporting and underreporting, or of positive and negative response effects. For attitudinal results, however, outside validation does not exist; instead, observed results are compared to a weighted average of the total. It does not make sense to attach signs to the differences since these signs would depend entirely on some arbitrary ordering of the answers. Hence, we can speak about the relative size of response effects for attitudinal data, but not about their direction.

Most of the studies in the published literature on response effects in attitudinal data relate primarily to interviewer or interviewer-respondent characteristics. These studies are discussed in detail in Chapter 4. In this chapter, we limit our discussion of response effects on attitudes to those effects unrelated to respondent or interviewer characteristics.

In addition to the data tables and discussions of them, specific studies are discussed in detail to illustrate the findings. These studies serve to exemplify and clarify the summary data; they are not a random sample of the studies. Our general conclusions come primarily from the summary tables, while the specific studies remind us of the limitations of these results.

In this chapter, we shall consider the average response effect for several of the primary task variables taken across a large range of studies. On the average, the results indicate small effects for any single variable. The large standard deviations indicate that the studies have highly variable results when one does not take combinations of variables into consideration. Thus, we shall first present and discuss the summary statistics for the single variables, and then consider the results obtained while looking at combinations of task variables. Table 2.1 presents the means and standard deviations of the response effects for selected task variables computed across the available studies. The full distribution of responses is reported in Tables B.1 through B.7, Appendix B.

CONDITIONS OF THE INTERVIEW AND
METHOD OF ADMINISTRATION

Where and how the interview is conducted affects responses on surveys (Table 2.1). On the average, there is a +.06 response effect for behavioral questions if the interview is administered in the home with no one else (other than the interviewer) present. There is a negative response effect (−.04) if others are present and the interview is administered out of the home.

While the total difference in means is about 9 or 10 standard deviation units, there is a large range of effects within each condition indicating that many other factors are also operating. Thus,

Table 2.1 Mean Response Effect in Standard Deviation Units by Selected Task Variable

Task Variable	Behavior			Attitudes		
	Mean Effect[a]	Standard Deviation	N	Mean Effect[b]	Standard Deviation	N
A. *Conditions of Interview:*						
In Home						
No one present	.06	.72	811	.12	.13	82
Other adults	—.02	.17	209	–	–	–
Out of Home						
No one present	.001	.71	503	.24	.36	314
Other adults	—.04	.62	464	.17	.15	89
B. *Method of Administration:*						
Face-to-face	.04	.57	3,014	.15	.20	887
Group	—.05	.70	345	–	–	–
Telephone	—.03	.20	75	.22	.36	75
Self-administered	—.11	.36	362	.22	.21	151
Mail/Diary	—.01	.14	115	–	–	–
C. *Threat of Interview:*						
Threatening	—.03	.79	892	.20	.22	141
Possibly threatening	.07	.33	804	.17	.21	479
Non-threatening	.01	.54	2,369	.16	.26	702
D. *Socially Desirable Answer:*						
Strong possibility	.10	.79	296	.22	.28	94
Some possibility	—.03	.31	466	.14	.15	168
Little possibility	—.002	.48	3,210	.17	.24	1,035
E. *Saliency of Interview:*						
Salient	.02	.38	1,574	.13	.15	530
Possibly salient	—.003	.77	852	.15	.19	207
Not salient	.01	.61	1,639	.20	.30	585
F. *Position of Question:*						
Early	—.02	.52	594	.12	.13	265
Middle	—.02	.21	518	.11	.12	89
Late	.06	.92	442	.15	.17	106
G. *Deliberate Bias or Deception:*						
Yes	.07	.71	341	.46	.51	121
No	.01	.56	3,659	.14	.16	1,164

[a] Response Effect $= \dfrac{\text{Actual} - \text{Validating}}{\text{Standard Deviation Validating}}$

[b] Response Effect $= \dfrac{\text{Actual} - \text{Grand Mean}}{SD_{GM}}$

the generalizations about behavioral items that follow cannot be made as strongly as those for attitudinal items, where the differences are slightly larger and the variations within conditions are smaller.

There is a small positive response effect (.04) for behavioral questions if the interview is personally conducted by the interviewer. If the interview is administered in any other way, the response effect is negative, although again the average effects are small, with the exception of the −.11 effect for self-administered questionnaires. There is a larger response effect for attitudinal questions if the questionnaire is administered by telephone or is self-administered than if it is a face-to-face interview.

Similarities of results in sections A and B of Table 2.1 might lead one to expect that there is a relationship between where and how the interview is conducted. An examination of the specific studies confirms this expectation. Most studies conducted in the home are face-to-face interviews. Those conducted away from home are primarily of two types: self-administered questionnaires given to groups of respondents, such as students or workers, and social psychological experiments conducted primarily with students.

The question arises whether the setting of the interview or the method of administration has the more important effect on response. The data clearly indicate that method of administration is the more important variable for behavioral data (Table 2.2). Controlling for both location of interview and method of administration, there are marked differences between the size of response effects for self-administered questionnaires and face-to-face inter-

Table 2.2 Mean Response Effect in Standard Deviation Units by Location of Interview and Method of Administration

Method of Administration	Behavior		Attitudes	
	In Home	Out of Home	In Home	Out of Home
Face-to-face	.05 (947)	.01 (430)	.14 (94)	.19 (363)
Self-administered	−.10 (73)	−.10 (256)	–	.17 (118)

views involving behavioral questions, regardless of whether responses were obtained in or out of the home. We cannot make the same comparison for attitudinal questions because there were too few studies using self-administered attitudinal questionnaires in the home. In the one comparison that can be made on attitudinal items, however, the mode of administration does not appear to make a difference in the size of the response effects for interviews given outside the home.

There are several studies (discussed below) that deliberately attempt to measure differences in responses on face-to-face and self-administered questionnaires. As far as we know, there are no studies that attempt to measure responses in and out of the home, controlling for other factors. Such studies might involve comparing workers' responses in a company setting to responses obtained at home, or students' responses in school to their responses at home, or shoppers' responses in a shopping center to their responses at home. If studies such as these used face-to-face interviews, we might be able to determine whether the differences in Table 2.2 are really a function of the location of the interview or of the different topics covered in these interviews.

POSITION OF QUESTION AND DELIBERATE
BIAS OR DECEPTION

Table 2.1 presents the data for two variables that have been given some attention in the literature. The first variable, position of the question, has by itself little biasing effect for behavioral items and a negligible effect for attitudinal items. There is a .06 mean response effect for behavioral questions placed late in the interview, compared with a −.02 average effect for questions in the early or middle part of the questionnaire.

There do not appear to be any sizable response effects associated with placement of questions after related questions. Table 2.3 indicates that the largest average effect (−.06) occurs for behavioral items that appear early in the interview, but are placed after questions with related content. Unfortunately, there were not enough studies of attitudinal items that could be coded for question placement relative to early questions to construct a similar table for attitudinal data.

The findings reported here confirm the analysis of a limited number of studies focusing on question order effects (Bradburn and Mason, 210). That analysis failed to show any consistent order effects, although individual studies did report significant order effects. In that report, the authors identified four theoretically plausible types of effects—saliency, redundancy, consistency, and fatigue—that might occur because of the position of the questions, but that operate in different directions to produce either overreporting or underreporting. It is possible that, in the studies we have surveyed, these different types of effects are operating in different studies and tend to cancel one another out. Considerably more research will have to be done before we can formulate any theory on position effects.

The second variable, which occurs in a few interview studies and in many social-psychological experiments, is the use of deliberate attempts to bias answers or to deceive the respondent about the true purpose of the study. In these studies, the magnitude of the response effect is likely to be far larger than that for experiments or surveys in which there is no attempt at deception. The results presented in Table 2.1 show a mean response effect of .01 for behavioral items if there is no deliberate deception, and a mean of .07 if there is deception. For attitudinal items, the mean response effect is .46 if there is deliberate bias or deception and only .14 if there is no deception. Obviously, it is easy to generate large response effects in a laboratory situation; there is no guarantee that the same effect will be found in the usual face-to-face interview in the home. Again, however, note that the standard deviation for

Table 2.3 Mean Response Effect in Standard Deviation Units by Position of Question Relative to Related Questions and in Total Questionnaire (Behavioral Items Only)

Position Relative to Related Question	Early	Middle	Late
After	−.06 (77)	−.04 (294)	.01 (95)
Not after	−.01 (141)	−.01 (99)	−.02 (118)

both behavioral and attitudinal items is very large when there is deliberate bias or deception. As with other task variables, the large variability in results when only one variable is taken into consideration suggests that consideration of response effects must be in terms of the combination of variables operating in any particular study.

DEGREE OF STRUCTURE

In the conceptual framework developed in Chapter 1, we hypothesized that the degree of structure in the interviewing situation would be an important variable in determining the accuracy or variance of the responses. We expected that the greater the degree of structure in the task, the greater the degree of accuracy in reporting behavior or the lower the response effect on attitudinal items. Table 2.4 presents the results of our analysis of studies reporting various forms of questionnaires that differed in the indicated structural features, cross-classified by form, place, and administration.

Contrary to our hypothesis, whether the question is closed-ended

Table 2.4 Mean Response Effect in Standard Deviation Units by Condition of Interview and Structure of Questions (Behavorial Items Only)

Condition of Interview	Structure of Question	
	Closed-ended	Open-ended
A. *Form of Interview:*		
Face-to-face	.03	.03
	(1,343)	(1,004)
Group	.05	−.06
	(108)	(136)
Telephone	−.03	[.06]
	(27)	(16)
Self-administered	−.24	.002
	(148)	(162)
B. *Place of Administration:*		
At home	.01	.05
	(342)	(378)
Outside home	−.14	.02
	(594)	(594)

or open-ended seems to have no general effect on responses to behavioral questions in face-to-face interviews and has a negative effect on self-administered questionnaires. It appears from Table 2.4 that there is a $-.24$ response effect on closed-ended questions in self-administered questionnaires, but no effect on open-ended questions. The self-administered questionnaire is more likely to be administered outside the home; thus, it is not surprising that there is a $-.14$ response effect for closed-ended questions asked outside the home. We do not know if these results are artifacts caused by other differences in the studies, since there are no studies testing both method of administration and question structure simultaneously. A possible explanation of this interaction relates to problems of self-presentation discussed later in this chapter.

QUESTION LENGTH

The number of words in a question gives an indication of the quantity, although not necessarily of the quality, of the stimulus received by the respondent. Recent psychological experiments have indicated that an increase in the quantity of the stimulus leads to an increase in the quantity of response, although, again, not necessarily to an increase in the quality (Cieutat, 162; Greenspoon, 328; Hildum and Brown, 363; Krasner, 454; Ogawa and Oakes, 597; Salzinger, 695; Shaffer, 731; U.S. Bureau of the Census, 837). In Table 2.5, we see that there is no general effect related to the number of words in the question in face-to-face interviews, but there is an effect in group and self-administered questionnaires. The shorter the question, the larger the negative bias. This is in direct contradiction to the general procedure of keeping questions on self-administered questionnaires as short as possible. This effect, however, should be studied under controlled conditions in order to understand its nature more fully.

PROBLEMS OF THREAT, SELF-PRESENTATION, AND SALIENCY OF QUESTIONS

Since the degree to which a respondent views an item as personal (and therefore possibly threatening) tends to be involved in considerations of self-presentation and saliency, we shall treat these variables together. First, let us look at the distribution of response effects for the variable we have called "threat" (Table 2.1). For each of the questions coded, the coder was asked to make a judgment about the relative threat posed by each question to the respondent's self-esteem or to the interviewer's appraisal of him. To a considerable extent, this variable may be confounded with another variable, social desirability, since admitting to behavior or opinions which lower the interviewer's esteem for the respondent would probably be considered socially undesirable. We instructed the coders to distinguish between questions that are largely personal and directly threatening to the respondent's self-esteem or are anxiety-provoking—for the most part, questions about illegal or deviant behavior, or about major health problems—and questions that do not appear to be manifestly threatening to the individual but contain the possibility of socially desirable answers about attitudes or behavior. In general, the threat items are more likely to be personal items, while the social desirability items are more distant from the individual.

Questions judged as presenting the possibility of a socially desirable answer show somewhat greater mean effects than do the threat questions (Table 2.1). The mean effect for behavioral items ranges from .10 for questions with a strong possibility of a socially desirable answer to −.002 for items rated as presenting little possibility of a socially desirable answer. Attitudinal items rated as pre-

Table 2.5 Mean Response Effect in Standard Deviation Units by Form of Interview and Length of Questions (Behavorial Items Only)

Number of Words in Question	Form of Interview		
	Face-to-Face	Group	Self-Administered
12 or less	.01	−.31	−.40
	(389)	(32)	(66)
13–22	−.04	[.06]	−.14
	(360)	(10)	(65)
23–32	−.003	–	[.01]
	(150)		(6)
33 or more	.01	.000	−.002
	(576)	(20)	(43)

senting a strong possibility of a socially desirable answer show somewhat greater average response effects than do items with little possibility. The variance around the means is high and suggests that strong effects are to be found only in combination with other variables rather than coming from threat or social desirability factors alone.

Table 2.1 indicates that, on the average, there are only small response effects for both threatening and non-threatening questions about behavior. For attitudinal items, there is little difference between the average effect for threatening items (.20) and the effect for the non-threatening items (.16). In both cases, the variance around the means is large.

Assessing response effects for attitudinal questions involving socially desirable answers is extremely difficult with the data at hand. In interpreting the results, several important facts must be kept in mind. First, questions coded as presenting a strong possibility of a socially desirable answer are more likely to involve controversial topics than questions coded as having little or no likelihood of a socially desirable answer. Concern over a social desirability factor usually comes when an investigator suspects that there is a pervasive social norm at work that is not in line with many people's "true" attitudes. Thus, the investigator expects that the responses given by the respondent will tend toward that norm even though his privately-held attitudes are different. Theoretically, concern about social desirability should be manifested on all attitudinal questions about which there exists a social norm (and this includes practically all attitudinal questions). Generally, however, investigators become worried about the biasing effects of social norms only when they believe that there are substantial segments of the population that do not, in fact, subscribe to those norms. Such cases would occur frequently when social change is accompanied by a normative change in the attitude of the population. The issues involved in such a process of change would, of course, be among the most controversial issues in society, and also those of greatest interest to students of social attitudes. Some contemporary examples would be attitudes toward sexual mores, changes in laws regulating drugs, and white respondents' attitudes toward racial integration.

We pointed out in Chapter 1 that the effect of increasing the possibility of social desirability in answer categories might result in actual reduction in the variance of responses because respondents would tend to choose answers closest to the social norms. Thus, we have a rather paradoxical situation in which we have reason to believe that the true distribution of opinion is quite broad (perhaps on the average broader than for items not classified as presenting a socially desirable answer), but that the effect of the variable we have been calling "social desirability" is to reduce the spread of opinion so that the distribution looks less variable than it really is. Insofar as differences in opinion are correlated with respondent characteristics such as education and income, differences between groups will also be attenuated. The aspects of the task that increase the saliency of the social norm, such as references to the opinions of respected figures or personal rather than self-administered interviews, would also tend to intensify the effect.

The reader will recall, however, that our measure of response effect is *relative* to our rough estimate of the true standard deviation, and therefore is not directly indicative of decreases in variance. Since the univariate comparison of questions according to their rating on the social desirability scale summarizes the data over a large number of studies that were also considering other variables, the more interesting comparisons are those made by taking the average response effects of questions with a strong possibility of a socially desirable answer under different conditions that increase or decrease the saliency of the social norm or the importance of presenting oneself in a favorable light.

Table 2.1 presents the average effects for the saliency of data for both behavioral and attitudinal questions. In general, we see practically no effects for behavioral reports, but again, a substantial spread of findings showing both positive and negative effects. For attitudinal items, however, the non-salient questions do show a somewhat larger average response effect (.20) than do salient (.13) or possibly salient (.15) questions. Such a finding would be consistent with the hypothesis that the respondent may do more guessing or engage in haphazard responses on questions of low saliency. The relationship between saliency and self-presentation will be discussed in a later section.

METHOD OF ADMINISTRATION AND PROBLEMS
OF SELF-PRESENTATION

Why should there be a difference in response effect between self-administered and face-to-face interviews? In Chapter 1 we hypothesized that the greater the problems of self-presentation provoked by the questions, the greater the response effects for behavioral questions would be. The more that the questioning process engages the respondent's desire to present himself in a favorable light, the more likely it is that the respondent will bend the report of his behavior in that direction. For attitudinal questions, we hypothesized that this tendency might actually work toward decreasing the variability of the responses because it could have the effect of getting respondents to converge upon the socially desirable answer. Because self-administered questionnaires are more private and do not require a direct revelation of self to another person who is physically present, we would expect that they would be less subject to problems of self-presentation than would face-to-face interviews. Presumably, telephone interviews and group interviews (in which a respondent could elicit social support for giving negative information about himself) would fall between the other two methods of administration on a dimension of privacy.

To some extent this difference is recognized by investigators in their choice of method of administration. In our review of the content of questionnaires, we found that studies of illegal behavior tended to use self-administered questionnaires to preserve anonymity. An example is a study by Clark and Tifft (168) on deviant behavior. In this study of 45 students, initial reports were subsequently checked by the use of a polygraph, and the anonymity of the respondent was carefully guarded. The results of the Clark-Tifft study are given in Table 2.6 and do indicate substantial under-reporting on approximately half the questions.

If one looks only at studies where both face-to-face and self-administered questionnaires have been used to measure the same items, the privacy hypothesis is confirmed. In a careful study of self-administered, face-to-face, and telephone interviews, Hochstim (367, 370) found a greater tendency on self-administered forms to report behavior that presents the respondent in a negative light. These results are given in Table 2.7. Thus, 44 per cent reported

Table 2.6 Estimated Net Underreporting for Self-Report Deviant Behavorial Items

Deviant Behavioral Items	Net Per Cent Underreporting	Per Cent Admitting Behavior
Taken little things (worth less than $2) that didn't belong to me	58	88
Skipped school	52	85
Speeded	38	85
Taken things of medium value (between $2 and $50)	30	45
Bought beer, wine, or liquor illegally	25	95
Masturbated	25	95
Falsified information on application form	25	58
Taken things from someone's desk or locker at school without permission	22	48
Gambled	18	80
Driven a car without a license	15	62
Driven in an unauthorized drag race	10	45
Had homosexual sex relations	10	22
Rape or attempted rape	5	15
Taken a car for a ride without the owner's knowledge	5	18
Used or sold narcotic drugs	5	10
Possessed pornographic material	5	50
Items with Less than 5 Per Cent Underreporting		
Run away from home		12
Attempted murder		0
Attempted suicide		2
Armed robbery		2
Gotten a female other than my wife pregnant		8
Bribery of a police officer or official		8
Visited a house of prostitution		18
Carried a razor, switchblade, or gun		12
Took part in a gang fight		10
Taken things of large value (over $50)		5
Broken into a home, store, or building		20
Struck my girl friend or wife		15
Witnessed a crime and did not report it		18
Defied my parents' authority		58
Vandalism		55
"Beaten up" on someone		10
Had premarital sex		55

Source: Clark and Tifft (168). Reprinted by permission of the American Sociological Association.

their health as excellent on the face-to-face interview as compared to 30 per cent on the self-administered form. This may reflect the almost automatic tendency to answer "Fine" when asked "How do you feel?" even if one doesn't feel very well. The understatement of the drinking of alcoholic beverages on the face-to-face interview as compared to the self-administered form clearly seems due to the presentation of a negative self-image.

A similar experiment by Thorndike, Hagen, and Kemper (807) compared 500 self-administered questionnaires and 500 face-to-face interviews on an inventory of psychosomatic symptoms. Respondents on the self-administered form reported approximately 15 per cent more psychosomatic symptoms than did respondents on the face-to-face interview. The largest difference was on the question "Have you frequently suffered from constipation?"—16 per cent of the respondents on the self-administered form responded "yes" compared to 8 per cent for the respondents on the face-to-face interview.

Table 2.7 Comparison of Women's Responses to Health Questions by Self-Administered, Telephone, and Face-to-Face Interviews

Item	Per Cent		
	Self-Administered	Telephone	Face-to-Face
Excellent health rating	30	37	44
	(977)	(518)	(284)
Discuss female medical problems with husband	68	52	47
	(490)	(266)	(129)
Discuss Papanicolaou test	40	31	32
	(490)	(266)	(129)
Never drink wine	46	44	55
	(507)	(282)	(157)
Never drink beer	51	49	59
	(507)	(282)	(157)
Never drink whiskey or liquor	36	34	47
	(507)	(282)	(157)

Source: Hochstim (367, 370).

In another study, Kahn (407) compared the responses of 162 male employees who were asked a series of questions about working conditions in both face-to-face interviews and self-administered questionnaires. One might expect the workers to express greater satisfaction in the face-to-face interview, and this was generally the case (Table 2.8). The greatest differences were found in respondents' perceptions of the company. On face-to-face interviews, 73 per cent stated that the company was well run and 64 per cent stated that it was a good place to work. On the self-administered form, only 40 per cent stated that the company was well run and 43 per cent that it was a good place to work. Workers were also more critical of their jobs and their foremen on self-administered questionnaires. The differences between face-to-face interviews and self-administered questionnaires were small on items relating to the work group. It is possible that these differences interacted with the location of the interview (in both cases, the work site) and that differences would have been smaller if the data collection had taken place in the home.

This tendency toward greater conformity in the more personal interviewing situation would imply that question cues for social desirability would have greater weight in attitudinal response effects for self-administered questions. The results presented in Table 2.9 confirm this hypothesis. For each study on which a response effect was calculated, each question was coded for the possibility of a socially desirable answer. This rating, like most on this variable, represents the coders' subjective impressions regarding the likelihood that one of the response categories to a question was distinctly more socially desirable than the others. In general, coders were instructed to be conservative and to code "strong possibility" only for questions that have figured prominently in the concern over socially desirable answers.

The average response effect for questions rated as having a strong probability of a socially desirable answer is .32 for self-administered interviews compared to .19 for face-to-face interviews. Where there was little or no possibility for a socially desirable answer, the difference between face-to-face and self-administered questionnaires diminishes to .04 standard deviation units.

Table 2.8 Attitudes of Employees to Working Conditions by
Face-to-Face Interviews and Self-Administered Questionnaires
(N = 162)

Attitudes of Employees	Per Cent Reporting	
	Face-to-Face	Self-Administered
Perception of Company:		
Machine replacement satisfactory	45	17
Machine maintenance satisfactory	64	19
Machine safety devices satisfactory	72	29
Enforcement of safety rules satisfactory	72	56
Traffic rules satisfactory	55	35
Safety instruction satisfactory	57	32
Better than most other companies	45	28
Good place to work	64	43
Well-run	73	40
Union made this a better place to work	42	64
Personal:		
Work makes me nervous sometimes	36	42
Good chance to use my skills	38	30
Prefer my present job to another	74	64
Dislike the kind of work I do	30	41
Dissatisfied with pay	28	25
Made little or no progress	10	21
Easy to make 100 per cent production	20	51
Hope to work here in five years	42	28
Perceived Characteristics of Foreman:		
Making production is very important to him	56	78
Keeps us well informed	23	22
Asks men how work should be done	15	26
Pulls for company, not the men	68	78
Interested in me aside from work	20	14
Interested in helping men get ahead	42	38
Lets me know how I'm doing	56	46
Very good at dealing with people he supervises	38	29
Gets along with me better than average	12	18
Knows the job	78	80
Does a good job	76	51
Perceived Characteristics of Work Group:		
Men get along better than most	21	19
Better than most in skill and knowledge	24	20
Work harder than most	25	24
Work planned better than most	13	6
Men stick together better than most	20	20
Men help each other better than most	33	35
I work harder than most	10	26

Source: Kahn (407).

A study by Knudsen, Pope, and Irish (451) concerning sex norms is an example of a study where socially desirable answers are likely. Women were asked whether premarital sex relations were all right with a man a woman plans to marry, with a man she loves, with a man she likes a lot, and with a man she is friendly with. The results indicate that less than 20 per cent of the respondents on face-to-face interviews stated that it was all right to have premarital sex, compared to 31 per cent of the respondents on the self-administered form. These results may also be influenced by the threat of self-disclosure, since in this case the respondents had all been premaritally pregnant.

Another study, by Sudman, Greeley, and Pinto (792), compared responses of Catholics on religious and ethical issues. In this study, one member in the household was interviewed face-to-face, while another member received a self-administered questionnaire. The results indicate that out of a total of 44 items, on ten items, respondents gave more socially acceptable answers on face-to-face interviews; on three items, respondents gave more socially acceptable answers on the self-administered questionnaire; and on the remaining items, there were no differences between the methods. This study illustrates that although a socially desirable answer may seem likely, in many cases there will be no difference in results between self-administered and face-to-face questions.

The data for behavioral items are not presented in Table 2.9

Table 2.9 Response Effect in Standard Deviation Units by Method of Administration and Possibility of Socially Desirable Answer (Attitudinal Items Only)

Possibility of Socially Desirable Answer	Method of Administration	
	Face-to-Face	Self-Administered
Strong possibility	.19	.32
	(58)	(22)
Some possibility	.11	.22
	(93)	(34)
Little or no possibility	.15	.19
	(734)	(91)

because we found no studies that compared face-to-face and self-administered questionnaires for the possibility of a socially desirable answer. There is, however, a study by Colombotos (177) that compares physicians' responses on face-to-face and telephone interviews. As one would expect, there is a tendency for physicians to give more socially acceptable answers on the face-to-face interviews (Table 2.10). For behavioral items, such as number of medical journals read, articles published, and reasons for going into medicine, there are differences of 14–20 percentage points between the two procedures. On items for which socially acceptable answers are unlikely (not presented in Table 2.10), no major differences are found.

A comparison of response effects during the early and late parts of the interview provides another indication of the socialization that occurs during the interview (Table 2.11). As may be seen from this table, the average response effect increases from −.02 to +.09 as the interview progresses on face-to-face interviews. On self-administered questionnaires, there is a slight decline as the interview progresses, possibly due to fatigue.

SELF-PRESENTATION AND THE STRUCTURE, LENGTH, DIFFICULTY, AND POSITION OF QUESTIONS

In order to pursue further the interrelation of different classes of

Table 2.10 Physicians' Responses on Face-to-Face and Telephone Interviews

Item	Per Cent	
	Face-to-Face (N = 68)	Telephone (N = 60)
Economic opportunity or social prestige were important in deciding to go into medicine	30	49
Father wanted me to be a doctor because of social prestige or economic opportunity	47	61
Read six or more medical journals	41	21
Have had three or more articles published in a medical journal	39	24

Source: Derived from Colombotos (177).

task variables, we investigated the self-presentation variable in relation to several of the task structure variables—the structure of the question, its length, its difficulty, and its position in the questionnaire. There is some interaction among the variables. If the question is threatening, the structure of the question, its position, length, and difficulty have differential effects on response. For the nonthreatening question, none of these variables are important. For threatening behavioral questions, there is a −.12 mean response effect for closed-ended questions and a +.12 mean response effect for open-ended questions (Table 2.12). For threatening attitudinal questions, there is a .22 average effect for closed-ended questions and a .16 average effect for open-ended questions. Although the difference is small, it suggests that the closed-ended question may increase the threat of the question because it forces the respondent to choose one from a number of alternatives. If true, this finding indicates that, if feasible, open-ended questions should be used for threatening subject matter areas to reduce threat.

Responses to open-ended questions appear to be unaffected by the possibility of a socially desirable answer (Table 2.13). For closed-ended questions on behavioral items, however, there is a .13 mean response effect if there is a strong possibility of a socially desirable answer and a small average effect (−.02) if there is no strong possibility of a socially desirable answer. For closed-ended attitudinal questions, there is a .23 average effect if there is a strong possibility of a socially desirable answer and a .16 mean

Table 2.11 Response Effect in Standard Deviation Units by Condition of Interview and Position of Question

Position of Question	Condition of Interview		
	Face-to-Face	Group	Self-Administered
Early	−.02	−.03	.03
	(505)	(40)	(26)
Middle	−.03	−.01	[.16]
	(433)	(50)	(12)
Late	.09	−.01	−.01
	(341)	(25)	(58)

effect if there is no possibility of a socially desirable answer. As with threatening questions, these results suggest that open-ended questions are preferable to closed-ended questions if there is a strong possibility of a socially desirable answer.

The results presented in Table 2.14 suggest that short questions have a strong negative effect on behavioral reports for threatening

Table 2.12 Mean Response Effect in Standard Deviation Units by Threat of Interview and Structure of Questions

Structure of Questions	Threatening	Possibly Threatening	Non-Threatening
		Behavior	
Closed-ended	−.12	.09	.002
	(417)	(558)	(761)
Open-ended	.12	.01	−.02
	(285)	(121)	(968)
		Attitudes	
Closed-ended	.22	.14	.17
	(102)	(134)	(443)
Open-ended	.16	.18	.11
	(33)	(132)	(106)

Table 2.13 Mean Response Effect in Standard Deviation Units by Structure and Social Desirability of Answer

Possibility of Socially Desirable Answer	Behavior		Attitudes	
	Closed-ended	Open-ended	Closed-ended	Open-ended
Strong possibility	.13	.01	.23	[.15]
	(239)	(28)	(87)	(5)
Some possibility	−.02	−.02	.14	.14
	(218)	(203)	(115)	(34)
Little or no possibility	−.02	−.01	.16	.15
	(1,286)	(1,076)	(652)	(224)

Table 2.14 Mean Response Effect in Standard Deviation Units by Threat of Interview and Length and Difficulty of Question

Item	Behavior			Attitudes		
	Threatening	Possibly Threatening	Non-Threatening	Threatening	Possibly Threatening	Non-Threatening
Number of Words in Question:						
12 or less	-.27 (100)	-.01 (37)	-.02 (419)	.19 (42)	.10 (113)	.11 (196)
13–22	-.05 (105)	-.06 (212)	-.04 (144)	.22 (48)	.12 (133)	.11 (129)
23–32	-.02 (97)	[.003] (19)	.01 (52)	.16 (23)	.13 (28)	.13 (84)
33 or more	-.003 (93)	.05 (113)	.00 (437)	[.28] (8)	.09 (46)	.09 (46)
Average Word Length of Question:						
3 letters or less	[.04] (15)	[.02] (13)	.17 (26)	[.33] (10)	.11 (38)	.12 (40)
4 letters	-.04 (250)	-.03 (278)	-.02 (626)	.17 (38)	.11 (140)	.09 (241)
5 letters	-.14 (130)	.02 (35)	.03 (270)	.19 (60)	.10 (123)	.15 (148)
6 letters or more	[-.77] (8)	.004 (64)	-.01 (88)	[.27] (13)	[.11] (19)	.08 (27)

questions. There is a −.27 average response effect for behavioral items if there are 12 words or less in the question but a zero response effect if there are 33 words or more. Thus, for threatening behavioral questions the accuracy of the response is improved by increasing the number of words in the question. Just the reverse is true for attitudinal questions, where the response effect increases as the number of words in the question increases. For questions with 12 words or less, the average response effect is .19 compared to .28 for questions with 33 words or more.

The number of letters per word in the question is used as a crude indicator of the difficulty of the question (Table 2.14). There is no consistent effect from this variable for attitudinal items. There are large effects for either very short or very long words, but these findings are based on a small number of cases and may not be reliable. For threatening behavioral questions, the average response effect ranges from −.04 if the word length is four letters to −.14 if the word length is five letters (and to −.77 if one wishes to include the small number of cases with six or more letters). Evidently, increasing the difficulty of the words in the question increases the threat of the question. This conclusion is based on a comparison of studies that differ in many respects and the results may be an artifact of these differences, but it would be useful to test this conclusion in a carefully controlled experiment.

If the subject matter of an interview is threatening, one would expect the greatest threat to occur at the beginning of the interview, with threat diminishing as the interview progresses and rapport is established between the interviewer and respondent. The limited data in Table 2.15 support this hypothesis. There is a −.21 average response for behavioral questions placed early in threatening interviews and a +.21 average response effect for questions placed late in threatening interviews. This difference suggests that the best responses for threatening behavioral questions would be obtained in the middle of the interview. For threatening attitudinal questions, the response effect increases from an average of .01 early in the interview to .28 late in the interview. There are small increases for non-threatening attitudinal questions as the interview progresses, but no differences for non-threatening behavioral items.

RESPONDENT AND INTERVIEWER CHARACTERISTICS
AND THREATENING QUESTIONS

Although Chapter 4 presents a detailed discussion of the characteristics of interviewers and respondents with regard to response
effects for attitudinal questions, we would like to mention briefly
some findings regarding the interaction between threatening questions and respondent and interviewer characteristics for behavioral
questions. The results presented in Tables 2.16 and 2.17 show
that young respondents and interviewers are most affected by
threatening behavioral questions. For non-threatening questions,
the differences become small and mixed. There is a $-.19$ mean
response effect for those under 25 years of age and for those with
13–15 years of school (that is, college students). Response effects
tend to be negative for male respondents and positive for female
(Table 2.16). The mean response effect for interviewers under 25
years of age on threatening questions is $-.48$, compared to $-.02$
for older interviewers (Table 2.17). For threatening questions, the

Table 2.15 Mean Response Effect in Standard Deviation Units by
Threat of Interview and Position of Question in Questionnaire

Position in Questionnaire	Threatening	Possibly Threatening	Non-Threatening
	Behavior		
Early	−.21	.02	.01
	(65)	(67)	(450)
Middle	−.02	−.04	−.004
	(106)	(214)	(198)
Late	.21	−.05	−.001
	(142)	(64)	(236)
	Attitudes		
Early	.01	.12	.07
	(48)	(138)	(79)
Middle	[.15]	.11	.10
	(11)	(34)	(44)
Late	[.28]	.15	.13
	(12)	(22)	(72)

mean response effect is negative for males ($-.10$) and positive for females ($.11$). Again, for non-threatening questions, there are no differences by age or sex of interviewer or respondent.

These results serve to warn against the uncritical generalization from college students to the general population on threatening behavioral issues. It should also be noted that several of the studies of college students involve the establishment of a threatening situation by use of deception in laboratory experiments. For example, in Sarason's studies (700) of serial learning of nonsense syllables using a Hull-type memory drum, a random half of his subjects received the following instructions:

Table 2.16 Mean Response Effect in Standard Deviation Units by Threat of Interview and Characteristics of Respondent (Behavioral Items Only)

Characteristics of Respondent	Threatening	Possibly Threatening	Non-Threatening
Age:			
Under 25	−.19 (130)	.07 (60)	.02 (649)
25–34	.28 (107)	.15 (48)	.04 (146)
35–44	−.11 (31)	.05 (160)	−.01 (357)
45–54	−.03 (28)	.06 (60)	.01 (101)
55–64	−.09 (31)	−.07 (21)	[−.24] (12)
65 and over	−.07 (26)	[−.11] (19)	−
Sex:			
Male	−.08 (310)	.032 (95)	−.02 (632)
Female	.08 (266)	.031 (100)	.03 (719)
Years of Education:			
8 or less	−.04 (44)	[−.02] (14)	.06 (174)
9–12	[.004] (19)	.06 (22)	−.04 (215)
13–15	−.19 (122)	−.03 (42)	−.01 (377)
16 or more	−	[.06] (14)	−.01 (73)

You seem to be having trouble with your test. Is anything wrong? Can you see the syllables clearly? How do you feel? You've been doing much worse than the other people who have worked on this task. In fact, yours is one of the lowest scores I've gotten so far, and you are one of the few people I've had who has not reached the college level on this test. That's why I asked if anything was the matter. You've only gotten _____ right. Usually people get that many right in half the time it's taken you.

In the college laboratory situation where the subjects are a captive audience, the level of threat can be increased and can have a large effect on responses, particularly in learning experiments. On the other hand, there is a limit to the level of threat possible in interviews administered in the home. If the threat level is *too* high, the effect is the respondent's refusal to cooperate at all rather than a response effect.

SALIENCY AND SELF-PRESENTATION

Let us next consider the interrelationship between the saliency of the question and the two variables relating to the problems of self-presentation. It is evident from the mean effects given previously in Table 2.1, that for attitudinal items, saliency and self-pres-

Table 2.17 Mean Response Effect by Threat of Interview and Age and Sex of Interviewer (Behavioral Items Only)

Age and Sex of Interviewer	Threatening	Possibly Threatening	Non-Threatening
Age:			
Under 25	−.48	−.06	−.02
	(58)	(55)	(321)
25–34	−.02	.11	−.004
	(24)	(62)	(67)
35–44	−.01	–	[−.031]
	(24)		(11)
Sex:			
Male	−.10	−.04	−.01 ·
	(164)	(20)	(484)
Female	.11	−.001	.01
	(143)	(178)	(362)

entation variables operate in opposite directions of response effect. It is probable that there is also an interrelationship between these two variables. It seems likely that items that are high in threat would also be highly salient, and although it is less clear, it is likely that there would be some relationship between saliency and social desirability. If this is true, the variables might be masking each other's effects. Controlling for both saliency and threat, we see in Table 2.18 that the response effect is .22 for attitudinal questions that are both threatening and non-salient, while the response effect is only .13 for items that are salient but not threatening. Note, however, that the case base for "threatening but not salient" is rather small and is based mainly on laboratory experiments in schools where a threatening situation is established and where the task is of little intrinsic interest to the subject. For behavioral items, there is a −.05 average response effect for questions that are both salient and threatening, but no sizable effect otherwise.

Some data presented in Table 2.18 are based on small samples, but they indicate that threat and the possibility of a socially desirable answer combine in response effects for attitudinal questions. There is a .32 mean response effect for items that both threaten the respondent and present a socially desirable answer. For all other combinations, the response effect is only about half as large. For behavioral questions, there is also a strong response effect (−.25) for items that are threatening and present a socially desirable answer. For non-threatening items where no socially desirable answer is possible, the response effect is −.01.

We should note the effects for the combination of threatening questions with the strong possibility of a socially desirable answer for both behavioral and attitudinal data, because they are considerably larger than the effects we have discussed so far. They indicate, as we suggested earlier, that the really strong response effects are most likely to be found in a combination of variables that act in the same direction.

TOPIC OF STUDY

Differential response effects are found for different topics studied, regardless of the conditions of the interview. These effects are probably related to variables such as threat, social desirability,

Table 2.18 Mean Response Effect in Standard Deviation Units by Threat, Saliency of Interview, and Possibility of Socially Desirable Answer

Item	Behavior			Attitudes		
	Threatening	Possibly Threatening	Non-Threatening	Threatening	Possibly Threatening	Non-Threatening
Saliency of Interview:						
Salient	-.05 (611)	.21 (266)	.01 (697)	.18 (97)	.12 (162)	.13 (271)
Possibly salient	.02 (218)	-.02 (358)	.00 (284)	[.36] (10)	.13 (79)	.15 (118)
Not salient	.00 (63)	.02 (188)	.01 (1,388)	.22 (34)	.22 (238)	.19 (313)
Possibility of a Socially Desirable Answer:						
Strong possibility	-.25 (128)	.44 (138)	.004 (30)	[.32] (17)	.24 (55)	.11 (24)
Some possibility	-.05 (133)	-.03 (197)	-.003 (136)	[.15] (15)	.13 (97)	.15 (56)
Little or no possibility	-.03 (576)	-.01 (455)	-.01 (2,163)	.19 (109)	.17 (322)	.16 (604)

and memory factors. Table 2.19 presents response effects in standard deviation units by subject of study. Here, for general information, we summarize these effects. We shall present a detailed discussion of memory factors in Chapter 3.

Voting.—The largest response effect in Table 2.19 is seen for studies of voting behavior where there is an average .41 effect. The size of the response effect is due both to the social desirability of voting and to the length of the recall period (some questions on the coded studies asked about voting behavior in the previous five years).

Financial.—In general, financial data on income and insurance are pretty well reported, although there are some small understatements of income from sources other than wages and salaries. Bank account holdings are understated, but these effects are balanced in the overall results in Table 2.19 by understatements in reporting the level of debt.

Both for savings accounts and for debt, the major source of response effect is failure to report at all. Lansing, Ginsberg, and

Table 2.19 Response Effect in Standard Deviation Units by Subject of Study

Subject of Study	Mean RE	σ	N
Behavior:			
Financial	.01	.28	456
Medical	−.01	.64	1,027
Household expenditures:			
Large	.07	1.08	172
Small	.02	.27	363
Media	−.01	.28	195
Demographic	.004	.17	277
Social behavior	−.03	.54	650
Voting	.41	.25	125
Attitudes:			
Foreign policy	.12	.15	86
National policy	.12	.20	128
Local policy	.12	.14	250
Race	.14	.12	321
Sex and family	.15	.19	276
Personality	.33	.41	225

Braaten (462) indicate that 24 per cent of the respondents in one study failed to report savings accounts and that 24 per cent in a different study failed to report car debts. The use of financial records such as income tax returns, checkbooks, and bank books reduces memory error on exact amounts if the account or debt is reported. The use of repeated interviews increases the accuracy of financial reporting by reducing the percentage failing to report.

Medical.—The results presented in Table 2.19 conceal the level of underreporting of medical problems because several of the studies compare alternative techniques for data collection without validating from outside sources. In general, there is only slight underreporting of hospital stays overnight or longer. Studies from the National Health Survey (830) indicate that 10 per cent of a sample of hospital stays selected from hospital records are not reported in an interview. The net underreporting is lower in this study since there is some overreporting due to telescoping effects.

In another National Health Survey study (832), 10 per cent of the number of physician visits for chronic ailments are also underreported. However, if *all* physician visits are measured (for example, visits for check-ups, short-term respiratory infections), then only 64 per cent are reported in an interview (832). Telescoping effects are not measured in this study, so the net underreporting may be more than 36 per cent.

The negative response effect is even larger ($-.50$ or more) if one attempts to compare physician records of conditions with respondent answers in an interview. Not all of this is response effect, since the doctor may not always inform the patient of the condition or the patient may not understand what the doctor is saying. Conditions most likely to be reported are those that are severe, costly, and require treatment. Recent effects of the condition, such as pain, emotional stress, days in bed, and visits to the doctor, are more important than routine medication or restrictions in diet.

Household expenditures.—Both large and small household expenditures are overreported on recall surveys, primarily due to telescoping effects. (The use of bounded recall procedures to eliminate telescoping is discussed in Chapter 3.) The effects are smaller since the presence of the item in the home acts as a reminder. This also explains why there is a larger positive effect for large items than for small items. The larger items are less likely to be forgotten because they cost more and are more visible in the home.

Media.—Since reading is considered a more socially desirable activity than watching television, we would expect that respondents on recall surveys would show a slight tendency to overstate the reading of magazines or newspapers and understate the total hours spent watching television. There is not much evidence that respondents report receiving or reading magazines or newspapers that they never read; rather, telescoping effects occur and there is an overstatement by those respondents who read a magazine or newspaper occasionally. In television measurement, the reverse occurs, and the few programs watched are likely to be forgotten in a recall interview. Television measurement studies currently avoid recall techniques and use either diaries or electrical measurement devices. Accurate readership studies focus on the respondents' attitudes toward the contents of a specific issue of a magazine to reduce the tendency to overstate reading. The results for media studies presented in Table 2.19 are not very revealing since they are based on comparisons of alternative techniques for data collection and not on outside validating information.

Demographic.—Several careful studies, particularly those by the U.S. Bureau of the Census, have indicated that there are very small or zero net response effects for items such as age, education, household composition, and occupation of household members. Most of these studies have involved reinterviews using more careful procedures and more highly-trained interviewers, and have also used record checks. There is a serious underestimation of the number of young black men who are not heads of families in the Census studies. This may be mainly due to the fact that, for a number of reasons, they are not included in any household listing. The mean effect for demographic characteristics is .004 in Table 2.19 and the standard deviation is the smallest of those for behavioral information, indicating that the distribution is heavily concentrated around zero.

Social behavior.—Most questions relating to social or antisocial behavior are either threatening or have a socially desirable answer. Since some of these questions tend to elicit overreporting and others underreporting, the average response effect tends toward zero

(−.03) when all studies are combined. Most of these studies were discussed earlier in the section dealing with effects due to problems of self-presentation.

Attitudes.—The results for questions dealing with race and with sex and family presented in Table 2.19 suggest that these questions elicit stronger general responses than do questions dealing with foreign, national, or local policy. The largest response effect is seen for personality studies, which include the psychological experiments with students using deception that have already been discussed, but also include studies of psychological well-being or mental illness. In the latter studies, the most important variables are the threat of the question and the possibility of a socially desirable answer. As an example, Phillips and Clancy (618) asked respondents to rate the degree of desirability of 22 items on a nine-point scale. The scale included such items as: "Do you feel somewhat apart or alone even among friends?" "Do you have personal worries that get you down physically?" and "Do you ever have trouble in getting to sleep or staying asleep?" Respondents were then grouped into three categories depending on how desirable they found the items to be. The results given in Table 2.20 indicate that respondents who see the items as relatively more desirable are much more likely to admit to them.

Conditions of the interview.—It is interesting to note in the results reported in Table 2.21 that medical and social behavior are better reported in the home than outside the home. Since both of these topics are threatening, this is not surprising. It may also reflect

Table 2.20 Symptom Scores on 22-Item Screening Instrument by Social Desirability of Items

Item	Item Desirability		
	Low (N = 39)	Medium (N = 41)	High (N = 35)
Per cent with 4+ symptoms	7.7	22.0	37.1
Mean number of symptoms (per cent)	0.8	2.6	3.4

Source: Phillips and Clancy (618). Reprinted by permission of the American Sociological Association.

the fact that the home interviews were face-to-face, while those out-side the home were self-administered. Results based on small sam-ples indicate that attitudes toward racial issues are most strongly expressed in the home, while attitudes toward sex are expressed most strongly outside the home.

Structure and position of questions.—Table 2.22 gives the re-sponse effects by topic of study for closed-ended and open-ended questions and for position of question. Financial data response effects are larger on closed-ended than on open-ended questions, as are reports on media usage. Open-ended questions yield larger response effects on medical and demographic data. The results are mixed for household expenditures, while the −.13 mean response effect on closed questions dealing with social behavior is a function primarily of these questions being on self-administered question-naires. Response effects for attitudes both on racial matters and on sex and the family are higher on closed-ended than on open-ended questions.

The results presented in Table 2.22 indicate that, whenever possible, media usage and demographic questions should be placed at the front of the questionnaire. Financial and medical data are best reported in the middle of the questionnaire; household expen-ditures are best reported at the end. These results are in line with

Table 2.21 Mean Response Effect in Standard Deviation Units by Condition of Interview and Subject of Study

Subject of Study	Behavior		Attitudes	
	In Home	Out of Home	In Home	Out of Home
Medical behavior	.15 (229)	−.30 (69)	−	−
Social behavior	−.003 (419)	−.27 (109)	−	−
Attitudes toward race	−	−	[.21] (14)	.14 (84)
Attitudes toward sex and family	−	−	.11 (63)	.35 (29)

Table 2.22 Mean Response Effect in Standard Deviation Units by Structure and Position of Question and Subject of Study

Subject of Study	Structure of Question		Position of Question in Questionnaire		
	Closed-ended	Open-ended	Early	Middle	Late
Behavior					
Financial	.05 (193)	-.02 (113)	[-.04] (18)	-.01 (70)	-.03 (117)
Medical	.05 (617)	.14 (215)	-.14 (137)	-.04 (274)	.36 (87)
Household expenditures:	—	—	[-.26] (19)	-.04 (56)	.002 (36)
Large	-.07 (64)	-.04 (65)	—	—	—
Small	.03 (166)	-.03 (100)	—	—	—
Media usage	.02 (126)	-.10 (35)	.00 (96)	[.003] (6)	-.05 (34)
Demographic	-.06 (70)	.03 (85)	.06 (24)	.07 (32)	-.03 (25)
Social behavior	-.13 (171)	-.001 (453)	—	—	—
Attitudes					
Attitudes on race	.11 (166)	.09 (21)	—	—	—
Attitudes on sex and family	.19 (174)	.08 (64)	—	—	—

the current procedures, which place less threatening questions early in the interview to give the respondent time to "warm up."

SUBJECT OF REPORT

One would expect the respondent to report more accurately about his own behavior than about that of other household members, and this is confirmed by the data presented in Table 2.23. What may be surprising is that, in general, reports about other household members are only slightly lower in response effect than are reports about self. Thus, on one of the studies of hospitalization discussed above (830), the respondent reporting about himself omitted 7 per cent of hospitalization episodes, while the respondent reporting on other household members omitted 14 per cent of the episodes. Similarly, in a study by Sudman and Ferber,[1] individual self-reports on clothing purchases were about 15 per cent higher than reports for other household members for a three-month recall. For longer time periods the differences were even smaller, averaging about 5 per cent. In the same study, reports by both husbands and wives about household furnishings did not differ from reports by wives only. Demographic information about other household members was reported with a high degree of accuracy.

Considering the cost savings relative to the response effects, collecting behavioral data from one household member about others in the household is a reasonable method, particularly for important behavior. For minor purchases, such as lunches or snacks, or phonograph records or tapes, however, reports by the housewife

[1] Seymour Sudman and Robert Ferber, *Experiments in Obtaining Consumer Expenditures in Durable Goods by Recall Procedures* (Urbana: Survey Research Laboratory, University of Illinois, 1970).

Table 2.23 Mean Response Effect in Standard Deviation Units by Subject of Report (Behavioral Items Only)

Subject of Report	Mean RE	σ	N
Self	.02	.50	2,104
Household	.04	.84	816
Other household members	−.01	.29	563

about her husband and children will be substantially underreported. One wonders whether household informants can report the attitudes of other household members reliably; to our knowledge, this has not yet been studied.

Threat and possibility of a socially desirable answer.—It has already been demonstrated that threat and the possibility of a socially desirable answer can have important response effects. The results in Table 2.24 indicate, however, that these effects are not found when individuals report about other household members. Thus, one might surmise that in some special situations when one is attempting to determine attitudes, the data from a household informant about others in the household may be more useful than direct self-reports about attitude. For behavioral data, however, self-reports are still a little better than informant reports.

Although there appear to be differences between reports about self and reports about household matters, these are due to the dif-

Table 2.24 Mean Response Effect in Standard Deviation Units by Subject of Report and Threat of Interview and Possibility of Socially Desirable Answer (Behavioral Items Only)

Item	Subject of Report		
	Self	Household	Other Household Members
Threat:			
Threatening	−.10	.14	−.02
	(540)	(187)	(138)
Possibly threatening	.18	−.04	−.02
	(388)	(274)	(121)
Non-threatening	.02	.04	−.001
	(1,160)	(355)	(304)
Socially Desirable Answer Possible:			
Strong possibility	.13	[−.18]	−.02
	(244)	(10)	(36)
Some possibility	−.03	−.09	.03
	(291)	(80)	(94)
Little or no possibility	.01	.01	−.02
	(1,528)	(659)	(432)

ferences in topics studied. For both types of reports, however, there are response effects of about the same magnitude due to the threat of the questions. While most of the threatening questions about households deal with financial matters (loans, welfare payments, income), there is an interesting study by McCord and McCord (532) that concerns parental attitudes toward their children. McCord and McCord found that interviews revealed less active rejection of sons than did observation procedures, and that boys showed less negative attitudes toward their parents on interviews than were observed. These results are given in Table 2.25.

Table 2.25 Parents' Attitudes toward Their Sons and Boys' Attitudes toward Their Parents (Per Cent)

Item	Observation Group (N= 250)	Interview Group (N=241)	Observation Group (N=216)	Interview Group (N=210)
	Mother		Father	
Attitudes toward Son:[a]				
Warm	50	46	30	32
Passive	32	44	46	55
Rejecting	18	10	24	13
	Observation Group (N=220)	Interview Group (N=208)	Observation Group (N=203)	Interview Group (N=187)
	Attitude toward Mother		Attitude toward Father	
Son's Attitudes toward Parents:[b]				
Favorable	82	91	59	74
Unfavorable	18	9	41	26

[a] "Warm" parents evidenced active affection for their children through open approval and pleasure in being with them; "passive" parents had little interaction with their sons although they may have been concerned for their welfare; "rejecting" parents openly demonstrated their dislike for their offspring. Agreement of two independent raters on a random sample of the observation group was 83 per cent for the mothers' and 77 per cent for the fathers' attitudes; on a random sample of the interview group, agreement was 84 per cent for the mothers' and 76 per cent for the fathers' attitudes.

[b] The boy's attitude toward his parent was considered "favorable" if there was some evidence of general approval and "unfavorable" if the boy appeared to fear, disapprove, or disdain his parent. Interrater agreement for the observation group was 93 per cent for attitude toward mother and 80 per cent toward father. For the interview group, interrater agreement was 88 per cent toward mother and 96 per cent toward father.

Source: McCord and McCord (532). Reprinted by permission. © Society for Research and Child Development.

Sex and education of respondent.—The major discussion of differences due to the sex of the respondent appears in Chapter 4. Here the reader may note that although there are differences between men and women reporting about themselves and other household members, there are no differences when they report about the household (Table 2.26). This non-finding supports the widely used practice of obtaining household information from any knowledgeable adult in the household regardless of sex.

Looking at years of education, the major response effect is for reports about self. Students in college are no different from other respondents when reporting about their households and other household members. In the school situation, it appears that only questions about self are threatening.

SUMMARY

How the interview is conducted has important implications on response effect. Differences between self-administered and face-to-

---

Table 2.26 Mean Response Effect in Standard Deviation Units by Subject of Report and Respondent Characteristics (Behavioral Items Only)

Respondent Characteristics	Subject of Report		
	Self	Household	Other Household Member
Sex:			
Male	−.06	.09	−.04
	(518)	(112)	(193)
Female	.05	.09	.04
	(461)	(187)	(198)
Years of Education:			
8 or less	.08	[−.05]	−.02
	(112)	(9)	(26)
9–12	.02	.02	.01
	(109)	(30)	(68)
13–15	−.08	.03	[−.04]
	(306)	(30)	(10)
16 or more	.002	–	−.02
	(39)		(42)

face interviews are particularly important. Many but not all of the differences between surveys conducted inside and outside the home are explained by the method of administration employed.

If the topic is threatening, more complete reporting may be obtained from self-administered rather than personal interviews. Self-administered forms may also be used for highly threatening questions dealing with possibly illegal behavior where anonymity is required. Where a socially desirable answer is possible on attitudinal questions, there is a greater tendency to conform on personal interviews than on self-administered questionnaires.

Large response effects are observed when college students, particularly males, are respondents or interviewers. The effects are particularly large in laboratory situations where there is a deliberate attempt to deceive the respondent.

Threat and saliency operate in opposite directions on response effect: the higher the threat, the greater the response effect, but the higher the saliency, the lower the response effect. The largest effects are seen, therefore, where threat is high and saliency is low. For threatening topics or for questions containing a socially desirable answer, the results suggest that closed-ended questions increase the threat and, therefore, the response effect. Open-ended questions are preferable in this situation, but may not always be feasible.

Finally, reports about other household members are only slightly less accurate than self-reports for important behavior (such as hospitalization episodes) and for demographic information. There is no improvement on questions relating to the household (such as household furnishings) if both husbands and wives respond as compared to responses from the wives only. The threat of the question appears to influence self-reports but not reports about other household members.

3

Effects of
Time and Memory Factors
on Response

INTRODUCTION

Although psychologists have conducted many experiments on forgetting[1] and the general shape of the memory curve is well-known, it is useful to specify, on the basis of survey results, what effects time and other interviewing variables have on the memory of behavior. There are two kinds of memory error, which operate in opposite directions. The first is the omission error, where the respondent forgets an episode entirely, whether it is a purchase of a product, a trip to the doctor, a law violation, or any other act. The second kind of error is the compression-of-time or telescoping error, where an event is remembered as occurring more recently than it did. Thus, a respondent who reports a trip to the doctor during the past seven days when the doctor's record shows it took place three weeks ago has made a telescoping error.

The examples suggest that we are primarily concerned with behavioral reports that can be validated. It is possible to ask respondents about past and present attitudes and to compare them, but the results are then a mixture of actual attitude change and memory error that cannot be separated.

Two principal methods have been used to improve memory: the use of available records, such as checkbooks or sales receipts, and

---

A slightly modified version of this chapter appears in *Journal of the American Statistical Association,* 68 (1973), 805–15.

[1] Donald A. Norman, ed., *Models of Human Memory* (New York: Academic Press, 1970); Norman J. Slamecka, *Human Learning and Memory* (New York: Oxford University Press, 1967).

the use of aided recall procedures where the possible answers are explicitly presented to the respondent. These methods, as we shall demonstrate, have opposite effects on memory errors. The use of records generally controls for overstatements due to telescoping errors, but has no effect or only a small effect on errors of omission. Aided recall, on the other hand, reduces the number of events that are omitted, but does not reduce (and may even increase) telescoping effects.

In this chapter, we attempt to quantify the effects of time on memory in the survey interview. A simple model is presented, based primarily on the experience of experimental psychologists. This model is then tested with real-world data. Finally, we discuss other characteristics of the interview, and of the respondent, that appear to have consistent effects on memory. These include the age of the respondent, whether the interview is face-to-face or self-administered, the threat of the interview, the position of the question in the questionnaire, and the structure of the question.

A SIMPLE MODEL OF THE EFFECT OF TIME ON MEMORY

Since total response error due to memory is the product of omissions and overstatements due to telescoping, a memory model is easily obtained by looking at the two component parts.

Omissions

A substantial literature in experimental psychology suggests that at least short-term and intermediate memory decays exponentially with time.[2] Although the same kinds of results are not available for long time periods, it seems reasonable to begin with a simple exponential model to explain the relative rate of omissions. We designate r_o as the fraction of all events reported, and $1 - r_o$ as the relative error due to omissions, then:

$$r_o = ae^{-b_1 t} \tag{1}$$

where b_1 determines the rapidity of decay and depends on such

[2] Wayne A. Wicklegren, "Multitrace Strengths Theory," in *Models of Human Memory,* ed. by Donald A. Norman, p. 76.

factors as the event's importance to the respondent, the characteristics of the respondent, and the conditions of the interview. Henceforth, we will refer to this parameter as the omission parameter.

The other parameter, *a,* is non-time related and depends on such factors as the degree of threat or social desirability of an event, or on the likelihood that the respondent is aware that an event has occurred. For example, regardless of forgetting, the purchase of alcoholic beverages is likely to be underreported because the respondent may feel that the interviewer will consider the purchases socially undesirable; or the purchase of phonograph records will be underreported by a mother who is not aware of what her children have bought.

Telescoping

If omission errors are not present or are corrected, it is often observed that the total number of events is overreported, particularly for frequently occurring events. The possibility of imaginary events being reported is low, since details of the event are usually required. Thus, a recall question might ask the respondent to give all the purchases of milk made during the past two weeks and to give the brand, price, and outlet name. Typically, overreporting occurs because the respondent telescopes time by including purchases made more than two weeks previously.

A telescoping error occurs when the respondent misremembers the duration of an event. While one might imagine that errors would be randomly distributed around the true duration, the errors are primarily in the direction of remembering an event as having occurred more recently than it did. This is due to the respondent's wish to perform the task required of him. When in doubt, the respondent prefers to give too much information rather than too little. Another example of this phenomenon may be found in crop surveys as reported by Mahalanobis (502). He found that serious overstatements of amounts planted were a function of plot size; the smaller the plot, the greater the overstatement. The error was due to ambiguous boundaries. Whenever the exact location of the boundary was not clear, the worker would count plants as inside, rather than outside, the boundary. The term "border bias" is sometimes used instead of telescoping.

The effect of telescoping is to increase the total level of events reported in a more recent period. Since this effect may not be obvious to those not familiar with the phenomenon, a hypothetical example will illustrate the process. Suppose a recall survey is conducted on February 4, 1972, asking the respondent about purchases of milk during the first four weeks of January. The respondent reports 20 purchases of milk during January on the following dates: January 5, 7, 9, 10, 11, 12, 13, 15, 16, 17, 18, 19, 21, 24, 25, 26, 27, 28, 29, and February 1. A check of dairy records indicates that these purchases were actually made on December 26, 27, 29, 31, January 4, 7, 9, 10, 12, 14, 15, 17, 18, 19, 21, 23, 25, 26, 27, and 29.

The user of the data obviously can do little with daily purchases, even if there are many households in the sample. Therefore, he obtains data summarized by one-, two-, three-, or four-week periods, as shown in Table 3.1. It may be seen that in each of the periods the reported purchases exceed the actual purchases and that the absolute error increases with time. The relative error (Reported Purchases/Actual Purchases −1) declines over time.

In surveys that require the respondent to report purchases made in a given time period, the most recent time period ordinarily is used. Thus, for a one-week recall period, the question would usually require the respondent to recall all purchases made in the previous week or in the last seven days. Except in methodological studies, the recall is for one time period only. Thus, if information is obtained for two weeks, it is not also obtained for one and four weeks.

Table 3.1 Actual and Reported Milk Purchases (Hypothetical Data)

Week	Cumulative Actual	Cumulative Reported	Absolute Error	Relative Error
1	5	7	2	.40
2	9	12	3	.35
3	14	18	4	.29
4	16	20	5	.25

Is there a simple model based on psychological experiments that can be used to describe the distribution of errors given in Table 3.1? Although psychologists have shown an increasing interest in perceptions of time duration in the last several years,[3] this work again relates to periods of short duration. For the recall periods used in survey research, the most useful concept is Weber's Law, which suggests that errors in perception of time will be a function of the logarithm of the time period. Weber's Law suggests that the net absolute error in the reported length of the time period is log b_2t where b_2 is a factor that translates calendar time to subjective time; we will refer to b_2 as the telescoping parameter.

The relative error in the length of time period reported is:

$$r_t = \frac{\log b_2t}{t} \qquad (2)$$

The net relative error due to both telescoping and omissions is:

$$R.E. = r_o (1 + r_t) - 1 \qquad (3)$$

Thus, in our example of milk purchases, if there were a .9 probability of a purchase being reported in the two-week period, the net relative error would be .9 (1.35) − 1 = .22.

It is possible for omission and telescoping errors to occur simultaneously during the recall process. Can anything be said about the relation between the omission parameter b_1 and the telescoping parameter b_2? As we shall demonstrate below, omission depends on the saliency of the question to the respondent: the more salient the event, the less likely it is to be omitted. All else being equal, more frequent events are more salient to the respondent, so that the omission rate is lower on frequently purchased nondurable goods than on infrequently purchased durable goods. Telescoping, however, appears to behave in the reverse manner: the more frequent the event, the greater the likelihood of confusion about dates.

[3] Paul Fraisse, *The Psychology of Time* (New York: Harper & Row, 1963); Robert E. Ornstein, *On the Experience of Time* (Baltimore: Penguin Books, 1970).

Individual events interfere with each other during the memory process. This suggests that the relation between b_1 and b_2 is of the form $b_1 b_2 = c$ (a constant that depends on the conditions of the interview). For the data given in the next section, the product of $b_1 b_2$ is reasonably constant.

It is also possible to specify the ratio between levels of reporting at periods t_1 and t_2. This is useful, since for some studies there may be information on levels of reporting for various time periods, but no outside validating information.

$$R(t_2/t_1) = \frac{t_1}{t_2} e^{-b_1(t_2-t_1)} \left(\frac{t_2 + \log b_2 t_2}{t_1 + \log b_2 t_1}\right) \qquad (4)$$

For the reader's convenience, Table 3.2 gives values of $e^{-b_1 t}$ for various values of b ranging from .01 to 1.0 and values of t ranging from 1 to 12. Table 3.3 gives the value of $(\log b_2 t)/t$ for values of b from 1 to 10 and values of t from 1 to 12, and Table 3.4 gives values of the ratio $R(t_2/t_1)$ for selected values of b_1, b_2, t_1, and t_2.

Some generalizations may be made from the model. First, the model implies that for long time periods there will be very substan-

Table 3.2 Values of $100e^{-b_1 t}$ for various values of b_1 and t

t	b_1												
	.01	.05	.10	.15	.20	.25	.30	.35	.40	.45	.50	.75	1.0
1	99	95	90	86	82	78	74	70	67	64	61	47	37
2	98	90	82	74	67	61	55	50	45	41	37	22	14
3	97	86	74	64	55	47	41	35	30	26	22	11	5
4	96	82	67	55	45	37	30	25	20	17	14	5	2
5	95	79	61	47	37	29	22	17	13	11	8	2	1
6	94	74	55	41	30	22	17	12	9	7	5	1	—
7	93	70	50	35	25	17	12	9	6	4	3	1	—
8	92	67	45	30	20	14	9	6	4	3	2	—	—
9	91	64	41	26	17	11	7	4	3	2	1	—	—
10	90	61	37	22	14	8	5	3	2	1	1	—	—
11	90	58	33	19	11	7	4	2	1	1	—	—	—
12	89	55	30	17	9	5	3	1	1	—	—	—	—

Table 3.3 Values of 100 $\frac{\log b_2 t}{t}$ for Various Values of b_2 and t

t	b_2												
	1	1.5	2	2.5	3	3.5	4	5	6	7	8	9	10
1	0	18	30	40	48	54	60	70	78	85	90	95	100
2	15	24	30	35	39	42	45	50	54	57	60	63	65
3	16	22	26	29	32	34	36	39	42	44	46	48	49
4	15	18	23	25	27	28	30	33	34	36	38	39	40
5	14	18	20	22	24	25	26	28	29	31	32	33	34
6	12	16	16	20	21	22	23	25	26	27	28	29	30
7	12	15	16	18	19	20	21	22	23	24	25	26	26
8	11	13	15	15	17	18	19	20	21	22	23	23	24
9	11	13	14	15	16	17	17	18	19	20	21	21	22
10	10	12	13	14	15	15	16	17	18	18	19	20	20
11	9	11	12	13	14	14	15	16	17	18	18	18	19
12	9	10	12	12	13	14	14	15	15	17	17	17	17

Table 3.4 Values of $100R(t_2/t_1)$ for Various Values of b_1, b_2, t_1, t_2

$t_1 = 1$ [a]	b_1					
	.05	.10	.25	.05	.10	.25
	b_2					
$t_2 =$	5	2.5	1	10	5	2
2	84	88	90	78	80	78
3	74	76	70	67	67	58
4	68	66	55	60	58	45
5	63	59	42	56	51	34
6	57	52	32	51	45	25
7	53	47	24	46	40	19
8	50	41	20	44	35	16
9	47	37	16	41	32	12
10	44	33	11	39	28	9
11	42	30	10	36	25	8
12	39	27	7	34	23	6

[a] Other values of R are derived from the relation:

$$R(t_j/t_r) = \frac{R(t_j/t_i)}{R(t_r/t_i)}$$

tial omission of events, regardless of telescoping; that is, the omission rate will overpower the overreporting due to telescoping. Some exceptions to this model may be noted. When there are very high initial overstatements, such as in reports of voting, the response error may still be positive after many time periods. In addition, the model implies that there is a time other than zero when omission and telescoping errors balance to produce the correct level. If one were interested only in net level of reporting, and not the details, this would be an optimum period to use for recall.

We must emphasize that this model describes recall of specific events. If, for example, the annual purchase of groceries was estimated by taking a one-week recall and multiplying it by 52, the estimate would be based on one and not 52 time periods and would probably be substantially overstated.

One major issue has thus far been ignored—the units of measurement for time. To some extent, this is arbitrary since changing time units will also change the values of the parameters b_1 and b_2 in the model. For very frequent events, such as purchasing of groceries or eating a meal away from home, a time unit of weeks seems reasonable. For less frequent events, such as a visit to the dentist or a purchase or sale of stocks, a time unit of a month could be used; for purchases of a home or car, a time unit of a year might be appropriate.

Illustrations of the Memory Model

In this section, we use the model to describe memory errors in reporting of purchases of durable and semidurable goods. The data are based on an experiment by Sudman and Ferber[4] using periods of average length of three, six, and nine months. Outside validating information was available on some purchases from a leading department store chain. This validating information makes it possible to estimate values of a, b_1, and b_2 for product types, and to compare the actual and observed levels of error. It is also possible to compare the observed values of the ratios $R(t_1/t_2)$ for all purchases with the expected values based on the model.

---

[4] Seymour Sudman and Robert Ferber, *Experiments in Obtaining Consumer Expenditures in Durable Goods by Recall Procedures* (Urbana: Survey Research Laboratory, University of Illinois, 1970).

One difficulty with the estimates is that they assume that a purchase reported by a respondent but not found in store records is an overstatement due to telescoping. While this is partially true, some of the differences may be due to errors of store name or other errors not related to time. Thus, the estimates of telescoping r_t are less reliable than estimates of omission errors. While omission data are generally satisfactory, they too present some problems. Items purchased as gifts were not shown in household reports of a product category, but were included in the store records. This is particularly troublesome for small household appliance purchases.

Table 3.5 gives the results for three categories—furniture and major appliances, housewares and small appliances, and auto service and supplies. In each case, the values of r_o and r_t, the omission and telescoping effects respectively, are computed from the validation data,[5] and estimates are made of a, b_1, and b_2. Since there are only three points, the fitting is done visually. The observed relative errors taken from the validation data are compared to the expected relative errors computed using formula (3). Similarly, the expected ratios $R(t_6/t_3)$ and $R(t_9/t_3)$ are computed from formula (4), while the observed ratios are based on all reported data.[6]

Given the measurement problems, the observed data seem to fit the model reasonably well. For each of the three durable and semi-durable categories the values of b_1 are in the range of .05 −.10, while the values of b_2 are in the range of 2.5–5.0. Note that in all three cases the product of $b_1 b_2 = .25$, confirming that b_1 and b_2 are inversely related.

The observed ratios $R(t_6/t_3)$ and $R(t_9/t_3)$ reflect not only omission errors but seasonal factors as well, since the Christmas shopping period occurred about two months before the study was conducted. Thus, gift items such as housewares and small appliances show lower than expected ratios, while furniture, rugs, and draperies show a close relation between observed and expected ratios.

The greatest variation in the three product groups is in the value of a, but these values appear reasonable based on prior knowledge

[5] *Ibid.*, pp. 45–46.
[6] *Ibid.*, pp. 10–11, 23.

Table 3.5 Observed and Predicted Values of Relative Errors and Ratios $R(t_1/t_2)$ for Furniture, Housewares, and Auto Supply Purchases

t	r_o	r_t	R.E. Observed	R.E. Expected	Total Observed	$R_{(t_i/t_3)}$ Observed	$R_{(t_i/t_3)}$ Expected
				Furniture, Rugs, Draperies, and Major Appliance Purchases			
3	.63	.29	−11	−14	111	−	−
6	.37	.23	−41	−41	73	.66	.69
9	.28	.20	−47	−58	56	.51	.49
			$a = .90$ $b_1 = .10$ $b_2 = 2.5$				
				Housewares and Small Appliances			
3	.30	.43	−28	−28	150	−	−
6	.30	.24	−45	−44	77	.51	.78
9	.25	.24	−52	−52	72	.48	.67
			$a = .60$ $b_1 = .05$ $b_2 = 5.0$				
				Auto Supplies and Service			
3	.24	.47	−32	−40	47	−	−
6	.28	.22	−48	−53	30	.64	.78
9	.26	.10	−70	−60	29	.62	.67
			$a = .50$ $b_1 = .05$ $b_2 = 5.0$				

of the products. The recall interview was conducted primarily with the housewife as the respondent. Many purchases of auto supplies and services are made by the husband or other household members, and the respondent is never aware of these. The value of a at .5 suggests that only about half of all actual purchases are known to the respondent, although this may also be a factor of the conditions of the interview. As mentioned earlier, the .6 value of a for housewares and small appliances is due in part to the fact that many such items are given as gifts. Other conditions of the interview and lack of knowledge by the respondent also are factors. As one would expect, the value of a for furniture is near 1.0, since the purchase of a major item is known to all household members.

The largest difference between an observed and expected value in Table 3.5 is found in the relative errors at $t = 9$ for furniture. The observed *R.E.* is -47 while the predicted *R.E.* is -58. We suspect that this is because the presence of the furniture in the house acts as a form of aided recall. We have no way of confirming this conjecture, but shall discuss aided recall later in this chapter.

Another example comes from the important study by Neter and Waksberg (586–588) on the use of bounded recall procedures to reduce telescoping in the reporting of large and small house repairs and alterations. This study is discussed in detail in the next section, since it is an application of the use of records. From the data it is possible to estimate values of b_1 and b_2 for expenditures under $100 and over $100. The value of b_1 is estimated from their Table 7, which compares three-month bounded recall to one-month bounded recall. The value of b_2 is estimated from their Table 1, which compares unbounded and bounded one-month recall.

These estimates are:

Small expenditures (under $100): $b_1 = .15$; $b_2 = 4$
Large expenditures: $b_1 = 0$; $b_2 = 3.5$

Data are also provided on levels of reporting for unbounded recall for periods of one, two, and three months (588, Appendix Table E, p. 52). From these results one can compute $R(t_2/t_1)$ and

$R(t_3/t_1)$ and compare to the expected values based on the model:

	Small Expenditures		Large Expenditures	
	Observed	Expected	Observed	Expected
$R(t_2/t_1)$	73	78	87	92
$R(t_3/t_1)$	55	63	88	87

The fit is reasonable and adds to our confidence in the model. It should be noted, however, that the number of points is limited, and that some of the same data are used in both fitting the parameters and testing the results.

Perhaps the most surprising result is the estimated value of zero for b_1 for large expenditures. This means that major household repairs or alterations are not forgotten, at least during a six-month period. If $b_1 b_2$ were constant, one would expect a value of $b_1 = .17$ for large expenditures, based on the values for small expenditures. As with large furniture items, we believe that the presence of the alteration in the house acts as a reminder to the respondent and inhibits forgetting. This does not insure that such expenditures would never be forgotten. It may mean that the natural time period for such expenditures is much longer than for small expenditures, and longer than the six-month period used in this study.

The memory model is subject to additional tests, even if outside validation data are not available. Comparison of diary reports and recall can yield the same kinds of comparisons using matched groups (see Quackenbush, 634; Sudman, 791). For example, if one wished to test the model on recall of grocery purchases, one might estimate that $a = 1$, $b_1 = .10$, and $b_2 = 4$, based on prior experience. Then one would expect the following relative errors of recall as compared to diary reporting:

Week:	1	2	3	4	5	6	7	8
Relative Error:	44	19	1	−13	23	−32	−40	−46

To summarize, the omission and telescoping phenomena observed in surveys can be described using relatively simple functions derived from experimental studies of memory decay and psychophysical experiments of perception errors that fit Weber's Law. The parameters of the functions relate subjective and objective time, and thus the omission and telescoping parameters are inverses of each other.

RESPONSE EFFECT BY LENGTH OF RECALL PERIOD AND SUBJECT OF STUDY

We now turn from our discussion of the memory model with particular examples to a general discussion of response effects related to time and other memory factors. The results come from the coding of the studies reported in the literature, as described in Chapter 1.

As one would expect, there is a decline in response effect from about .04 for a one-week period to −.06 for periods longer than three months. Obviously, the data make more sense when also classified by subject of study, and these results are given in Table 3.6. The expected initial overreporting followed by declines through time are generally observed. The data for large and small household expenditures agree fairly well with the examples given earlier. Financial data recall does not decline as sharply. This may be because the natural recall period is longer (quarterly or annually) or be-

Table 3.6 Response Effect in Standard Deviation Units by Length of Recall Period and Subject of Study

Length of Recall Period	Subject of Study				
	Large Household Expenditures	Small Household Expenditures	Financial	Medical	Voting
1 week or less	.35 (54)	.09 (135)	—	—	—
2 weeks	[.16] (8)	.03 (36)	—	—	—
3–4 weeks	[−.31] (11)	[−.06] (18)	—	—	—
1 month	.23 (73)	.06 (189)	.07 (143)	−.02 (338)	.40 (48)
2–3 months	—	[−.25] (17)	.10 (135)	.01 (26)	[.35] (12)
4–12 months	−.09 (48)	−.03 (70)	−.05 (45)	−.15 (46)	[.26] (8)

cause aided recall is more likely. The voting data show the initial effects of social desirability, and the initial overreporting of .40 only decreases to .26 for the period of 4–12 months.

The results of Table 3.6 confirm (although perhaps weakly) the theoretical model we have developed. There is a general decline in response effect. The initial or early overreporting is probably a function of both telescoping and giving a socially desirable answer as in the voting studies.

AIDED RECALL AND THE USE OF RECORDS

Two principal methods have been used by survey researchers to improve respondents' memories—aided recall and records. Aided recall procedures attempt to stimulate memory by providing specific cues, such as pictures, lists, or copies of magazines. In consumer expenditure studies, the unaided recall question might be "What groceries did you buy this week?" while the aided recall question might be "Did you buy any presweetened cereals?" In media readership studies, aided recall procedures involve showing the respondent a list of magazines and newspapers and asking whether he happened to see any of them in the specified period, while the unaided recall question might be "What magazines did you happen to see this week?"

It seems pretty clear that the use of aided recall should and does increase the level of reported activity (Table 3.7). It does not necessarily follow, however, that aided recall will always improve the accuracy of reporting. Although aided recall may reduce omissions, it may increase, or at least not decrease, telescoping effects and may thus lead to net overreporting.

It is often difficult to determine from reading reports of past studies whether aided recall procedures have been used. One possible surrogate for aided recall might be the use of structured closed-ended questions that prod the respondent's memory. The results in Table 3.7, however, indicate no overall difference between closed-ended and open-ended questions. Some additional discussion of open-ended and closed-ended questions is found later in this chapter in the section dealing with the conditions of the interview.

If the respondent refers to available records, however, we find that effects occur that are just the reverse of the effects produced by aided recall (Table 3.7). Telescoping effects are eliminated if a record is available, since the date of the event is on the record. There will also be some decrease in omissions, but this decrease will generally be smaller. On the average, the use of records reduces response by approximately 10 per cent, while aided recall increases response by the same percentage.

We do not mean to suggest that the level of reported events is the only factor to consider. The use of records gives substantially more reliable information about the details of the event, such as the price of a purchase and the place where the purchase was made. A study by Horn (376) in the Netherlands, for example, indicated that 47 per cent of respondents who consulted records gave the correct balance in their savings accounts, while only 31 per cent of respondents who did not consult records gave the correct balance.

If data are threatening or if the respondent is asked to report on others in the household for whom he does not have complete information, the use of records does not improve underreporting and can make it worse. This is seen for medical expenditures (which may be considered threatening) in Table 3.8. The use of records improves accuracy in the reporting of financial data by decreasing the level of overreporting. For small household expendi-

Table 3.7 Response Effect in Standard Deviation Units by Availability of Records, Structure of Questions, and Aided Recall

Item	Average Response Effects		
	Net Mean	σ	N
Records Available:			
Yes	−.03	.28	896
Uncertain	.03	.24	333
No	.06	.78	939
Structure of Questions:			
Closed-ended	−.001	.42	1,750
Open-ended	.01	.64	1,376
Recall:			
Aided	.13	1.31	208
Unaided	−.02	.48	1,209

tures, the reverse pattern is seen—the use of records increases the level of reporting. These results are based on only a few observations, but they suggest that for small purchases, the reminder and information effects of records may be greater than the telescoping effects.

Observing the effects of aided recall and the use of records separately, one naturally wonders what the effect on memory would be of using both techniques simultaneously. If there were no interactions, the net effect would be to yield data with a response effect near zero. Unfortunately, the number of cases where both have been used is so small that no meaningful generalizations can be made. Again, this seems a natural problem for controlled experimentation.

AIDED RECALL, USE OF RECORDS, AND LENGTH OF THE RECALL PERIOD

Based on the model of exponential memory decay, one would expect that differences between aided and unaided recall procedures would become more important as the length of the recall period increases and that, similarly, differences between events where records are and are not available would also increase with time. These expectations are confirmed for availability of records (Table 3.9), but there is insufficient data to make any generalizations

Table 3.8 Response Effect in Standard Deviation Units by Availability of Records, Aided Recall, and Subject of Study

Subject of Study	Records Available			Recall	
	Yes	Uncertain	No	Aided	Unaided
Financial	.02	.03	.14	–	–
	(149)	(39)	(73)		
Medical	.09	.01	.12	.34	.02
	(435)	(143)	(259)	(86)	(566)
Small household expenditures	.09	.06	.08	[.04]	.005
	(46)	(95)	(47)	(18)	(133)
Media usage	–	–	–	.003	.004
				(76)	(57)

about time and aided recall. For periods of two weeks or less, the average difference in response effect between events where records are and are not available is −.04, while for periods of more than three months, the average difference in response effect is −.13.

BOUNDED RECALL PROCEDURES

Probably the best single study of telescoping effects on memory was conducted by Neter and Waksberg (586–588) for the U.S. Census Bureau. They not only measured telescoping but also proposed a procedure, bounded recall, for eliminating this type of error. Bounded recall procedures involve a series of interviews with the same panel of respondents. At the beginning of the bounded interview, which is the second or later interview, the respondent is told about the expenditures reported during the previous interview, and is then asked about additional expenditures made since then. The interviewer also checks the new expenditures reported with previous expenditures to make sure that no duplication has occurred.

Both bounded and unbounded recall procedures were studied for periods ranging from one to six months, with different household members designated as respondents: head, wife, joint interview with head and wife, or any knowledgeable adult. No significant differences were found in the reports of different respondents in a given household. Since conditioning effects due to the repeated interviewing make it difficult to study telescoping effects, Neter and

Table 3.9 Response Effect in Standard Deviation Units by Length of Recall Period and Availability of Records

Recall Period	Availability of Records		
	Available	Uncertain	Not Available
0–2 weeks	.04	.125	.08
	(176)	(120)	(380)
3–13 weeks	−.06	−.08	.02
	(59)	(49)	(55)
14 or more weeks	−.09	−.01	.03
	(430)	(160)	(129)

Waksberg give two sets of estimates in their tables, one assuming conditioning losses and one assuming no conditioning losses.

Table 3.10 (based on 588, Tables 1 and 3) gives estimates of recall error for periods of one and six months by comparing bounded and unbounded recall. These results are consistent with the memory model presented earlier. For larger jobs, there is

Table 3.10 Relative Differences in Household Repair Jobs and Expenditures Due to Recall Error, as Estimated from Unbounded and Bounded One- and Six-Month Recalls, by Size of Job—February 1960–March 1961

Size of Job (in Dollars)	Per Cent Difference (Bounded Recall as Base)				Standard Error of Per Cent Difference	
	Household Repair Jobs		Expenditures			
	If No Conditioning Losses	If Conditioning Losses	If No Conditioning Losses	If Conditioning Losses	Jobs	Expenditures
One-Month Recall:						
Total	39.7	15.4	55.2	39.1	4.0	17.0
Under 20	30.1	8.0	34.2	3.9	4.0	6.0
Under 10	29.3	9.0	34.9	9.7	5.0	7.0
10–19	33.0	4.7	33.5	− 1.4	8.0	13.0
20–99	62.4	28.4	71.0	32.7	7.0	8.0
20–49	52.3	19.6	56.5	17.2	8.0	9.0
50–99	89.6	53.1	86.6	51.0	13.0	16.0
100 and over	56.2	56.2	53.5	53.5	18.0	24.0
100–499	61.1	61.1	76.2	76.2	20.0	26.0
500 and over	31.4	31.4	35.6	35.6	37.0	48.0
Six-Month Recall:						
Total	− 0.6	−17.9	18.8	6.5	4.0	17.0
Under 20	−11.8	−26.8	2.6	−20.5	4.0	6.0
Under 10	−20.3	−32.8	−10.8	−27.5	5.0	7.0
10–19	15.2	− 9.3	15.0	−15.1	8.0	13.0
20–99	21.0	− 4.3	23.8	− 3.9	7.0	8.0
20–49	17.6	− 7.6	19.8	−10.3	8.0	9.0
50–99	30.4	5.3	28.0	3.6	13.0	16.0
100 and over	31.8	31.8	19.5	19.5	18.0	24.0
100–499	24.2	24.2	30.9	30.9	20.0	26.0
500 and over	65.7	65.7	10.5	10.5	37.0	48.0

Source: Neter and Waksberg (588).

no evidence of omissions, and the telescoping effect decreases over the six-month period. For small repairs, the omission rate increases over time so that one-month bounded recall is higher than six-month unbounded recall.

The principal problem with bounded recall procedures is that while they correct for telescoping effects, they do not eliminate the errors due to omissions. This was found in the Neter–Waksberg study to be the case for small household repair expenditures.

Our conclusion is that bounded recall is an extremely effective procedure for eliminating telescoping for major expenditures where b_1 is near zero and where b_2 is large. For smaller expenditures, where omissions are the most serious error, other procedures, such as the use of diaries, seem preferable. For example, the Census Bureau has been using bounded recall procedures to measure the number and characteristics of trips away from home. These bounded recall procedures should prevent telescoping of major trips and vacations, but should prove ineffective in reducing the omission rate in reports of short, minor trips.

AGE OF RESPONDENT

A full discussion of respondent characteristics related to response effects is presented in Chapter 4. Of all the respondent variables, however, only age is related to memory. The survey results relating age and memory, given in Table 3.11, are confirmed by experimental studies.[7] The table shows no difference in response effect for periods of 13 weeks or less and 14 weeks or more for respondents under age 55. For respondents over 55, the underreporting increases from $-.08$ to $-.16$ as the time period extends to more than 13 weeks. The availability of records, which reduces telescoping but not omissions, has a much larger effect on respondents over age 55, although this result is based on a very small number of observations.

CONDITIONS OF THE INTERVIEW

In this section we discuss briefly four conditions of the interview that seem to be related to memory: (1) whether the questionnaire

---

[7] Pierre Lecomte du Noüy, *Biological Time* (New York: Macmillan, 1937).

is administered face-to-face or self-administered, (2) the threat of the interview or question, (3) the position of the question in the questionnaire, and (4) whether closed-ended or open-ended questions are used. All of these are surrogates for the interaction between the respondent and interviewer, which cannot be measured directly.

Method of Administration

Since remembering events in the distant past can be hard work, one would expect that the presence of an interviewer who prompts and encourages the respondent would result in better memory than would the use of a self-administered questionnaire. Table 3.12 confirms this hypothesis. There is also a suggestion that, on the other hand, telescoping is greater for face-to-face interviews. On self-administered questionnaires, there is a .01 response effect for a recall period of two weeks or less, and a −.20 effect for periods of 14 weeks or more. For face-to-face interviews, there is a .07 effect for periods of two weeks or less and a −.05 effect for periods of 14 weeks or more.

Similarly, there is a .15 response effect for aided recall for face-to-face interviews, and no effect for self-administered question-

Table 3.11 Response Effect in Standard Deviation Units by Age of Respondent and Length of Recall Period, and Availability of Records

Item	Age of Respondent	
	Under 55	55 or Older
Recall Period (Weeks):		
0–13	.02	−.08
	(1,203)	(65)
14 or more	.02	−.16
	(498)	(39)
Records Available:		
Yes	−.02	−.20
	(302)	(39)
Uncertain	.05	−
	(191)	
No	.04	[.04]
	(464)	(17)

naires. Note that the small sample for self-administered question-naires suggests that self-administered forms do not readily lend themselves to aided recall procedures. As expected, the availability of records affects face-to-face interviews by reducing telescoping effects. For self-administered forms, the results bounce around meaninglessly. This is partly a function of the specific studies pro-viding the data. The self-administered studies where no records were available were for recall periods of more than one year. Nevertheless, it is more likely that available records will be used if an interviewer probes than if the respondent is on his own.

Threat of the Interview or Question

As there is no direct information on how threatening or how salient the interview was to the respondent, we attempted to infer

Table 3.12 Response Effect in Standard Deviation Units by Method of Administration and Length of Recall Period, Aided Recall, and Availability of Records

Item	Method of Administration	
	Face-to-Face	Self-Administered
Recall Period (Weeks):		
0–2	.07 (1,217)	.01 (208)
3–13	.03 (94)	–
14 or more	−.05 (646)	−.20 (68)
Recall Aided:		
Yes	.15 (188)	[.00] (16)
No	.01 (927)	−.34 (113)
Records Available:		
Yes	−.03 (711)	−.13 (39)
Uncertain	.04 (272)	[.04] (6)
No	.11 (793)	−.28 (114)

this from the subject matter of the questionnaire. Thus, this code duplicates, to some extent, the results for memory by subject of study discussed earlier. Threatening subjects were described as those dealing with taboo or sensitive topics: sex, drinking, crime, financial data, or serious illnesses.

One would expect a priori that the greater the threat, the greater the number of omission errors and the more negative the response effect will be as the recall period increases. This is confirmed in Table 3.13, which shows no differences in response effect between threatening and non-threatening topics for recall periods of two weeks or less, but shows a .15 unit difference ($-.18$ to $-.03$) for periods of 14 weeks or more.

Aided recall has a much greater effect if the interview is threatening. For threatening interviews, there is a .56 unit difference

Table 3.13 Response Effect in Standard Deviation Units by Threatening Interview and Length of Recall Period, Aided Recall, and Availability of Records

Item	Threatening Interview		
	Yes	Possibly	No
Recall Period (Weeks):			
0–2	.01	.17	.02
	(408)	(217)	(1,323)
3–13	−.01	.08	−.12
	(68)	(59)	(115)
14 or more	−.18	−.03	−.03
	(145)	(417)	(220)
Recall Aided:			
Yes	.37	[−.09]	−.02
	(82)	(9)	(117)
No	−.19	−.02	.03
	(192)	(433)	(580)
Records Available:			
Yes	−.15	−.003	−.01
	(137)	(73)	(328)
Uncertain	−.02	.03	.26
	(370)	(87)	(238)
No	.02	.04	−.01
	(377)	(173)	(369)

between aided and unaided recall (.37 to −.19). For non-threatening interviews, the difference is only .05 units (−.02 to .03).

The availability of records also shows a strong effect for threatening interviews, but a mixed effect or no effect for non-threatening interviews. Threatening interviews have a −.15 effect if records are available and a .02 effect if they are not.

The reader may wonder why we do not discuss the relation between saliency and memory. Theory would make one expect that memory would be better for highly salient items. The data relating saliency and memory, however, show no meaningful trends. This failure to confirm our theoretical expectation may be due to a lack of sensitivity in our saliency measure, which was based on the coder's subjective estimate of how salient the topic was to the respondent. It would certainly be possible to measure saliency directly by asking the respondent such questions as "How important is this topic to you?" This is another area that needs additional research.

Position of Question in the Questionnaire

Two general, and to some extent opposing, hypotheses have been suggested about response effects and the position of the question in the questionnaire. The first hypothesis says that rapport increases throughout the interview so that the respondent performs his task better at the end than at the beginning. (This could also be explained by the respondent's greater experience.) The other view is that fatigue sets in, and leads to a decline in performance at the end of an interview.

Table 3.14, which relates memory to the position of the question in the questionnaire, tends to support the first hypothesis. There is no evidence of any increase in omission errors as the interview concludes. Rather, the response bias becomes smaller as the interview progresses. While there are no differences for recall periods of less than two weeks, for periods of 14 weeks or more, response bias decreases from −.15 early in the interview to −.01 late in the interview. These results do not indicate that fatigue could never be a factor. Most survey researchers have been concerned about fatigue, and in our search of the literature, we rarely found interviews that lasted longer than one and one-half hours. For interviews of this length, there is no evidence of a fatigue factor, but it could become a serious problem in interviews lasting more than two hours.

Results based on a small sample indicate that aided recall has no effect at the start of an interview, but has a large (.57) effect late in the interview. The availability of records also has a larger effect late in the interview than it does at the beginning. For questions late in the interview, there is a difference of .34 units (−.04 to .30) if records are or are not available. Early in the interview, the difference is .13 units (−.17 to −.04).

Closed-ended and Open-ended Questions

It is not clear in advance what the net effect on memory of using closed-ended or open-ended questions will be. Although closed-

Table 3.14 Response Effect in Standard Deviation Units by Position of Question in Questionnaire and Length of Recall Period, Aided Recall, and Availability of Records

Item	Position of Question in Questionnaire		
	Early	Middle	Late
Recall Period (Weeks):			
0–2	.03	.02	−.01
	(198)	(125)	(194)
3–13	−.05	−.03	−
	(32)	(59)	
14 or more	−.15	−.05	−.01
	(112)	(255)	(51)
Recall Aided:			
Yes	−.001	−	.57
	(72)		(53)
No	.04	−.04	.004
	(99)	(354)	(181)
Records Available:			
Yes	−.17	−.04	−.04
	(102)	(254)	(106)
Uncertain	−.03	−.01	−.02
	(30)	(89)	(24)
No	−.04	−.002	.30
	(142)	(46)	(107)

ended questions, if very specific, can serve as aided recall procedures, open-ended questions with probing by the interviewer can obtain reports of events that the respondent might exclude from a more specific question. The results in Table 3.15 suggest that both telescoping and omission errors are smaller for open-ended than for closed-ended questions. For closed-ended questions, there is a .05 response effect for recall periods of two weeks or less, and a −.08 response effect for periods of 14 weeks or more. For open-ended questions, the range is from −.02 for periods of two weeks or less to −.03 for periods of 14 weeks or more, with an unexplained dip to −.09 for periods of 3–13 weeks.

Aided recall has a much larger effect on open-ended questions, as one would expect, since closed-ended questions are already a form of aided recall. The .46 unit effect is due primarily to a large

Table 3.15 Response Effect in Standard Deviation Units by Closed-ended and Open-ended Questions and Length of Recall Period, Aided Recall, and Availability of Records

Item	Type of Question	
	Closed-ended	Open-ended
Recall Period (Weeks):		
0–2	.05	−.02
	(867)	(597)
3–13	−.02	−.09
	(137)	(34)
14 or more	−.08	−.03
	(159)	(99)
Recall Aided:		
Yes	−.01	.46
	(126)	(166)
No	−.06	−.02
	(615)	(303)
Records Available:		
Yes	−.07	.002
	(395)	(229)
Uncertain	.05	.01
	(144)	(68)
No	.07	.06
	(466)	(354)

study of contraception by Poti, Chakraborti, and Malaker (624); but even with this study omitted the results would be the same, although the magnitude of the effect would be substantially reduced.

The availability of records reduces telescoping on both open-ended and closed-ended questions, but has a slightly larger effect on closed-ended questions. On open-ended questions, there is zero response effect if records are available, and a .06 response effect if they are not. For closed-ended questions, the response effect is −.07 if records are available, +.07 if they are not.

SUMMARY

Memory effects in surveys can be described by a function that is the product of effects due to omissions and telescoping. The model has the advantage of having only three parameters to fit, and appears to describe real-world data reasonably well.

The use of aided recall procedures increases response effect by an average of about .10 units, while the use of records and bounded recall procedures reduces response effect by the same amount. Thus, records and bounded recall procedures are most appropriate for major events where omissions are unimportant and telescoping is the major source of error. Aided recall is most helpful for less important events and for longer recall periods when telescoping effects have become small. Even with aided recall, however, the omission rate may be very high under these conditions, and other methods, such as diaries, should be used.

Among respondent characteristics, only age, as expected, is related to memory. The conditions of the interview that reduce memory error for longer recall periods are the use of face-to-face rather than self-administered questionnaires, questions placed at the end rather than the beginning of the interview, and the use of open-ended rather than closed-ended questions. Finally, the more threatening the study or question, the higher the omission rate will be.

4

The Effect of Respondent and Interviewer Characteristics on Response to Attitudinal Questions

In Chapter 2 we considered a variety of variables relating to the task in which the interviewer and respondent are engaged. In the conceptual framework outlined in Chapter 1, we noted that, in addition to the task variables, there were reasons to expect that certain characteristics of interviewers, either alone or in relation to the characteristics of the respondent, might be sources of variance. The work of Katz (413) and the classic work of Hyman (389) and his associates at NORC alerted users of survey data to such possibilities and demonstrated empirically that such effects exist. Since then many survey organizations have attempted to minimize these response effects by matching interviewer and respondent characteristics whenever possible. Thus, one is told that young people should be interviewed only by other young people, women by women and men by men, and racial and ethnic groups only by interviewers of the same race or ethnicity.

In this chapter, we examine the studies we have analyzed to determine what generalizations can be derived from the substantial number of studies that have investigated the effects of interviewer characteristics on responses. We began our analysis with the presumption that interviewer effects would be substantial. The results presented in this chapter, however, indicate that the picture is much less clear. In many cases, characteristics of respondents and interviewers have no apparent effect on response; in other cases, the response effect depends on the special subject matter of the study;

even when a response effect due to interviewer and respondent characteristics is present, it is small in relation to the size of response effects due to other factors. To some degree, then, the concentration of attention on interviewer and respondent characteristics has been due more to the ready availability of this information rather than to the size of the response effect.

The measure of response effect used in this chapter is the same as that used earlier; that is, it is a standardized score based on deviations from the grand mean of the samples studied. In this chapter we shall be discussing only attitudinal studies, for which there is no outside validating information; thus, observed results are compared to a total mean which sometimes must be constructed from the weighted total of the subsamples. We remind the reader that when dealing with attitudinal data it does not make sense to attach signs to the differences observed since these signs would depend entirely on some arbitrary ordering of answers. For a detailed discussion of the construction of this measure of response effect, the reader is referred to Chapter 1.

Unlike behavioral data, for which a small response bias is clearly more desirable than a large one, it is not self-evident that a smaller response effect will always be more desirable for attitudinal data. While it might be argued that a large response effect indicates that some respondents are really opening up to interviewers (as in the case where blacks are interviewed by black rather than white interviewers on attitudes toward integration), it might also be argued that a large response effect indicates that the respondent is giving the interviewer the answer he thinks the interviewer expects. For example, if one were considering matching the sex of the respondent and the interviewer, it is uncertain whether women interviewed by women would be more "truthful" or less "truthful" than women interviewed by men. Generally, we shall refrain from making value judgments about the size of the response effects due to various combinations of characteristics.

While this measure of response effect does not allow us to decide whether responses are biased or not, it does allow us to compare response effects for, say, race of interviewer and respondent to effects for sex of interviewer and respondent, and to determine which characteristics are more important as sources of variance.

The principal variables considered here are the age, sex, race, and education of the respondent and the age, sex, race, and education of the interviewer. Other interviewer variables, such as social class, party affiliation, and experience, are discussed only briefly because the data are limited. Other interesting variables, such as religion, anxiety, conformity, and hostility, are omitted because of insufficient data.

If there are separate response effects due to respondent characteristics or to interviewer characteristics, then it makes sense to discuss interaction effects only if the observed responses differ significantly from the sum of the separate effects. Therefore, in this chapter we first examine respondent characteristics and interviewer characteristics to see if there are any separate effects before considering the interactions between respondent and interviewer characteristics.

Unfortunately, there is some possibility of confusion about the definition of the word "interaction." As used in this chapter, interaction refers to the social process that occurs during the interview as the interviewer and respondent carry on their respective roles of asking and answering questions. This interaction is not identical to statistical interaction found in the standard analysis of variance. Our data do not permit the standard ANOVA procedures, although they do suggest that such procedures, if they had been employed in the published studies, would have been most valuable.

CHARACTERISTICS OF RESPONDENTS

If the title of this section were interpreted broadly, it would consist of a survey of most of the literature in the behavioral sciences, since the chief factor studied is the relationship between behavior and attitudes, on the one hand, and respondent characteristics on the other. For most surveys, respondent characteristics are the "true" sources of variance that we observe; other sources, such as task variables and interviewer characteristics, are treated as part of the "error" variance. Because we thought that some of the more interesting response effects would show up as an interaction between interviewer and respondent characteristics rather than as a function of interviewer characteristics alone, we coded the respondent characteristics in studies where such information was available in addition to interviewer characteristics.

The sample of studies discussed here, then, is not a representative sample of all studies that have examined variation in response according to respondent characteristics. Rather, the sample is biased to some unknown degree, toward those types of questions and interviewing situations which were of interest to researchers doing studies of interviewer effects on response. In order to set general standards for comparing the size of response effects, we present some basic data on average response effects by the major respondent characteristics.

Certainly one would not expect any major response effects when summarizing over all studies except insofar as the particular sample of studies contains examples of questions on which there are valid differences according to the particular respondent characteristics. The results do show some differences worth discussing (Tables 4.1 and 4.2).

Table 4.1 Response Effect in Standard Deviation Units on Attitudinal Questions by Characteristics of Respondent (Average Response Effect)

Characteristics of Respondent	$\overline{X}$	σ	N
Age:			
Under 21	.23	.32	405
21–24	.25	.28	32
25–34	.20	.16	41
35–44	.17	.22	75
45–54	.07	.07	90
55 and over	.20	.17	28
Sex:			
Male	.15	.21	167
Female	.13	.14	264
Race:			
White	.13	.19	408
Black	.17	.14	264
Years of Education:			
8 or less	.32	.32	30
9–11	.17	.28	91
12	.15	.12	10
13–15	.26	.38	269
16 or more	.14	.26	91

Table 4.2 Mean Response Effect in Standard Deviation Units on Attitudinal Questions by Cross-Classification of Characteristics of Respondent

	Characteristics of Respondent			
	Sex			
	Male		Female	
Age:				
Under 25	.28		.14	
	(57)		(200)	
25–34	[.28]		[.20]	
	(18)		(5)	
35–44	[.07]		[.08]	
	(4)		(10)	
45–54	.05		—	
	(72)			

	Race			
	White		Black	
Age:				
Under 21	.13		.14	
	(222)		(42)	
21–24	.21		[.13]	
	(20)		(8)	
25–34	[.11]		[.17]	
	(10)		(8)	
35–44	[.16]		[.16]	
	(6)		(6)	
45–54	[.18]		[.11]	
	(8)		(8)	
55 and over	[.28]		[.06]	
	(8)		(8)	
Years of Education:				
8 or less	.36		[.24]	
	(22)		(7)	
9–11	.20		.16	
	(35)		(43)	
12	[.14]		—	
	(5)			
13–15	.08		—	
	(123)			
16 or more	.12		—	
	(85)			

	Years of Education			
	8 or Less	9–12	13–15	16 or More
Age:				
Under 25	.32	.15	.25	—
	(26)	(83)	(242)	
25–44	—	[.08]	[.34]	[.42]
		(5)	(14)	(17)
45–54	—	—	—	.05
				(72)

Table 4.1, which gives the distribution of response effects as well as the mean and standard deviation for age, sex, race, and education of respondent, shows that the largest effect among these four variables is for years of education. The largest response effect of .32 is found among those with eight years or less of school. An examination of the cross-classification between education and age in Table 4.2 makes clear, however, that these results refer not to poorly-educated adults but to children who are still in school. Similarly, the next largest response effect of .25 is for those under 25 years of age with 13–15 years of school. This group consists almost entirely of students still in college. Thus, these response effects are probably due to the conditions of the interview rather than to the characteristics of respondents, although there is no way to separate out these effects. It would seem reasonable to hypothesize that adult respondents with less than eight years of school might be more subject to interviewer effects than adults with more education, but there do not appear to be adequate data to test this hypothesis.

The differences in Table 4.1 by sex, race, and age are small and do not indicate any general response effects. The slightly higher response effects for respondents age 24 and under are again a result of their student status. The strange dip in the 45–54 age group is the result of two very atypical surveys—one of physicians and the other of respondents in Chile and Uruguay.

"Don't Know" or "No Opinion" Responses

Our coding scheme for response effects did not include "don't know" or "no opinion" answers, but from other published data we can say something about consistent differences in responses by respondent characteristics (Table 4.3). The data for Table 4.3 are taken from the *Public Opinion Quarterly*'s "The Polls" from 1965–1971. All results taken from this source were treated alike since sample sizes were not given. The number of cases (N) refers to the number of different questions asked (a question was counted several times if it was asked on several different studies).

As one might expect, the percentage of "don't know" responses declines as education increases. Smaller increases in "don't know" responses are also observed with increasing age; some of this is

Table 4.3 Mean Percentage of "Don't Know" and "No Opinion" Answers on Attitudinal Questions by Characteristics of Respondent

Subject	Education				Age				Sex		
	College	High School	Grade School	N	Under 30	30–49	50 or More	N	Male	Female	N
Free speech (34:3)	3.4	3.9	8.9	14	5.0	4.9	6.4	8	3.6	5.4	13
Capital punishment (34:2)	7.8	10.8	11.6	5	7.4	9.2	9.6	5	7.6	11.9	16
Vietnam war (34:1)	6.4	9.4	15.8	32	8.1	11.7	15.3	15	9.2	15.8	16
Middle East (33:4)	19.5	31.1	40.9	15	19.3	21.3	23.7	3	13.0	22.5	4
Racial problems (32:3,4)	10.7	11.9	17.1	15	10.6	12.4	14.9	15	12.4	15.8	8
Civil rights demonstrations (31:4)	5.3	8.3	12.3	6	10.0	9.0	11.0	3	10.5	13.8	4
Birth control (31:2 and 30:3)	8.8	13.2	21.7	15	10.9	14.8	20.7	15	17.5	14.7	17
Morality (30:4)	2.0	5.0	8.5	2	3.0	5.0	7.5	2	9.1	7.7	15
Religion (29:1)	10.2	11.2	10.8	4	4.4	4.4	4.8	5	11.1	8.9	8
Cancer (30:2)	3.0	6.0	11.0	1	30.3	25.0	24.7	3	—	—	—
Anti-Semitism (29:4)	7.9	10.0	16.4	7	6.5	7.0	8.5	2	—	—	—
Women's role (35:2)	8.7	12.3	—	—	—	—	—	—	11.0	11.8	43
All subjects	—	—	18.5	116	9.9	11.6	14.6	76	10.4	12.0	144

Source: *Public Opinion Quarterly;* numbers within parentheses indicate volume and number.

probably a function of the correlation between age and education.

Perhaps the most interesting differences in Table 4.3 are found between males and females (although they are the smallest). Again, some of this may be due to differences in education level, although on some topics, such as birth control, the percentage of "don't know" answers is higher for men. We suggest another explanation that relates to the roles played by men and women. In our society it is more acceptable for a woman to admit that she does not know than it is for a man. This is not a major difference—the average percentage "don't know" is 10.4 per cent for men and 12 per cent for women—but it is found consistently except on questions such as birth control which are far more salient to women.

Combinations of Characteristics

Examining the effect of combinations of respondent characteristics in Table 4.2, we observe differences between male and female respondents under age 35. For respondents under age 25, primarily students, the response effect for males is .28, which is double the effect for females. This difference indicates that male students are more likely to be influenced by the interviewer or the interviewing situation than are female students. The difference between sexes is smaller in the 25–34 year age group (.28 to .20), but is still in the same direction. The difference between sexes disappears for older adults, but this result is based on a very few studies.

Most of the studies providing the data for Table 4.2 refer to topics that have very little saliency to respondents. An extreme example of this is a study by Berg and Rapaport (73) of student answers to an imaginary questionnaire in which nine sets of answers were provided, but no questions (Table 4.4). The instructions given to the subjects were:

This is an experiment to determine how well you can guess the answers to questions when you do not know what the question is. The experimenter will call off the Roman numeral for each question, and he will imagine the correct answer. You are merely to circle one of the alternatives in each case. Just select whatever answer enters your mind without trying to think heavily about it. *Please do not begin until the signal is given. Remember,* circle one alternative only. (p. 476)

Two sets of answer sheets were prepared to reduce order effects. The results, as shown in Table 4.4 (computed from Tables 1 and 2 of the Berg–Rapaport paper) clearly indicate the presence of response effects and some differences by sex. These sex differences are not present on all questions, so it is hard to understand why Berg and Rapaport attribute these differences to the sex of the

Table 4.4 Distribution of Responses to Imaginary Questionnaire

Question Numbers and Answer Categories		Per Cent	
		Male	Female
I.	Heads	52	67
	Tails	48	33
II.	1	14	6
	2	26	28
	3	45	52
	4	15	14
III.	Yes	51	51
	Uncertain	24	23
	No	25	26
IV.	X	57	63
	Y	43	37
V.	Very satisfied	11	14
	Satisfied	52	51
	Dissatisfied	25	25
	Very dissatisfied	12	10
VI.	First	40	40
	Second	30	37
	Third	30	23
VII.	True	60	70
	False	40	30
VIII.	A	21	18
	B	40	36
	C	24	31
	D	15	15
IX.	Agree	44	43
	Indifferent	27	34
	Disagree	29	23
	N	(188)	(186)

Source: Berg and Rapaport (73). Reprinted by permission of The Journal Press.

examiner rather than to the sex of respondent. In any event, there were no controls for examiner. For eight of the nine questions, the female respondents were farther from a random response than were the males. The reasons for these differences are unclear.

No other combination of respondent characteristics is meaningfully related to response effect. The difference in Table 4.2 between whites and blacks with eight years of education or less is due to the fact that the white sample consists only of studies of elementary school children while the black sample consists of some studies of adults as well as a study of Maori children in New Zealand.

Respondent Characteristics and Conditions of the Interview

Some of the task variables discussed in Chapter 2 interact with respondent characteristics in causing response effect. These are: the threat of the question, the method of administration, the structure of the question, the length of the question, and the social desirability of the answer. Although the case bases become small in some of the tables, the results at least suggest some areas that need further research.

Threat of question.—Threatening questions deal with attitudes toward such behavior as sex, contraception, and drinking. Among respondent characteristics, only sex appears to be related to the threat of the question. Table 4.5 indicates that the response effect is twice as high for women as for men if the question is threatening (.18 to .09) while the reverse is the case for non-threatening ques-

Table 4.5 Mean Response Effect in Standard Deviation Units on Attitudinal Questions by Threat of Question and Sex of Respondent

Sex of Respondent	Threat of Question		
	Threatening	Possibly Threatening	Non-Threatening
Male	[.09] (9)	.16 (83)	.15 (75)
Female	.18 (26)	.15 (101)	.11 (137)

tions (.11 to .15). It may well be that women find questions on sex attitudes more salient as well as more threatening than men do. An example of this type of question is a question from the F-scale used by Hyman (389) in a study of interviewer effects: "prison is too good for sex criminals; they should be publicly whipped or worse"; he found that women were more likely than men to agree to the question.

Another example, reported by Benney, Riesman, and Star (68), is from a study of attitudes toward mental health. In this study, the respondent was asked to consider the behavior of a young woman named Betty Smith who stays in her room and shuns boys and parties, and to speculate about why she does this. A tabulation was made of responses that included sexual interpretations. The results indicate that women under age 40 were somewhat more likely to make sexual interpretations than women over age 40, although the differences were not large; 12 per cent of the women under age 40 made sex references as compared to 9 per cent of the rest of the sample.

Method of administration.—As has been shown in Chapter 2, differences between face-to-face and self-administered interviews are often larger than differences due to respondent or interviewer characteristics. Here we consider whether there are any interactions between characteristics of respondents and method of administration. For interviews on attitudes administered face-to-face, there are no significant differences associated with respondent characteristics. For self-administered forms, however, there are major differences by sex and race, as shown in Table 4.6. The response effect is .43 for males on self-administered forms compared to .24 for females. For whites, the response effect is .47 compared to .17 for blacks. We have no studies of attitudes that employ both face-to-face and self-administered forms and that also provide race and sex information. Thus, response effects by method lack comparability. It seems likely, however, that white respondents and males, both black and white, find self-administered questionnaires less inhibiting than face-to-face interviews, particularly when a socially desirable answer is possible.

Structure of questions.—It was seen in Chapter 2 that closed-ended questions that explicitly state alternatives have a higher response effect than open-ended questions that allow the respondent to shape his own answer. Are there characteristics of respondents that interact with closed-ended questions? Table 4.7 suggests that effects due to closed-ended questions are high for students, particularly those in elementary school, and that women are slightly more likely to be influenced by question structure than are men.

Some of the sex differences may be due to different interpretations of the question, as pointed out in a study by Crutchfield and Gordon (199). They used the following closed-ended question during World War II:

After the war, would you like to see many changes or reforms made in the United States, or would you rather have the country remain pretty much the way it was before the war?

After asking the question they probed extensively to learn how the question was being interpreted. The intended frame of reference for the question was domestic changes or reforms; about one-third of the respondents interpreted the question with a different frame of reference. Women tended more frequently than men to answer in terms of immediate personal conditions, immediate war conditions,

Table 4.6 Mean Response Effect in Standard Deviation Units on Attitudinal Questions by Method of Administration and Sex and Race of Respondent

Characteristics of Respondent	Method of Administration	
	Face-to-Face	Self-Administered
Sex:		
Male	.12	.43
	(100)	(17)
Female	.13	.24
	(177)	(21)
Race:		
White	.12	[.47]
	(271)	(19)
Black	.15	[.17]
	(215)	(12)

and a desirable state of affairs in general, while men answered mainly in terms of the intended reference.

Length and difficulty of question.—As we pointed out in Chapter 2, the length of the question may influence response in two ways: (1) the longer the question, the more difficult it may be for the respondent to understand it; and (2) the longer the question, the greater the interviewer influence and the longer the respondent answer will be. The results in Table 4.8 indicate that two respondent characteristics, race and education, interact with question length. The sharpest effect is noted for race, where there are no differences between white and black respondents if there are 12 words or less in the question and a difference of only .03 units if there are 17 words or less, but where there is a much larger effect for blacks than whites (.21 to .08) if there are 28 words or more. Similarly, for education, the response effect is largest for respondents with a high school education or less if the number of words in the question is 18 or more.

These results may illustrate what Lenski and Leggett (471) call

Table 4.7 Mean Response Effect in Standard Deviation Units on Attitudinal Questions by Structure of Question and Sex and Education of Respondent

Characteristics of Respondent	Structure of Question	
	Closed-ended	Open-ended
Sex:		
Male	.09	.17
	(101)	(39)
Female	.13	.12
	(118)	(31)
Years of Education:		
8 or less	[.51]	[.08]
	(17)	(13)
9–12	.17	[.02]
	(94)	(4)
13–15	.24	[.18]
	(132)	(91)
16 or more	.14	[.08]
	(87)	(4)

respondent deference and what others have called acquiescence or conformity; that is, a tendency to answer "yes" to a question, particularly when the question is ambiguous and difficult to understand. The example Lenski and Leggett give is based on two questions measuring anomie:

1. It's hardly fair to bring children into the world, the way things look for the future.
2. Children born today have a wonderful future to look forward to.

(Note that these questions both have fewer than 18 words, but are highly ambiguous.) Respondent deference has occurred if the respondent answers "yes" to both of these statements. Lenski and Leggett (471) found that race and education were the chief characteristics related to deference, with race being the more important of the two. The results are given in Table 4.9 (based on Lenski and Leggett's Table 1). In this case, the interviewers were virtually all middle-class whites, so there is no way of knowing if the situation would have been different if black interviewers had been used.

Another example of deference is reported by Hare (352), based

Table 4.8 Mean Response Effect in Standard Deviation Units on Attitudinal Questions by Length of Question and Race and Education of Respondent

Characteristics of Respondent	Number of Words in Question			
	12 or Under	13–17	18–27	28 or More
Race:				
White	.13	.11	.10	.08
	(100)	(57)	(96)	(74)
Black	.13	.14	.20	.21
	(89)	(36)	(50)	(48)
Years of Education:				
12 or less	.14	[.10]	[.37]	–
	(69)	(8)	(12)	
13–15	.08	.08	.09	–
	(43)	(45)	(41)	
16 or more	–	–	.05	.04
			(26)	(46)

on two experiments with white and black mothers and white male interviewers, who were usually identified as "doctors." Black women were much higher on deference in both experiments and were more likely to give inconsistent "yes-yes" responses when items were reversed.

Possibility of a socially desirable answer.—Among attitudinal questions, the strongest possibility of a socially desirable answer is found in questions dealing with racial, religious, and ethnic attitudes. Many social critics have suggested that the polls' showing of a decline in prejudice toward minorities does not reflect any real change in underlying feelings, but reflects instead an awareness that prejudiced answers are no longer socially acceptable. Another topic where the respondent may feel that some answers are more acceptable than others is attitudes toward sexual behavior, including premarital sex and birth control, although here the socially acceptable answer is by no means as obvious.

Thus, it is not surprising to find that sex and race of respondents interact with social desirability (Table 4.10). If there is a strong possibility of a socially desirable answer, the response effect is almost twice as large for women as for men (.18 to .10). If there

Table 4.9 Percentage of Respondents Giving Mutually Contradictory Answers to Questions Regarding Children's Future, by Extent of Formal Education and Race

Extent of Formal Education	Whites		Negroes	
	Percentage giving mutually contradictory answers	No.	Percentage giving mutually contradictory answers	No.
Some college education	2	105	14	14
High school graduates	3	182	17	18
High school attenders, nongraduates	7	123	12	34
Eight grades or less formal education	9	111	32	37
All respondents	5	521	20	103

Source: Lenski and Leggett (471). Reprinted from "Caste, Class and Deference in the Research Interview," *American Journal of Sociology* 65 (1960), 464, by permission of the University of Chicago Press. Copyright 1960 by the University of Chicago.

is little possibility of a socially desirable answer, the response effect is larger for men than for women (.18 to .13). If there is a strong possibility of a socially desirable answer, the response effect is larger for whites than for blacks (.22 to .15), while the reverse is the case if there is little possibility of a socially desirable answer (.12 to .16).

Summary.—Among respondent characteristics, none is very important when examined separately. Some of the interactions between respondent characteristics and interview conditions are interesting, although not large in comparison to some effects of the interviewing situation and of memory errors. The largest effects are noted for male students in either elementary school or college, but these are probably as much a function of the interviewing situation as of the characteristics of the respondent. Elementary school students are particularly influenced by closed-ended questions and by questions with many words.

Sex differences interact with the threat of the question, the method of administration, the structure of the questions, and the possibility of a socially desirable answer. Response effects are larger for females on threatening, closed-ended questions where a socially

Table 4.10 Mean Response Effect in Standard Deviation Units on Attitudinal Questions by Possibility of a Socially Desirable Answer and Sex and Race of Respondent

Characteristics of Respondent	Possibility of Socially Desirable Answer		
	Strong Possibility	Some Possibility	Little or No Possibility
Sex:			
Male	[.10]	.08	.18
	(14)	(40)	(111)
Female	.18	.11	.13
	(28)	(53)	(181)
Race:			
White	.22	.10	.12
	(50)	(76)	(274)
Black	.15	.22	.16
	(24)	(20)	(209)

desirable answer is possible. Response effects are larger for males on self-administered than on face-to-face questionnaires.

Response effects are larger for black than for white respondents on face-to-face interviews and where the question is more difficult. They are larger for white respondents where a socially desirable answer is possible. Several studies indicate that deference is higher for black than for white respondents.

There are consistent patterns in the fractions of respondents giving "don't know" or "no opinion" answers. The likelihood of a "don't know" answer is higher for older people and for those with less education, and is also slightly higher for women than for men except on topics such as birth control and morality.

CHARACTERISTICS OF INTERVIEWERS

Relatively less information is available for interviewers than for respondents, and the results that are available tend to be more specialized. For example, there is so little information on interviewers over age 45 that hardly anything can be said about them. Similarly, there is no information on interviewers with less than some college education because, until recently, most interviewers were white, middle-aged, middle-class women with some college education. Males, blacks, and lower-class interviewers have been used in special situations where there was a desire to match characteristics or to test the effect of differences.

A large number of studies report results for interviewers who are college students, and as seen in Table 4.11, these interviewers cause much larger response effects than do other interviewers. For interviewers under age 25 (mainly college students), the average response effect is about .35 compared to about .13 for other interviewers. The same result is observed if one looks at interviewers' years of education, where most of the interviewers with 13–15 years of school are currently college undergraduates.

As with respondents, where the largest response effects were also noted in the student group, much of this may be a function of the interviewing situation and the type of questions asked, as discussed in Chapter 2. Note that most of the respondents interviewed by undergraduate interviewers are themselves undergraduates. Another factor may be the inexperience of the interviewers. As noted in Table 4.11, the response effect is twice as high for inexperienced as for experienced interviewers, and many of the inexperienced interviewers are college students.

Table 4.11 also indicates that higher social status interviewers induce a larger response effect than do lower social status interviewers. One thinks immediately of the Katz (413) study, but we defer the discussion of that study to the next section. In order for interviewer status to affect the respondent, the respondent must be aware of the interviewer's status. While in surveys of the general public this may be difficult or impossible for the respondent to determine, it is highly pertinent in a school situation where respondents and interviewers are students and status is generally known.

Table 4.11 Response Effect in Standard Deviation Units on Attitudinal Questions by Characteristics of Interviewer (Average Response Effect)

Characteristics of Interviewer	$\overline{X}$	σ	N
Age:			
Under 21	.32	.38	118
21–24	.38	.46	85
25–34	.13	.15	51
35–44	.13	.16	86
Sex:			
Male	.18	.19	299
Female	.15	.22	102
Race:			
White	.14	.13	429
Black	.14	.12	183
Years of Education:			
13–15	.28	.36	150
16	.15	.18	222
17 or more	.17	.31	225
Social Status:			
Higher	.19	.32	53
Lower	.09	.06	32
Experience:			
Experienced	.09	.11	376
Not experienced	.16	.15	94

An example of the effect of interviewer status is given by Das (203). He used 48 male Indian students and attempted to measure the relation between suggestibility as measured by the amount of body sway and the status of experimenter. The four levels of prestige were I: Head, Psychology Department, II: Laboratory Assistant, III: Attendant of the Department, and IV: Unidentified. Body sway increased with prestige of experimenter from 1.66 inches for the unidentified experimenter to 2.21 inches for the Head of the Psychology Department.

The other way the social status of an interviewer can influence response is in the degree to which it affects how the interviewer perceives the respondent's answers. Particularly on issues related to social class, the interviewer could unconsciously distort respondent views to bring them into closer agreement with her own. To our knowledge, this conjecture has never been tested, although it would be easy to do so using tape recorded interviews as described by Hyman (389).

The interviewer's sex and race have no general effect on response nor do any other combinations of interviewer characteristics. There is only fragmentary information on interviewer characteristics related to respondent "don't know" answers. In general, one would expect the same relationships as were seen between respondent characteristics and "don't know" answers. Hanson and Marks (348) indicate that on questions similar to those used by the Census Bureau, the percentage of "don't know" answers ranges from 1 to 2 per cent for interviewers under age 50, but rises to about 4 per cent for interviewers over age 50. They also find the expected inverse correlations between the percentage of "don't know" responses and scores on the Enumerator Selection Aid test, which includes items on reading comprehension, map reading, and the ability to follow instructions similar to those used by the Census.

The "don't know" rate was 14.1 per cent for the lower-class inexperienced interviewers in the Katz (413) study, and only 10.5 per cent for the upper-class experienced interviewers. While information on sex differences of interviewers is fragmentary, what there is suggests a higher "don't know" rate for female than for male interviewers. For ten questions, the "don't know" rate is 23.5 per cent for male interviewers and 24.8 per cent for females.

Interviewer Characteristics and Conditions
   of the Interview

As with respondent characteristics, there are some interviewer characteristics that interact with the conditions of the interview, such as the method of administration, the structure of the questions, the possibility of a socially desirable answer, and the position of the question in the questionnaire. In studies where interviewer and respondent characteristics are matched, it is not possible to distinguish between respondent characteristics, interviewer characteristics, and interactions; thus, in this section we will treat chiefly those effects that have not been implied earlier.

Method of administration.—As seen in Table 4.12, there is a steady decline in response effect on face-to-face interviews as the

Table 4.12 Mean Response Effect in Standard Deviation Units on Attitudinal Questions by Method of Administration and Characteristics of Interviewer

Characteristics of Interviewer	Method of Administration	
	Face-to-Face	Self-Administered
Age:		
Under 21	.28	[.14]
	(96)	(16)
21–24	.18	[.43]
	(67)	(8)
25–34	.12	–
	(49)	
35–44	.08	[.41]
	(70)	(14)
Sex:		
Male	.17	.37
	(205)	(26)
Female	.10	[.38]
	(78)	(4)
Years of Education:		
13–15	.24	[.07]
	(128)	(4)
16	.13	.15
	(153)	(65)
17 or more	.15	.39
	(136)	(21)

age of the interviewer increases. A different pattern emerges for self-administered questionnaires, where the education of the interviewer appears to be the more important factor. There is a sharp rise in response effects as the education of the interviewer increases. A plausible explanation, similar to that for the body sway example given above, is this: most self-administered questionnaires coded in this study were administered in school settings where the status of the experimenter depends primarily on his level of education. The sex of the interviewer appears to be irrelevant for self-administered forms, but male interviewers elicit a slightly larger response effect than do female interviewers in face-to-face interviews.

Structure of questions.—Although closed-ended questions have a greater influence on respondents than do open-ended questions, they reduce the possibility of interviewer effects by providing greater structure. It is not surprising, therefore, that for closed-ended questions there are no significant differences by interviewer characteristics (Table 4.13). Open-ended questions are less struc-

Table 4.13 Mean Response Effect in Standard Deviation Units on Attitudinal Questions by Structure of Question and Characteristics of Interviewer

Characteristics of Interviewer	Structure of Question	
	Closed-ended	Open-ended
Sex:		
Male	.17	.14
	(165)	(117)
Female	.14	[.26]
	(80)	(4)
Race:		
White	.14	.13
	(260)	(142)
Black	.15	[.08]
	(150)	(6)
Years of Education:		
13–15	.26	.27
	(68)	(60)
16	.14	.13
	(155)	(55)
17 or more	.18	.10
	(127)	(84)

tured and allow greater interviewer variability in probing, in providing other subtle cues, and in recording the answer. A study by Clark (169) measured the effect of the sex of the interviewer on responses in terms of sexual imagery by male students on a Thematic Apperception Test. Half of the tests were administered by a male experimenter and the other half by a female experimenter who was dressed attractively and wore perfume. All testing was done at night in an office to make the female's presence less formal; further, the female experimenter had trouble with the projector on the first TAT picture in order to enable her to request the males to come to her assistance. As a result, 70 per cent of the males interviewed by the female experimenter were below average in their mention of sex-related themes compared to 31 per cent of those interviewed by the male experimenter. When only themes related to sex-related guilt were included, 83 per cent of those interviewed by the female were below the average compared to only 45 per cent of those interviewed by the male. In this case, it is clear that the sex of the experimenter is related to the topic.

The results presented in Table 4.13 suggest that the response effect obtained by white interviewers is higher than that obtained by blacks on open-ended questions, although here again the topics are mainly racial attitudes and the number of studies is small. The largest response effect on open-ended questions is found for interviewers with 13 to 15 years of school, primarily undergraduate students. The presence of this effect has already been mentioned several times, but it is interesting to note that the effect seems stronger and more direct for open-ended than for closed-ended questions.

Possibility of a socially desirable answer.—The sex and the race of the interviewer do interact with the possibility of a socially desirable answer (Table 4.14). The response effect is slightly larger for white than for black interviewers if there is a strong possibility of a socially desirable answer, while the reverse is true if there is little possibility of a socially desirable answer. This agrees with the findings discussed earlier for respondents.

The results for interviewers by sex are the opposite of those found for respondents. If there is a strong possibility of a socially desirable answer, the response effect is more than twice as large for male as for female interviewers (.23 to .10). If there is little possibility of a socially desirable answer, there is no significant difference between male and female interviewers. As an example, in the Benney, Riesman, and Star (68) mental health study discussed above, 59 per cent of respondents interviewed by female interviewers indicated that they thought that overindulgence in sex led to mental disturbances, compared to 50 per cent of respondents interviewed by male interviewers.

Position of question in questionnaire.—If the interviewer is successful, rapport between respondent and interviewer should build steadily during the interview. This increasing rapport could cause larger response effects late in the interview. Thus, for this variable, considering respondent and interviewer characteristics jointly yields more interesting results. The interactions between position in the questionnaire and characteristics of respondents and interviewers are given in Table 4.15. For black respondents and interviewers, response effects increase as the interview progresses, indicating that rapport is increasing. For white respondents and interviewers, the position of the question in the questionnaire makes no difference.

For students and others with 12 years of school or less, response effects increase as the interview progresses; for respondents with

Table 4.14 Mean Response Effect in Standard Deviation Units on Attitudinal Questions by Possibility of a Socially Desirable Answer and Sex and Race of Interviewer

Characteristics of Interviewer	Possibility of Socially Desirable Answer		
	Strong Possibility	Some Possibility	Little or No Possibility
Sex:			
Male	.23	.15	.17
	(28)	(56)	(213)
Female	[.10]	[.12]	.16
	(6)	(15)	(79)
Race:			
White	.18	.13	.13
	(40)	(47)	(330)
Black	[.14]	[.21]	.14
	(18)	(7)	(154)

13–15 years of school, they decrease, but no effects are observed for respondents with 16 or more years of school.

Opposite trends are again observed by sex of respondent and interviewer. For female interviewers there is a sharp increase in response effect as the interview progresses, while for female respondents there is a slight decline. For male respondents there is a small increase in response effect as the interview progresses,

Table 4.15 Mean Response Effect in Standard Deviation Units on Attitudinal Questions by Position of Question and Characteristics of Respondent and Interviewer

Characteristics of Respondent and Interviewer	Position of Question in Questionnaire		
	Early	Middle	Late
Sex of Respondent:			
Male	.04	–	[.09]
	(69)		(5)
Female	.11	.07	.06
	(41)	(40)	(41)
Race of Respondent:			
White	.07	.09	.08
	(118)	(50)	(56)
Black	[.11]	.20	.24
	(10)	(20)	(44)
Years of Education of Respondent:			
12 or under	.10	.15	.18
	(23)	(21)	(20)
13–15	.11	.07	.06
	(41)	(40)	(40)
16 or more	.04	–	[.08]
	(68)		(6)
Sex of Interviewer:			
Male	.11	.08	.12
	(40)	(42)	(62)
Female	[.05]	[.17]	[.27]
	(4)	(18)	(16)
Race of Interviewer:			
White	.11	.11	.14
	(50)	(55)	(67)
Black	[.10]	[.16]	.20
	(10)	(15)	(27)

but there are no trends for male interviewers. Again we must consider interviewer and respondent characteristics jointly.

Summary.—Because interviewers, until recently, have possessed a limited range of characteristics (being generally white, middle-aged, middle-class women with some college), only one factor seems highly related to response effect. Inexperienced, undergraduate college student interviewers elicit much higher response effects than do older experienced interviewers employed by survey organizations. These effects are larger on face-to-face than on self-administered interviews. The status of the interviewer is important primarily in school situations where it is easily recognized.

The sex of the interviewer influences response effects in several ways, but primarily when the topic of the study is highly sex-related. Female interviewers elicit a larger effect on responses than do male interviewers if the question is open-ended and occurs late in the interview; males elicit a larger effect than females if there is a strong possibility of a socially desirable answer.

On open-ended questions, white interviewers elicit a larger response effect than black interviewers, but there is no difference by race for closed-ended questions. Response effects for white interviewers are larger if there is a strong possibility of a socially desirable answer than if there is little possibility; for black interviewers it makes no significant difference whether there is a strong possibility or little possibility of a socially desirable answer.

The "don't know" rate declines as the education and experience of an interviewer increases. Limited data suggest also that the "don't know" rate is slightly higher for female than for male interviewers and for the small number of interviewers above age 50.

INTERACTIONS BETWEEN RESPONDENT AND INTERVIEWER CHARACTERISTICS

We have examined the effects on response of respondent characteristics and of interviewer characteristics; we now turn to a consideration of the response effect interactions between the age, sex, race, education, and social status of respondents and the age, sex, race, education, and social status of interviewers. Most of the topics of the studies in our sample are related directly to the characteristics; thus, for example, studies reporting on sex interactions have typically dealt with sexual questions, studies reporting on age inter-actions have dealt with generation differences, and studies on race interactions have dealt with attitudes toward racial issues. When the respondent-interviewer demographic characteristics are not related to the subject of the study, either there are no data or the response effects are negligible.

We shall attempt to differentiate between interaction effects and effects that are the sums of the separate main effects due to respondent and interviewer characteristics. It may be helpful to consider interviewers as constrained respondents; that is, one would usually expect interviewer characteristic effects to be in the same direction as respondent characteristic effects, but smaller. As an example, black respondents generally have less favorable attitudes toward the police than do white respondents. Similarly, black inter-viewers have less favorable attitudes than do white interviewers. We would expect, however, a larger difference between black and white respondents than between black and white interviewers, since the structure of the questionnaire and the interviewing situation limit the direct interviewer effect.

We say that an interaction has occurred when this situation is reversed, and effects due to interviewer characteristics are not in the same direction as those for respondent characteristics and are larger. An example of this is the result on the question mentioned earlier, "prison is too good for sex criminals . . ." (Hyman, 389), where a higher percentage of female respondents agree with the statement, but where a higher percentage of respondents inter-viewed by male interviewers also agree with the statement.

Other interaction effects are possible. If one had an independent estimate of the ratio of interviewer to respondent effects, it would be possible to predict the expected joint effect due to the sums of the main effects. Significant deviations from the expected effect, then, would also be interactions. It should be obvious from the examples that the distinction between interactions and the sum of main effects is possible only on a study-by-study basis and not over summary response effects.

As far as we know, there are no studies that have been designed with sufficient controls to separate clearly the effects of the social interactions between interviewer and respondent from the other effects. For example, to separate these effects in a study of the response effects of the racial characteristics of respondents and interviewers, one would want to compare responses of respondents to interviewers of the same race, different race, and on self-administered forms.

Social Class Differences: The Katz Results

The earliest study on the joint effects of interviewer and respondent characteristics was by Katz (413). He measured the effect of the social status of the interviewer by comparing a group of nine Gallup interviewers to a group of eleven working-class interviewers. The procedure involved rather loose quota sampling, so that some of the differences may have been due to sample execution rather than to the joint characteristics of the interviewers and respondents. Thus, middle-class interviewers may have had a greater tendency to reach and interview middle-class respondents, while working-class interviewers may have interviewed working-class respondents. There were also differences in the levels of interviewing experience and in other variables between the two groups of interviewers.

On questions relating to labor issues, Katz found, not surprisingly, that working-class interviewers obtained more pro-labor responses, particularly from union members, than did middle-class interviewers. These results are presented in Table 4.16 (based on Table 1 in the Katz paper, but revised to omit the "no opinion" and "don't know" answers and to split out union and non-union respondents). On war issues (the study was conducted in Pittsburgh during March, 1941), the Gallup interviewers obtained slightly more interventionist responses than did working-class interviewers, a finding which corresponds with the known relation between social class and interventionist attitudes prior to World War II. On questions relating to government ownership of electric companies, steel mills, and banks, the differences were slight between the two groups of interviewers.

There was an average difference of 12 percentage points between Gallup and working-class interviewers when interviewing union respondents on labor questions. The differences between the interviewers when interviewing non-union respondents on labor questions averaged 7 percentage points. This is best seen for the question asking whether the respondent favored the closed shop. While there was only a 2 percentage point difference

Table 4.16 Comparison of Gallup and Working-Class Interviewers on Labor Questions, Government Ownership, and War Issues by Percentage

Question	Union Respondent		Non-Union Respondent	
	Gallup Interviewer	Working-Class Interviewer	Gallup Interviewer	Working-Class Interviewer
Labor:				
Favor law against strikes in war industries	68	54	77	67
Employers will play fair if a strike law	64	59	75	68
Favor use of force by strikers	50	62	44	34
Favor closed shop	67	80	36	38
Favor law against sit-down strikes	67	53	75	64
Labor will do better job running defense	46	61	29	33
Government Ownership:				
The government should own—				
electric companies	49	56	46	46
steel mills	32	43	33	30
banks	53	48	59	36
War Issues:				
Foreign organizations should be outlawed	95	86	95	76
German workers worse off under Hitler	83	83	84	72
England will win war	83	77	83	69
U.S. should stop helping England and try to stay out	24	30	29	32
U.S. should send England munitions	82	72	81	76
U.S. should send England warships	45	34	41	40
U.S. should send England American pilots	20	17	18	17
U.S. should declare war	9	5	7	3

Source: Katz (413).

between Gallup and working-class interviewers for non-union respondents, 80 per cent of union respondents interviewed by working-class interviewers favored the closed shop compared to 67 per cent of union respondents interviewed by Gallup interviewers. We remind the reader that it is not possible to tell from these results which group of interviewers obtained the "true" results. It is possible that pro-union attitudes were either overreported to working-class interviewers or underreported to Gallup interviewers, or that some of both was occurring.

The joint effects found in this study can best be explained as the sum of main effects rather than as interactions between interviewer and respondent characteristics. Generally, the ratio of interviewer to respondent effects is about .2, and the deviations from this average on individual questions are small enough to be attributed to chance rather than to interactions.

Joint effects are smaller and approach zero for questions dealing with government ownership and war issues. The average difference between Gallup and wage-earner interviewers was 7 percentage points when interviewing union respondents and 8 percentage points when interviewing non-union respondents.

To summarize, the Katz study demonstrated response effects due to the interviewer's social class, and joint response effects on labor questions due to the social class of the interviewer and the respondent. Surprisingly, we have not been able to uncover other studies conducted since then that consider the effects on attitudes of the social class of the interviewer and the respondent.

The interviewing procedures used in the Katz study are certainly far different from the typical survey today. In that study, male interviewers, half of whom were under age 25, interviewed people walking down the block. Today, most interviewers are older women and the interviewing is much more carefully controlled. In fact, most survey organizations train their interviewers to minimize social class differences by dressing appropriately for the area where the interviewing occurs, and by structuring the questionnaire. Nonetheless, since response effects are also a function of what the interviewer hears and records, we would expect that social class response effects would still be found if a careful study were to be conducted. To avoid still further confounding with race, such a study might be conducted in Appalachia or with Appalachian white migrants.

Age Interactions

The data on response effect interactions between age of interviewer and respondent are available mainly for respondents under age 21 (that is, students). As seen in Table 4.17 and as we have noted earlier, the highest response effects are found when both the interviewer and respondent are under age 25. Some of this may also be due to the conditions of the interview. Given the limited data, however, one is hard-pressed to either prove or disprove an interaction effect due to respondent and interviewer age. It would be useful to have studies where interviewers are under age 25 and respondents are older and retired, and other studies where interviewers are over age 65 while respondents' ages vary.

Perhaps the best of the limited studies on age interactions is by Ehrlich and Riesman (245). The limitations of this study include the fact that the respondents were all high school girls and that the interviewing was done in the schools. The results given in Table 4.18 indicate that younger interviewers (age 40 and under) tended to obtain slightly more peer-oriented and slightly fewer adult-oriented answers, while the oldest interviewers (over age 53) were perceived as authority figures. These results were only true for girls 16 and over. Younger girls' responses did not vary consistently by interviewer age.

In this study, the answers to questions were categorized in terms of whether or not the adult's expectation or demand was flatly rejected. Four of the questions were as follows:

1. "Now, I'm going to show you some pictures about a girl, her parents, and her friends. In each picture someone has just said something, and another person's going to answer. What do you think the answer would be?"
Picture 1. (A girl is going out the door, parents are sitting on couch. Girl says: "I'm going over to Mary's house—all the girls are going to be there!")
Ask: What would the parents say?
Picture 2. (Same as Picture 1. Parents say: "All right, but don't just go down to the drugstore to see if boys are hanging around!")

Table 4.17 Mean Response Effect in Standard Deviation Units on Attitudinal Questions by Characteristics of Respondent and Interviewer

Characteristics of Respondent	Characteristics of Interviewer			
	Age			
Age:	Under 21	21–24	25–34	35–44
Under 21	.30 (116)	.66 (24)	.23 (20)	.14 (76)
21–34	—	—	[.07] (5)	—
35–44	—	—	[.08] (16)	—

	Sex	
Sex:	Male	Female
Male	.28 (51)	[.12] (12)
Female	.14 (184)	.10 (28)

	Race	
Race:	White	Black
White	.10 (221)	.13 (49)
Black	.19 (112)	.14 (128)

	Years of Education		
Years of Education:	13–15	16	17 or More
12 or less	.13 (30)	.17 (30)	[.08] (14)
13–15	.47 (60)	[.72] (6)	—
16 or more	—	[.08] (4)	—

Table 4.18   Mean Percentage of Responses to Questions from Ehrlich and Riesman Study by Age of Respondent and Interviewer

Age of Interviewer	Age of Respondent		
	13 or Less	14–15	16+
	Question 1: Mean Percentage of "Girl Goes" Responses		
24–40	18 (31)[a]	17 (34)	27 (26)
41–52	10 (46)	19 (49)	24 (47)
53+	10 (23)	23 (23)	10 (25)
	Question 2: Mean Percentage of "Would Not Tell Parents Later" Responses		
24–40	40 (30)	39 (34)	36 (26)
41–52	44 (46)	28 (49)	29 (48)
53+	43 (23)	42 (23)	30 (25)
	Question 3: Mean Percentage of "Wouldn't Return" Responses		
24–40	11 (29)	21 (33)	36 (25)
41–52	8 (44)	14 (47)	25 (43)
53+	12 (22)	14 (22)	19 (24)
	Question 4: Mean Percentage of "Not See," "Not Tell," or "Nothing" Responses		
24–40	8 (30)	19 (33)	24 (24)
41–52	11 (44)	16 (44)	23 (46)
53+	8 (23)	17 (22)	13 (23)

Source: Ehrlich and Riesman (245). Reprinted from "Age and Authority in the Interview," *Public Opinion Quarterly* **25** (1961), 44, by permission of *Public Opinion Quarterly*.

[a] Figures in parentheses are the number of interviewers in each cell. The number of interviewers in a given cell varies slightly from question to question because questions 3 and 4 were asked only of a random two-thirds of the sample.

Ask: What would the girl say?
Picture 3. (The girls are at Mary's. From the group comes the caption: "Let's go down to the drugstore—maybe the fellows are there!")

Of this sequence, only picture 3 is used in the re-analysis, for which the question was "What would the girl say now?"

2. "If the girl decided to go along with her friends to meet the boys, do you think she'd tell her parents about it later?"

3. "A girl has a very good job away from home. She gets a letter from her mother saying her mother is lonely and asking the girl to move back home. What does she say?"

4. "While she is giving your class a test, your teacher is called out of the room. She asks you to take over the class and to make sure that nobody cheats. You see a close friend of yours copying from someone else's paper. What would you do?"

On these four questions, there was an average difference of 13 percentage points between the youngest and oldest interviewer groups. It seems likely, however, that there were no differences on most of the other questions in the questionnaire, although these are not reported. The interactions by age, then, are highly specific to age-related issues, to girls in a narrow age band (16–18), and to a particular interviewing situation (in the classroom) where adult authority might be expected to be more salient.

Sex Interactions

Since sex is a dichotomous variable, one would expect that there would be ample results in all four cells to measure response effect interactions, but the data are still too limited to test this expectation. The sex of the interviewer is given only when a study specifically intends to measure sex effects or when the interviewers are all the same sex. Most of the studies have examined the effects on women's responses to male and female interviewers on sexually related topics. But, as seen in Table 4.17, the largest response effect (.28) is found when both respondents and interviewers are male, and only small differences are found between females interviewed by male and by female interviewers. Again, some of these results may be due to the conditions of the interview, particularly among male students interviewed in school.

These results are illustrated by the Benney, Riesman, and Star (68) study mentioned above. Table 4.19 (their Table 4 summarized) gives the percentage of sex responses to the "Betty Smith" question by sex of interviewer and respondent. Although the percentage of sex responses is highest for males interviewed by males, this figure differs by only about 4 percentage points (13 to 9 per cent) from that for females interviewed by males.

Hyman (389) reports the results of an Audience Research Institute study on preferences for movies. Preferences were determined by responses to cards on which the story was summarized in about 50 words. The results given in Table 4.20 indicate that there was an average difference of 11 percentage points between men and women when respondents were interviewed by members of their own sex, and an average difference of 8 percentage points when respondents were interviewed by members of the opposite sex. This difference of 3 percentage points is not an interaction effect as in the example above, but is derived as the sum of the separate main effects due to the sex of the interviewer and the sex of the respondent.

Race Interactions

In recent years, greater emphasis has been placed on matching interviewers and respondents by race than on any other type of

Table 4.19 Percentage of Sex Responses to "Betty Smith" Question by Sex of Respondent and Interviewer

Interviewer	Respondent	
	Male	Female
Male	13 (273)	9 (259)
Female	9 (1,433)	9 (1,504)

Source: Benney, Riesman, and Star (68), "Age and Sex in the Interview," *American Journal of Sociology* **62** (1956), 150. Permission for use granted by the University of Chicago Press. Copyright 1956 by the University of Chicago.

matching. The general results shown in Table 4.17, which reflect a wide range of studies, do not show very large differences. The largest response effect is for blacks interviewed by whites, and this is related to the studies of deference or conformity mentioned earlier.

Several of these studies were with black children in classrooms and used unstructured materials such as pictures and dolls (Vaughan, 843; Trent, 814). These studies indicate some shift toward the selection of figures similar in color to that of the interviewer, although the differences are not very impressive. A study of college students by Summers and Hammonds (794) indicates that even on a self-administered anonymous questionnaire, white students were more willing to admit racial prejudice when the administrator was white than when the administrator was black.

Table 4.20 Results of Story Tests by Sex of Interviewer as Related to Sex of Respondent

Name of Picture	Percentage Favorable to Picture				Percentage Differences between Men and Women Respondents	
	Male Respondents		Female Respondents			
	Interviewed by:		Interviewed by:		Interviewed by:	
	Men	Women	Men	Women	Own Sex	Opposite Sex
General Lee of Virginia	45	38	30	34	11	8
Guardian of the Forest	24	25	21	14	10	4
They Can't Do This to Me	21	24	27	28	7	3
Two Weeks with Pay	10	13	22	24	14	9
They Knew What They Wanted	10	14	14	18	8	0
Lawrence of Arabia	27	32	28	18	9	4
Helen and Warren	5	11	17	19	14	6
The Great McGinty	24	23	13	12	12	10
Lucky	22	17	10	9	13	7
Lucky Partners	11	18	20	24	13	2
Mr. and Mrs. (Test 1)	16	14	26	29	13	12
Mr. and Mrs. (Test 2)	20	19	31	32	12	12

There have not been any large-scale studies of the effects of black interviewers on white respondents.

A larger study of 840 black residents in North Carolina shows no differences between black and white interviewers for items with low or moderate threat, but shows differences of about 10 percentage points for high threat items such as approval or disapproval of sit-ins (Williams, 900). Table 4.21 summarizes the results of this study. An almost identical study was conducted 20 years earlier in Memphis by the National Opinion Research Center, in which 1,000 black adults were interviewed, half by white and half by black interviewers. The results reported by Hyman (389) are given in Table 4.22. Differences averaged about 15 percentage points on sensitive items such as "Is the army fair to Negroes now?" "Are labor unions fair or unfair to Negroes?" and "Would Negroes be treated better or worse if Japan conquered the U.S.A.?" There is no way of knowing, on these two studies, if the joint response effect is the sum of interviewer and respondent effects (as seems likely) or is due to interaction effects.

The most recent study in this area is by Schuman and Converse (721). About 500 interviews with black households were conducted in the Detroit area using professional black interviewers and white students from the Detroit Area Study. Of 130 questions examined, the race of the interviewer explains 2 per cent or more of the variance for 15 per cent of all questions, and 32 per cent of those questions dealing with racial opinions (Table 4.23).

Schuman and Converse distinguish between questions with some racial content and questions dealing primarily with militant protest and hostility to whites. Much larger response effects were found for questions dealing with militancy and hostility toward whites (Table 4.24). On the 12-item militancy scale created for this study, race of interviewer accounts for a quarter of the variance. On the other hand, only five of 76 nonracial questions have at least 2 per cent of their variance explained by race of interviewer. Thus, response effects due to respondent and interviewer race depend very heavily on the content of the question.

Education Interactions
As may be seen in Table 4.17, the results available for education

Table 4.21 Low or Moderate and High Threat Potential Items by Race of Interviewer

Items	White Interviewer		Negro Interviewer		Differences between Proportions	Significance[a] of Difference between Proportions
	Per Cent	Number	Per Cent	Number		
Low or moderate threat potential items:						
Respondents over 40 years of age	37.9	235	34.1	593	3.8	No
Respondents bothered when something unexpected happens	79.5	215	75.5	563	4.0	No
Respondents reporting one or no jobs in the household	57.8	255	50.4	571	7.4	No
Respondents not registered to vote	49.3	221	48.4	574	0.9	No
Respondents attending church weekly or more	46.0	235	40.7	590	5.3	No
Respondents belonging to less than two organizations	78.1	233	71.7	587	6.4	No
High threat potential items:						
Want less than a college degree for son	29.8	225	26.1	588	3.7	No
State that politicans are more important than the voters	60.8	227	38.9	552	21.9	Yes
State that it is not a good idea to make changes in the way our country is run	17.8	242	9.1	570	8.7	Yes
Report that they do not read a daily newspaper	47.6	233	33.8	588	13.8	Yes
Report that they do not read a Negro newspaper	55.6	235	42.7	592	12.9	Yes
Disapprove of sit-ins	23.9	188	15.2	538	8.7	Yes
Say that a Negro mother should send her daughter to a Negro school	56.7	122	48.1	568	8.6	Yes

Source: Williams (900). Reprinted by permission of the American Sociological Association.
[a] Statistical significance is determined at the .05 level of significance, using a two-tailed test.

Table 4.22 Classification of Questions Asked of Negro Respondents by the Degree of Significance of Difference in Answers to Negro and White Interviewers in Memphis, Tennessee (1942)

Question	Category Tested	Percentage of Negroes Giving Answer Indicated to:	
		Negro Interviewers (N = about 500)	White Interviewers (N = about 500)
		A. Difference between Responses to Negro and White Interviewers Significant at .001 Level	
Is enough being done in your neighborhood to protect the people in case of air raid?	Yes	21	40
Do you think this country will win the war?	Yes	59	79
If we win, do you think the Negroes will be treated better, worse, or the same?	Better	34	44
Would Negroes be treated better or worse if Japan conquered the U.S.A.?	Worse	25	45
Would Negroes be treated better or worse if Germany conquered the U.S.A.?	Worse	45	60
Is the army fair to Negroes now?	No	35	11
Is the navy fair to Negroes now?	No	23	11
Have Negroes, right now, as good a chance as whites to get defense jobs?	Yes	39	52
Who is most to blame for this? (Asked of those answering "No" above)	Government	8	2
Are labor unions fair or unfair to Negroes?	Fair	30	47
Is it important to concentrate on winning the war or on democracy at home?	Winning the war	39	62
Who would a Negro go to to get his rights?	(White people?)	16	6
	(Police?)	2	15
	(Law courts?)	3	12
	(Nobody?)	26	13

Question	Answer		
What Negro newspaper do you usually read?	None	35	51
Who do you think should lead Negro troops?	Negro officers	43	22
B. Difference between Responses to Negro and White Interviewers Not Significant at .001 Level but Significant at .01 Level			
Do you think Negroes are better off or worse off than before the war (in what way)?	Less economic discrimination	21	28
Which do Negroes feel worst about now?	(Housing?)	8	14
	(Discrimination in public places?)	8	4
Does anyone in your family own an automobile?	Yes	20	13
C. Difference between Responses to Negro and White Interviewers Not Significant at .01 Level			
About how much longer do you think the war will last?	Less than one year	28	33
Do you think Negroes are better off or worse off than before the war?	Better off	38	42
Which do Negroes feel worst about now?	(Job discrimination?)	33	28
	(Wages?)	43	46
Have Negroes right now just as good a chance as whites to get defense jobs?	(Managers?)[a]	21	15
(Who is most to blame for this?)	(Labor unions?)[a]	7	4
Which is fairer (to Negroes) CIO or AF of L?	CIO[a]	36	29
Where do you get most of your news about the war?	Talking to people[a]	13	9
What radio station do you usually listen to?	WREC[a]	52	44
What was the highest grade you completed at school?	High school or better[a]	19	14

Source: Hyman (389). Reprinted from *Interviewing in Social Research,* p. 165, by permission of the University of Chicago Press. Copyright 1956 by the University of Chicago. All rights reserved.
[a] Difference significant at .05 level.

interactions are limited to the findings mentioned earlier, which indicate that the largest response effects are found when students are both the respondents and the interviewers. Even if more results were available, it is unlikely that it would be possible to disentangle education from social class, race, and age variables.

Summary

The principal finding in this section is that response interactions due to the characteristics of respondents and interviewers are not general but depend very specifically on the topic of the question. Social class differences of interviewers affect union members when the issues are labor-oriented, but not otherwise. Age interactions are seen on questions relating to adult authority when the respondents are female students age 16 to 18, but no consistent differences are observed for younger girls, and there is no evidence of age effects for adults. Sex interactions have been found for some sex-related questions, but the highly specialized nature of the questions suggests that there are probably no interactions by sex on most questions.

Black respondents are shown on several studies to give much more militant answers to black than to white interviewers on racial questions, but even here the differences are smaller on items not dealing with militancy or hostility toward whites, and the differences disappear altogether on nonracial questions.

Table 4.23 Categories of Questions Affected by Race of Interviewer

Category	Number of Questions	Variance Explained by Race of Interviewer (Per Cent)			
		2 Per Cent or More	1–2 Per Cent	Less than 1 Per Cent	Total
Total questions analyzed	130	15	11	74	100
Racial opinions	40	32	5	63	100
Racial facts	14	14	29	57	100
Nonracial opinions	29	3	11	86	100
Nonracial facts	47	8	11	81	100

Source: Schuman and Converse (721). Reprinted from "The Effects of Black and White Interviewers on Black Responses in 1968," *Public Opinion Quarterly* 35 (1971), 5, by permission of *Public Opinion Quarterly*.

Table 4.24 Questions with Racial Content Showing Greatest Difference by Race of Interviewer

Question	Answer Tested vs. Others	Per Cent by Race of Interviewer		Per Cent Difference	Per Cent Variance Explained (E^2)
		White	Negro		
	2.0 Per Cent or More Variance Explained				
Do you personally feel that you can trust most white people, some white people, or none at all?	Trust most whites	35	7	28	12.5
Would you say that because of the disturbance Negroes in Detroit now feel more ready to stand up for their rights, less ready to stand up for their rights, or that there hasn't been much change?	More ready	61	84	−23	4.9
Some people feel that last summer's disturbance was a step forward for the cause of Negro rights. Other people feel that it was a step backward for the cause of Negro rights. Which opinion comes closest to the way you feel?	Step forward	30	54	−24	4.7
Do you think Negro parents can work better with a Negro teacher than with a white teacher?	Yes, better with Negro teacher	14	29	−15	4.4
Suppose there is a white storekeeper in a Negro neighborhood. He hires white clerks but refuses to hire any Negro clerks. Talking with him about the matter does no good. What do you think Negroes in the neighborhood should do to change the situation?	Nothing	26	10	16	4.1
What do you think is the most important thing the city government can do to keep a disturbance like the one last summer from breaking out again in Detroit?	Use of force, police	35	18	17	3.9

(Table 4.24 continued)

Table 4.24 Continued

Question	Answer Tested vs. Others	Per Cent by Race of Interviewer		Per Cent Difference	Per Cent Variance Explained (E^2)
		White	Negro		
		2.0 Per Cent or More Variance Explained			
Some leaders want to organize Negroes into groups to protect themselves against any violence by whites. Do you think this is worthwhile or not?	Yes, worthwhile	18	35	−17	3.2
In your church, has money ever been collected at Sunday service for the Civil Rights movement?	Yes, money collected	30	46	−16	2.9
Do you think city officials in Detroit are more willing to listen to Negro demands since the disturbance, less willing to listen, or hasn't there been much change?	More willing	59	79	−20	2.7
Do you think Negro teachers take more of an interest in teaching Negro students than white teachers do?	Yes, Negro teachers take more interest	26	41	−15	2.5
Were there any white students in the schools you attended?	Yes	49	33	16	2.5
Do you think many policemen would use this right (to stop and search on suspicion) unfairly against Negroes?	Yes	70	83	−13	2.4
Some people say there should be Negro principals in schools with mostly Negro students because Negroes should have the most say in running inner city schools. Would you agree with that or not?	Yes, agree	26	42	−16	2.4

	2.0 Per Cent or More Variance Explained		
If you were treated impolitely in a downtown store in Detroit, how would you feel . . . very angry, a little angry, or would you not let it bother you?	Very angry	27	42	−15	2.4
How do you feel we should refer to last July's disturbance in Detroit: Should it be called a riot, a rebellion, or what?	Rebellion or revolt	50	68	−18	2.0

	0.05 Per Cent or Less Variance Explained		
Have you ever taken part in any kind of nonviolent protest for civil rights?	Yes	25	25	0	0.00
Now that Martin Luther King is gone, who do you think is the single most important Negro leader in the country?	Abernathy	58	58	0	0.00
Some people are saying that the assassination of Martin Luther King will drive Negroes and whites further apart. Others think that it will bring them closer together. Which do you think will probably happen? ("No change" is recorded when volunteered.)	Bring together	66	70	− 4	0.00

(Table 4.24 continued)

Table 4.24 Continued

Question	Answer Tested vs. Others	Per Cent by Race of Interviewer		Per Cent Difference	Per Cent Variance Explained (E^2)
		White	Negro		
	0.05 Per Cent or Less Variance Explained				
Do you and the white families that live around here visit in each other's homes, or do you only see and talk to each other on the street, or do you hardly know each other?	To white interviewers, respondents report less close contact and less no contact				0.00
If using (laws and persuasion, nonviolent protest) doesn't work (to gain rights) then do you think Negroes should be ready to use violence?	Yes, use violence	23	23	0	0.00
Do you think you were ever refused a job or laid off from a job because of being Negro?	Yes	26	27	− 1	0.01
Do you think there are many, some, or just a few places in the city of Detroit where a Negro could not rent or buy a house because of racial discrimination?	Many places	36	37	− 1	0.00
Do you feel that you personally have missed out on getting the kind of job you want and are qualified for because of race?	Yes	26	27	− 1	0.03
Do you think you have ever been discriminated against when you were trying to buy or rent a particular house or apartment?	Yes	25	27	− 2	0.04

Source: Schuman and Converse (721). Reprinted from "The Effects of Black and White Interviewers on Black Responses in 1968," *Public Opinion Quarterly* **35** (1971), 54–56, by permission of *Public Opinion Quarterly.*

CONCLUSIONS AND IMPLICATIONS FOR
INTERVIEWER SELECTION

Although the results of this chapter have shown many examples of response effects due to respondent and interviewer characteristics, one is ultimately struck by the narrowness of the findings. Response effects occur when the respondent has not arrived at a firm position on the issue and when the subject of the study is highly related to the respondent or interviewer characteristics. In a report of black attitudes in Detroit, Schuman and Converse (721) suggest that:

... interviewer effects may be partly a frame-of-reference phenomenon. Given the amorphous and shifting nature of human attitudes and beliefs, the race of the interviewer (and of the Other more generally) may crystallize attitudes in a direction not previously known for certain even to the respondent. (p. 68)

On the other hand, careful studies of response effects on voting preferences in presidential elections show no interviewer effects (Hyman, 389). It is also instructive to compare two questions from the Schuman and Converse study. The first is a very general attitudinal question and has a large response effect. The second is a quite specific behavioral question and there is *no* effect.

1. Do you personally feel that you can trust most white people, some white people or none at all?
2. Have you ever taken part in any kind of non-violent protest for civil rights?

The difference here may be due to the difference between attitudinal and behavioral reports or to the difference between general and specific questions. Since so few studies of interviewer effects deal with behavioral items, we cannot tell.

That respondent and interviewer characteristics influence response only when the subject of the study is highly related to these characteristics is evident from the data in this chapter. In none of the published studies, for example, is there any report that the sex of the interviewer and respondent affects political or racial attitudes, nor do we find any such response effects in our analysis. Since the published results typically report only significant differences, there are probably studies that have been conducted, but not reported, showing no response effects when the subject of the study is not related to characteristics.

Some survey organizations have been greatly concerned about respondent and interviewer characteristics and have attempted to solve the perceived problem either by eliminating the interviewer entirely or by matching respondent and interviewer characteristics. Neither of these solutions seems satisfactory to us; in fact, either may intensify rather than improve the problem.

Comparing the results of this chapter to those in Chapter 2, it is evident that, generally, the task variables are more important than respondent and interviewer characteristics. Differences between self-administered and face-to-face interviews are generally larger than differences due to respondent and interviewer characteristics. In some cases, results on self-administered forms may be better than face-to-face interviews as, for example, when diaries are used instead of recall interviews to obtain purchasing behavior. In other cases, when probing is required, face-to-face interviews may be better than self-administered forms. In any event, one does not eliminate response effects by using a self-administered form, and may frequently increase them.

As we have indicated, matching of interviewers has no effect on response unless the issues are highly related to the respondent and interviewer characteristics. Of course, there may be other reasons for matching. The use of black interviewers in black areas for a study of medical needs may make it easier to obtain cooperation from community groups, obtain qualified interviewers, and reduce travel costs, as well as providing work for people in the area. It will not, however, increase the respondent's willingness to cooperate or change his reporting of medical needs.

If the issues of the survey are highly related to interviewer and respondent characteristics, such as on a study of racial attitudes, matching these characteristics will conceal response effects without necessarily providing the "true" answers. It is possible that black respondents will try to give answers to black interviewers that are more militant than the views they actually hold because they think it is expected, while they will conceal some of their militancy when interviewed by white interviewers. The "true" answer, if it exists, may be somewhere in between.

What is the best solution in this sort of situation? We suggest that the best alternative would be to measure response effects by designing the survey such that respondent and interviewer characteristics are both matched and unmatched in random subsamples of the total sample. If the response effects are small, they may be ignored and the combined results used. If the response effects are large, they should be reported, and included as one of the variables in the analysis. For some purposes, response effects may be considered as "noise" or random variation. In these cases, survey error will be a function of both sampling and response errors, and estimates, significance tests, or Bayesian decision rules should use total error rather than sampling error alone.

Some control of response effects due to interviewer characteristics can be achieved by using carefully trained and experienced interviewers who are less likely to misperceive and miscode respondent answers or to suggest an answer by verbal or nonverbal methods. Ultimately, the quality of a survey depends on the interviewer's ability and not on the interviewer's characteristics.

5

Summary and Implications for Further Research

We have presented a conceptual framework which we hope will have general utility for the study of response effects in social research. We have conceptualized the research interview as a social encounter that has many characteristics in common with social conversations but that is much more highly structured and focused on the particular task of seeking and giving information. The interview is, as Bingham and Moore (85) have pointed out, a "conversation with a purpose." We believe that the structured characteristics of the situation contribute in important ways to the magnitude and variance of the responses obtained and that it is the task of methodological research on response effects to study the nature and magnitude of these effects.

We have identified what we believe to be the three conceptually distinct sources of variance in the given situation: (1) the variables that derive from the nature and structure of the task, (2) the variables that derive from the characteristics of the interviewers, and (3) the variables that derive from the characteristics of the respondent. Given the purposes of most social research, the variables associated with respondent characteristics generally have been conceptualized as part of the "true" variance in responses, while variance due to differences in task structure or interviewer characteristics have been seen as part of the "error" variance. Task variables are further divided into three large classes: (1) variables relating to the structure of the task and the method of administration, (2) variables relating to problems of self-presentation on the part of the respondent, and (3) variables relating to the saliency of the task to the respondent. We have used this framework to organize a systematic review of methodological studies in order to derive tentative generalizations about the relative magnitude of sources of response effects and, where possible, to clarify the interrelationships among different types of variables. We hope that the effects of our systematic application of such a conceptual framework will be to sharpen the analysis of problems involved in studying response effects and to provide greater clarity in future research. In addition, we have some hope that future research, by working within a systematic framework, will result in greater cumulative knowledge about response effects in social research.

In this chapter we shall summarize briefly our conclusions about the relative importance of the different sources of variance. It seems useful to consider three types of questions separately: (1) non-threatening behavioral questions, (2) threatening behavioral questions, and (3) attitudinal questions. For each of these interview situations, we shall discuss procedures for minimizing response effects, or in the case of attitudes, for determining how important response effects are. We shall also summarize a few of the major new methodological studies that could be done to begin to fill the many large gaps that still remain, and briefly discuss the methodology of our literature review and its implications for additional bibliographic research.

NON-THREATENING BEHAVIORAL QUESTIONS

A comparison of the results of Chapters 2, 3, and 4 indicates that memory factors are the most important factors influencing response for non-threatening behavioral questions, with average response effects of about .15 standard deviation units. Other task variables are of some importance for non-threatening behavioral questions, with response effects averaging about .05 units, while interviewer and respondent demographic characteristics are of little or no importance, with response effects near to zero. The ranking of importance seems indisputable, but the magnitude of the differences is difficult to interpret since it varies widely according to the characteristics of the individual study.

Response effects in non-threatening behavioral studies can be reduced by using procedures discussed in Chapter 3 for reducing memory errors. For frequent events of low saliency, the best procedure for reducing the number of omitted events is the use of diaries. For less frequent events of higher saliency, recall may be improved by shortening the length of the recall period. Omissions are substantially lower for periods of a month or less than they are for longer periods. While both the use of diaries and the use of shorter recall periods may increase the expense of data gathering, the improvement in the quality of the results will more than repay this added cost. A good example of this technique is the national Consumer Expenditure Survey conducted during 1972–73 by the U.S. Bureau of the Census. The new procedure includes two-week diaries and quarterly recall to replace the annual recall survey used previously.

One additional method of reducing omissions is the use of aided recall. Checklists and detailed questions will enable the respondent to report events just below the surface of consciousness.

For frequent non-salient events, the use of diaries is the best method for reducing overstatements due to telescoping. For less frequent events, the use of bounded recall procedures is highly effective. The use of records, such as checkbooks, bills, and bank books, also increases the accuracy of response.

THREATENING BEHAVIORAL QUESTIONS

Response effects are generally larger for what we have called threatening behavioral questions than for non-threatening behavioral questions. We account for this difference by hypothesizing that problems of respondent self-presentation are of greater importance for threatening behavioral questions. Task variables are the most important factors influencing response, with response effects averaging about .24 standard deviation units. Memory variables are next in importance, averaging about .18 units, while respondent-interviewer variables are least important, averaging near zero—with two important exceptions: when both respondents and interviewers are college students, especially male, there is an average response effect of about .15 units; for studies of sexual behavior, the sex of the respondent and interviewer is important, with average response effects of about .20 units.

The best and most widely used method for reducing response effects for threatening questions is the use of self-administered questionnaires, which, in some cases, insure anonymity, and which remove the threat of a direct disclosure to another person of what may be considered socially unacceptable behavior. It is unclear whether the respondent feels less threatened in the home or in a group setting where many people are filling out the form simultaneously, thus insuring anonymity. If the interview is in the home, it is vital that no other household member be present. Away from home, a neutral setting such as a church or community center is better than a school or work location where lines of authority have been established previously.

Certainly anyone who wishes an accurate measure of socially unacceptable behavior should avoid the use of student interviewers and respondents in the classroom or school laboratory situation, where the level of threat is very high. If interviewers are used, they should be experienced and highly trained. The threatening questions should be put near the end of the interview so that the interviewer has a chance to establish good rapport with the respondent. As with non-threatening questions, the use of shorter time periods will reduce both omissions and telescoping, although, on the average, these events are probably more salient to the respondent than are non-threatening events.

ATTITUDES

Task variables are more important causes of response effects in attitudinal studies than are respondent-interviewer characteristics, except when these characteristics are highly related to the attitudes being measured, as, for example, in studies of racial or sex-role attitudes.

It might appear that self-administered questionnaires would always be preferable to face-to-face interviews for collecting attitudinal data, but there are many situations where an interviewer is indispensable—where probing is required; where some questions are asked or skipped, depending on the answers to previous questions; or where the sequence of questions cannot be revealed to the respondent because it would influence the answers. Self-administered questionnaires cannot be sent by mail to a general population sample since effects due to sample biases toward those most interested in the subject and those with more education will be more serious than response effects.

As we suggested at the end of the last chapter, the most important concern with attitudinal questions is not to reduce response effects, since in some cases this may worsen rather than improve the results, but to stabilize the attitude measurement under different kinds of interviewing conditions. Unstable attitudes imply that different data gathering methods should be used so that the variability may be measured and taken into account in the analyses performed on the data.

There are several important factors to consider in selecting interviewers—previous experience, interpersonal skills, clerical ability, and for cost reasons, geographic location—but the perfect matching of interviewer and respondent characteristics is neither possible nor necessary on most surveys. Thus, for example, on questions dealing with the war in Vietnam, matching interviewers and respondents by race or sex would probably have little effect on the results. Only for those studies in which interviewer characteristics are directly and publicly (i.e., visible to the respondent) related to the attitudes being measured does interviewer-respondent matching appear to be important.

We have summarized here only those effects that our secondary analysis of studies indicates are fairly certain to be important in designing a study. This is not meant to suggest that no other variables are important, nor to neglect the conclusion that a combination of variables may have very important effects where they do not have strong effects when they appear singly. In particular, the reader should be sensitive to the fact that response effects often work in different directions, so that in any single study there may be offsetting factors which tend to cancel one another out. Survey researchers need to develop a much greater awareness of the complex interaction of types of task variables and their potentially offsetting effects.

In any single study there may be questions which are threatening as well as those that are non-threatening, questions about behavior as well as questions about attitudes. Since questions may be differentially affected by the various kinds of variables, it is clear that there will never be any easy and simple rules for designing a perfect survey instrument. In actual studies, compromises will have to be made among methodological options to insure the best overall results. In many instances this may require a battery of methods that are applied to comparable subsamples of the overall sample.

One inescapable conclusion of our research is that a much greater flexibility of effort is required and that social research would profit from the greater use of a methodological mix within each study. Such a conclusion, of course, was pointed out years ago by Campbell and Fiske (137), who noted that the contribution of method variance to the measurement of psychological traits may be greater than the differences among the traits themselves. The lessons to be derived from their work, however, appear to have had little impact on the practice of survey research. We hope that the review of the methodological literature presented here will hasten the day when the choice of methods is not based entirely on cost considerations, but also includes self-conscious attention to problems of relationships between the method and response effects.

SUGGESTED ADDITIONAL RESEARCH

Throughout this monograph we have suggested additional research because of the sparseness of or ambiguities in the published data. Here we list some of the more important of these studies. The order below is not meant to be our ranking of the importance of these projects, although it does reflect some of the priorities we derive from our review.

The effect of the interaction of method of administration and level of threat on response.—This study was suggested in part by the difficulty our coders had in determining the threat level of various questions. A study is now being conducted at the National Opinion Research Center that will compare face-to-face, telephone, self-administered, and randomized response procedures on four subject matter areas selected on an a priori basis as having different threat levels. The low threat topics are owning a library card and voting. The higher threat topics are having been convicted of drunken driving and having declared bankruptcy. Outside validation is available for each of these topics. Respondents will be asked after the formal interview to rate how threatening they found each of the topics.

The effect of interview location on response.—A study of workers in the plant and at home, or of students at school and at home, or of shoppers at a shopping center and at home, would add to our knowledge of interview location effects. The topics should be varied so that responses to high and low saliency questions can be related to location of interview. For example, questions could be asked both at work and at home about attitudes toward one's employer as well as more general questions unrelated to work. Similarly, questions about school discipline or about attitudes toward a shopping center could be compared to more general questions when they were asked at different locations. Comparisons might also be made between face-to-face and self-administered forms when given in different places.

The effects of using open-ended and closed-ended questions on response to threatening questions.—More work needs to be done on measuring the effect of the number of words in the question and the word length or difficulty for open-ended and closed-ended questions about threatening topics. In addition, open-ended and closed-ended questions could be compared in and out of the home and using face-to-face and self-administered forms.

The use of other household members to report attitudes.—Such a study would have to control the level of threat. It is possible that for non-threatening attitudinal questions, there would be only small differences between a respondent's attitudes and the reports of those attitudes by another household member. On threatening questions, where we expect greater concern with self-presentation on the part of the person giving his own attitudes, it is possible that there would be a greater discrepancy between self-report and the report of others. It would also be useful to administer both face-to-face and self-administered forms to both respondents. Naturally, such a study would have to be concerned about topics that are relatively salient and for which there would be an expectation that other household members would know the target respondent's attitudes.

Order effects on attitudinal questions.—For threatening questions dealing with racial or sexual attitudes, a study could be conducted in which the placement of these questions varied from early to late in the questionnaire. It would also be valuable to compare self-administered forms and face-to-face interviews for which the interviewer and respondent are matched or unmatched on the variable studied.

Cross-national research.—While extensive efforts were made to include research on response effects conducted at research centers abroad, the fact remains that the overwhelming proportion of the research reviewed in this monograph comes from the United States. The degree to which our findings may be generalized beyond our own cultural context is questionable. Indeed, the conceptual framework within which we have been analyzing the studies suggests that cultural differences that affect the definition of the interview situation may have important consequences for the generalizations we have made here about the relative magnitude of different sources of response effects. For example, Elizabeth Noelle[1] has suggested that some of the variables relating to problems of self-presentation, which we have suggested are important in the United States, are of less importance in Germany where people have a different view of the way they present themselves to strangers. Variables relating to method of administration, on the other hand, may be relatively more important in Germany because of greater problems in securing the cooperation of respondents. Since there may be marked differences among people in different countries in conceptions of what it means to give information to strangers, how one presents oneself in public, or willingness to talk about particular "private" topics with anyone, careful comparative studies are imperative before we can know how generally true specific findings may be. To our knowledge, there has been practically no cross-national methodological research. We hope that this situation will not continue.

Obviously this is not a comprehensive list, but reflects some of our own future research interests. Given the conclusions above, it is not surprising that most of these studies relate to task variables. Interviewer characteristics, which we believe to be less significant than task variables, and memory factors have been intensively studied. Regardless of his interests, however, the methodological researcher need have no concern that there is nothing left to do.

---

[1] Personal communication.

THE CODING OF STUDIES AS A RESEARCH STRATEGY

Other researchers faced with the problem of codifying large bodies of literature may be interested in our evaluation of the coding process we used. Did the results repay the expenditures of time and money involved? We think that they did, and if we had to do it again, we would do it pretty much the same way.

The careful coding and analysis of published studies is, of course, much cheaper than conducting new studies, and gives results over a far wider spectrum. The problems of comparability that we have mentioned frequently are the price one must pay for this rich mine of secondary data. The careful analysis of secondary data highlights gaps in the literature and indicates where carefully controlled experiments may be performed most fruitfully.

Most readers will compare these procedures to the more typical reviews of the literature, in which the reviewer cites the literature, summarizes the results of the studies one by one, and sometimes attempts an evaluation of individual studies. The formal coding methods that we used are a good deal more costly and time consuming than the typical literature review. They do, however, have three main advantages:

1. By looking at all possible studies, not only those specifically designed to prove a hypothesis or those that are most interesting or best known, one gets a less biased indication of the importance of a variable. Suppose, for example, that interviewer characteristics are important only in isolated cases while the method of administration is almost always important. Such a fact can best be detected when all studies, or a carefully selected probability subsample of all studies, are examined.

2. The necessity of coding forces one to be careful in the definitions that are used. The codes that are given in Appendix A went through repeated revisions that helped to clarify what was meant by general terms such as "interviewing conditions" and "threat." Thus, even when the reader may feel that the final definition is still inadequate, he has been alerted to the problem. Formal procedures help reduce fuzzy thinking.

3. Formal procedures allow us to rank the independent variables influencing response in order of importance, although nothing very meaningful can be said about the distance between ranks. This

is probably the most important advantage of formal procedures. In the informal review of the literature, one generally finds a series of variables that are statistically significant, but statistical significance is not at all the same thing as importance. Even if it is possible to identify important variables using informal procedures, it is generally not possible to rank them.

Formal procedures are time consuming, but the marginal cost of coding compared with the cost of finding the source and reading it to see if it is germane is not very large. In addition, if the codes and coding instructions have been properly devised, the coding can be delegated to graduate students or highly skilled coders (even with well-devised codes this is not a job for an inexperienced coder).

The quality of the results will depend, of course, on the coding structure that has been established. If important factors are omitted from the structure, they can never show up in the results. It is better to begin with as broad a structure as possible and to have blank cells where there are no data available than to find oneself with lots of data that do not fit. Nevertheless, after we completed the coding, some studies had to be omitted because they just did not fit our structure. As an example, we completely ignored studies that dealt with response reliability. This was a deliberate decision, however, and, as with our other decisions, can be seen in the specific codes used.

A brilliant reviewer using informal procedures may well do a better job than a pedestrian reviewer using formal methods, but we would conclude that the brilliant reviewer could do better still if he combined his intuitive grasp of the field with the more formal methods.

Appendix A
Coding Instructions

General

1. Do not use secondary sources unless original source is unavailable. If secondary source is used, there must be some information about methodology.

2. Omit anecdotal data, or results based on one or two respondents.

3. Note that reliability is a separate issue that we are not concerned with on this study. Thus, if on two successive waves, a panel gives answers that differ between waves, we would only be concerned with mean changes as indicating lack of validity. Of course, reliability, that is, no mean changes, would be no evidence of validity. Note, however, that differences between interviewers on the same survey when assignments have been randomized are to be included as indicating interviewer effects.

1–4 *Sequence Number for Source*
      This number will be assigned serially by the coder, who will also keep a running list of sources. If multiple coders are used, then each coder will be assigned a block of numbers.

5–6 *Sequence Number for Finding within Source*
      Since many studies will report multiple findings based on different questions or subsamples, the within-source sequence number is necessary to differentiate these. No list of these need be kept separately.

7–8 *Book or Journal in Which Report Is Found*
      00   Book or monograph

01   Doctoral Dissertation
02   American Journal of Public Health
03   American Journal of Sociology
05   American Sociological Review
06   Applied Statistics
08   British Journal of Social and Clinical Psychology
10   Child Development
11   U.S. Department of Agriculture
16   Human Relations
17   Industrial Relations Center, U. of Minnesota
18   International Journal of Opinion and Attitude Research
19   Journal of Abnormal and Social Psychology
20   Journal of Advertising Research
21   Journal of the American Dietetic Association
22   Journal of the American Statistical Association
23   Journal of Applied Psychology
24   Journal of Business
26   Journal of Consulting Psychology
27   Journal of Experimental Psychology
29   Journal of Marketing
30   Journal of Marketing Research
31   Journal of the National Cancer Institute
32   Journal of Personality
33   Journal of Personality and Social Psychology
34   Journal of Psychology
35   Journal of the Royal Statistical Society
36   Journal of Social Issues
37   Journal of Social Psychology
39   Milbank Memorial Fund Quarterly
41   National Center for Health Statistics
42   Pediatrics
43   Personnel and Guidance Journal
45   Population Studies
48   Psychological Review
49   Public Health Reports
50   Public Opinion Quarterly
51   Rural Sociology
53   Science

56 Social Forces
57 Social Psychiatry
58 Sociometry
59 Southern Cooperative Series Bulletin
62 Journal of Negro Education
63 Western Political Quarterly
64 Journal of Retailing
65 Journal of Genetic Psychology
66 Journal of Educational Psychology
67 American Journal of Psychology
68 Journal of Nervous and Mental Disease
69 Comprehensive Psychiatry
70 Cancer
71 Proceedings of the American Statistical Assn., Social
    Statistics Section
72 British Journal of Psychiatry
73 Journal of Michigan State Medical Society
74 Journal of the American Institute of Criminal Law
    and Criminology
75 School and Society
76 Journal of Projective Techniques
77 Archives of Psychology
78 Review of Economics and Statistics
79 Perceptual and Motor Skills
80 Psychological Reports
81 Journal of Educational Measurement
82 Unpublished Manuscript
84 Journal of Consulting and Clinical Psychology
85 Journal of Counseling Psychology
86 Journal of Educational Research
87 Psychological Monographs
88 Educational Administration and Supervision
89 Journal of Educational Method
90 American Journal of Mental Deficiency
91 Calcutta Statistical Association Bulletin
93 Bulletin of the the International Statistical Institute
94 University of California Publications in Psychology
95 Journal of Parapsychology
99 Other

9 *Type of Research*
   1 Survey
   2 (Laboratory) experiment
   3 Actual behavior
   8 Not given
   9 Not applicable
      These 8 and 9 codes will be used this way in all columns.

10–11 *Year of Study*
   Code last two digits of year in which study was done. If unavailable, code year in which published. If nothing else is known, some estimate of the quality of a study may be inferred from its date.
   99 Not given

12 *Researcher's Background*
   1 Sociology
   2 Psychology
   3 Personnel
   4 Market research
   5 Economics or business
   6 Survey research
   7 Other (political science) (public health) (psychiatry) (medicine)

13 *Researcher's Reputation*
   0 Unknown
   1 Graduate student
   2 Some earlier publications
   3 Many publications, an acknowledged specialist

14 *Type of Sample*
   0 Judgment, convenience, college students
   1 Limited geography, probability sample
   2 National probability or quasi-probability sample

15 *Size of Sample*
   1 Under 25

2   25–49
3   50–99
4   100–199
5   200–399
6   400–999
7   1,000 & over
8   Not given
9   Not applicable

16   *Methodological Details Given in Report*
0   None
1   Some, limited
2   Full or almost full detail

17   *Type of Validating Data*
0   No source given or other study where no details are available, or where quality is obviously shoddy

1   Internal, i.e., comparisons between interviewers who have random assignments, comparisons between earnings and expenditures accounting for change in assets or external between two studies of reasonable quality

2   *Outside* source of validation such as hospital or doctors' records, bank records, employment records, or comparison to a survey of very high validity (i.e., using diary records to validate recall)

18   *Overall Quality of Research*
This score ranging from 0 to 9 is determined by summing the scores in columns 13, 14, 16, and 17 and thus depends on:
a.   Researcher's reputation
b.   Type of sample
c.   Methodological details given
d.   Type of validating data

19 *Source of Data*
    1   Ordinal source
    2   Secondary source (use only if original source is un-
        available)

20 *Type of Data*
    1   Behavior (includes purchasing) (medical care)
    2   Attitudes
    3   Expectations
    4   Ability
    5   Personality (happiness, neurosis)
    6   Ownership, debts, savings
    7   Demographic (age, etc.)

21 *Subject of Report*
    1   Self (respondent)
    2   Household or family
    3   Other members of household (i.e., housewife for hus-
        band or children)
    4   Other individuals
    5   Environment
    6   Interviewer

22 *Time Period*
    1   Past
    2   Present
    3   Future (expectations)

23–24 *Length of Time Period*
    Express as numbers of weeks   (00 for present)
    77 for 77 weeks or more
    88 not given   6 months = 26 weeks
    99 not applicable   3 months = 13 weeks

25 *Threatening Interview*
    1   Yes—deals with taboo behavior (sex, drinking) or
        with financial or serious illnesses

2 Possibly threatening
3 Clearly non-threatening

26 *Salient*
  1 Salient—deals with respondent's or household's important behavior or with current issues of great interest
  2 Possibly salient—major political issues not immediately current
  3 Clearly non-salient—deals with issues that respondent does not know or care about, minor purchases, minor foreign or domestic problems

27 *Evaluation of Respondent's Interest by Interviewers or Experimenters*
  1 Highly interested and cooperative
  2 Mildly interested
  3 Not interested, not cooperative

28 *Records Available for Behavior*
  1 Records available
  2 Uncertain
  3 Records not available
  9 Not applicable

29 *Aided Recall*
  1 Aided recall
  2 Not aided recall

30 *Method of Administration*
  1 Face-to-face
  2 Group
  3 Phone (personal not face-to-face, recorded)
  4 Self-administered, interviewer or experimenter present
  5 Mail, self-administered, no one present (anonymous, unsigned)
  6 Diary

31 *Length of Interview or Experiment*
Count number of quarter hours. Thus, an hour-and-a-half interview could be coded 6.

7 1¾ hours or more
8 Not given
9 Not applicable

32 *Structured or Unstructured Questions*
1 Closed-end question
2 Open-end question
3 No specified wording—interviewer varies at will

33 *Position of Question in Questionnaire*
1 Early, first ⅓
2 Middle ⅓
3 Late, last ⅓
4 No standard version of questionnaire
9 Not applicable

34 *Position of Question Relative to Related Questions*
1 After related questions
2 Not after related questions
3 No standard wording to questionnaire
4 Before related questions
5 Not before related questions

35 *Deliberate Bias in Questionnaire Question Wording or Deception in Experiment*
1 No deliberate bias
2 Deliberate bias in question wording
3 Deliberate bias in experiment-deception

36 *Length of Question*
(The number of words divided by 5)

1 7 or under
2 8–12

3   13–18
4   19–22
5   23–28
6   29–32
7   33 words or more
8   Not given
9   Not applicable

37   *Length of Words in Question*
This is intended as a naive estimate of the difficulty of the words. The number of letters in all words is divided by the number of words to give an average that is rounded to the nearest whole number.

7   7 or more letters/word
8   Not given
9   Not applicable

38   *Is a Socially Desirable Answer Possible*
Some behavior is clearly socially desirable such as giving to charity. Some attitudes are also socially desirable such as patriotism and love of mother. Most items of behavior, however, that refer to consumption choices such as car driven or favorite food have no socially desirable answer. Note that a negative response to socially undesirable behavior (such as child beating) is a socially desirable answer.

1   Socially desirable answer not possible
2   Some possibility of socially desirable answer
3   Strong possibility of socially desirable answer

39   *Is Respondent Anxious?*
1   Respondent anxious
2   Respondent not anxious

40   *Respondent's Age*
1   Under 21

2   21–24
3   25–34
4   35–44
5   45–54
6   55–64
7   65 and over

41   *Respondent's Sex*
1   Male
2   Female

42   *Occupation of Household Head in Respondent's Household*
(If retired or currently unemployed, use previous occupation if available. If student or never employed, use not applicable.)

1   Professionals, Managers, and Proprietors
2   Clerical and Sales
3   Craftsmen
4   Farmers and Farm Laborers
5   Operatives
6   Service Workers
7   Laborers
8   Not given
9   Not applicable, student, never employed

43   *Relative Household Income*
This is relative rather than absolute because income has changed so substantially in the last 50 years. If absolute income figures are given, they may be converted to percentiles by reference to *Statistical Abstracts.*

1   Lowest ⅕
2   Second ⅕
3   Third ⅕
4   Fourth ⅕
5   Highest ⅕

44 *Respondent's Education*
   1   8 years or less
   2   9–11 years
   3   12 years
   4   13–15 years
   5   16 years
   6   17 years or more

45 *Race or Ethnicity of Respondent*
   0   White, not specified
   1   Negro
   2   English, Scotch, Welsh
   3   French, German, Scandinavian
   4   Irish
   5   Italian
   6   Polish, Russian, or Eastern European
   7   All other
   8   Not given
   9   Not applicable

46 *Religion of Respondent*
   1   Protestant
   2   Catholic
   3   Protestant or Catholic
   4   Jewish
   5   Other
   6   None

47 *Misc. Respondent Characteristics*
   1   Respondent behaved in unusual way for his sex
   2   Lived in neighborhood more than 10 years
   3   Lived in neighborhood 3–10 years
   4   Lived in neighborhood less than 3 years
   5   Childhood in city or town
   6   Childhood in rural area
   7   Public housing resident
   0   Non-public housing resident

48 *Misc. Respondent Characteristics* (cont.)
   1   Unfavorable attitude toward borrowing
   2   Middle attitude toward borrowing
   3   Favorable attitude toward borrowing
   4   Low conformity
   5   Middle conformity
   6   High conformity

49 *Misc. Respondent Characteristics* (cont.)
   1   Low personal effectiveness
   2   Middle personal effectiveness
   3   High personal effectiveness
   4   Union member
   5   Yea sayer
   6   Nay sayer

50 *Political Preference*
   1   Democrat
   2   Republican
   3   Independent
   4   Not registered

51 *Household Size*
   1   One member
   2   2 members
   3   3 members
   4   4 members
   5   5 members
   6   6 members
   7   7 or more members

52 *Is Respondent Hostile?*
   1   Respondent hostile
   2   Respondent not hostile
   3   Respondent neutral

53 *Interviewer's or Experimenter's Age*
   1   Under 21
   2   21–24

3   25–34
4   35–44
5   45–54
6   55–64
7   65 and over

54   *Interviewer's Sex*
1   Male
2   Female

55   *Occupation of Household Head in Interviewer's Household*
Normally, this would be the interviewer's husband, but it might be the interviewer's father or the interviewer himself.

1   Professionals, Managers, and Proprietors
2   Clerical and Sales
3   Craftsmen
4   Farmers and Farm Laborers
5   Operatives
6   Service Workers
7   Laborers
8   Not given
9   Not applicable, student, never employed

56   *Interviewer's Education*
1   8 years or less
2   9–11 years
3   12 years
4   13–15 years
5   16 years
6   17 years or more

(NOTE: Interviewer's Household Income omitted since it is not available.)

57   *Race or Ethnicity of Interviewer*
0   White, or not specified
1   Negro

2 English, Scotch, Welsh
3 French, German, Scandinavian
4 Irish
5 Italian
6 Polish, Russian, or other Eastern European
7 All other
8 Not given
9 Not applicable

58 *Religion of Interviewer*
1 Protestant
2 Catholic
3 Protestant or Catholic
4 Jewish
5 Other
6 None

59 *Misc. Interviewer Variables*
1 Interviewer behaved in unusual way for her sex
2 Interviewer's spouse behaved in unusual way for his sex
3 Interviewer refuses to interview Negroes (stereotype) or lower class
4 Interviewer known to respondent
5 Interviewer agrees with respondent
6 Interviewer differs with respondent
7 Interviewer expects answer

60 *Misc. Interviewer Variables* (cont.)
1 Interviewer social class highest
2 Interviewer social class high
3 Interviewer social class low
4 Interviewer social class lowest
5 Interviewer briefed (trained)
6 Interviewer not briefed

61 *Misc. Interviewer Variables* (cont.)
1 Interviewer knows results

2 Interviewer does not know results
3 Interviewer embarrassed by questions
4 Interviewer not embarrassed by questions
5 Interviewer experienced
6 Interviewer not experienced

62 *Is Interviewer Hostile?*
1 Interviewer hostile (blames respondent)
2 Interviewer not hostile (approves)
3 Interviewer neutral

63 *Is Interviewer Anxious?*
1 Interviewer anxious
2 Interviewer not anxious

64 Blank

65 *Relative Length of Interview*
1 More than 50 per cent above average
2 10–50 per cent above average
3 Average 90–110 per cent of average
4 51–90 per cent of average
5 50 per cent or less of average

66 *Conditions of Interview*
1 Respondent and interviewer in home, no one else present
2 Some distractions (children, TV), no adults present
3 Other adults present
4 Outside home (street, office), no one else present
5 Outside home, some distractions
6 Outside home, other adults present
7 In home, only spouse present

67 *Evidence of Interviewer or Respondent Cheating*
1 None
2 Interviewer cheating

3 Respondent cheating
4 Both cheating

68–69 Blank

70 *Direction of Response Error or Variance*
0 None
1 Positive
2 Negative
3 Indeterminate

71–73 *Magnitude of Relative Error*
Since many different types of studies will be included, absolute errors become meaningless. Some form of relative error is necessary. The most useful form seems to be to compare the size of the bias to the size of the standard deviation. (At the least, this solves the problem of computing a relative bias when the validating mean is zero.) Thus, Rel error is defined as:

$$\frac{(\text{Actual} - \text{Validating})}{s}$$

The validating measures are clear if outside sources are used. (Note these outside sources need not be perfect, only better than the response being measured. Thus, diaries may be used as validators for recall studies.) If internal comparisons are used, then a weighted average of these should be used as the validating criterion and differences computed as relative errors (e.g., differences in responses by different interviewers when assignments have been randomized).

For proportions $s = \sqrt{pq}$

For continuous data, $s = \sqrt{\dfrac{\Sigma x_i^2 - \dfrac{(\Sigma x)^2}{n}}{n-1}}$

74 *Cause of Error If Known*
    1 Respondent error
    2 Interviewer error in asking question
    3 Interviewer error in coding or transcribing answer
    4 Combination of factors

75 *Social Desirability of Error*
    1 No relation to social desirability
    2 Error in direction of socially desirable response
    3 Error in direction of socially undesirable response

76–77 *Topic of Study*
    01 Financial (including employment)
    02 Medical (including mental health)
    03 Large household expenditures
    04 Small household expenditures
    05 Media usage (movies)
    06 Demographic (age, education)
    07 Social behavior
    08 Voting
    11 Attitude on foreign policy
    12 Attitude on national policy
    13 Attitude on local policy
    14 Attitude on race relations or prejudice
    15 Attitude on sex behavior, family

78–79
    00 Rel Error based on mean
    99 Rel Error based on standard deviation
    01–98 Use for percentage data. Percentage from which
           σ is computed.

Appendix B

Full Distribution of Responses from Table 2.1

Table B.1 Response Effect in Standard Deviation Units by Conditions of Interview (Per Cent of Studies Showing Indicated Magnitude of Effects)

Response Effect in Standard Deviation Units	In Home		Out of Home	
	No one Present	Other Adults	No one Present	Other Adults
	Behavior[a]			
−.51 or more negative	4.8	1.0	8.9	7.3
−.26 to −.50	5.8	9.6	14.8	8.2
−.11 to −.25	12.7	12.0	11.1	11.9
−.06 to −.10	9.5	10.0	7.4	9.9
.00 to −.05	18.4	16.2	12.7	14.0
.01 to .05	13.4	18.1	8.9	14.0
.06 to .10	10.8	14.4	6.0	8.8
.11 to .25	13.1	15.8	11.3	12.4
.26 to .50	6.8	2.9	10.9	7.5
.51 or more positive	4.7	0.0	8.0	6.0
Total	100.0	100.0	100.0	100.0
N	811	209	503	464
Mean Effect	.055	−.019	.001	−.036
Standard Deviation	.718	.173	.710	.624

[a] Response effects for behavioral measures $= \dfrac{\text{Actual} - \text{Validating}}{s_v}$

(Table B.1 continued)

Table B.1 Continued

Response Effect in Standard Deviation Units	In Home		Out of Home	
	No one Present	Other Adults	No one Present	Other Adults
	Attitudes[b]			
.00	18.3	–	3.5	0.0
.01 to .05	18.3	–	25.2	25.8
.06 to .10	18.3	–	17.8	16.9
.11 to .25	35.4	–	22.6	36.0
.26 to .50	7.3	–	19.1	19.1
.51 or more	2.4	–	11.8	2.2
Total	100.0	–	100.0	100.0
N	82	–	314	89
Mean Effect	.124	–	.243	.167
Standard Deviation	.132	–	.356	.147

[b] Response effects for attitudinal measures $= \dfrac{\text{Actual} - \text{Grand Mean}}{s_{GM}}$

Response Effects in Surveys

Table B.2 Response Effect in Standard Deviation Units by Method of Administration (Per Cent of Studies Showing Indicated Magnitude of Effects)

Response Effect in Standard Deviation Units	Face-to-Face	Group	Phone	Self-Administered	Mail/Diary
			Behavior		
−.51 or more negative	4.5	8.1	4.0	9.4	0.9
−.26 to −.50	6.6	9.0	1.3	10.8	4.3
−.11 to −.25	12.3	12.5	21.3	9.9	8.7
−.06 to −.10	8.8	7.8	9.3	10.5	7.8
.00 to −.05	19.7	13.9	24.1	17.7	32.2
.01 to .05	13.1	13.9	18.7	11.9	18.3
.06 to .10	8.9	6.7	5.3	11.0	16.5
.11 to .25	12.6	13.6	10.7	9.4	8.7
.26 to .50	8.0	8.1	4.0	4.7	2.6
.51 or more positive	5.5	6.4	1.3	4.7	0.0
Total	100.0	100.0	100.0	100.0	100.0
N	3,014	345	75	362	115
Mean Effect	.036	−.049	−.025	−.112	−.009
Standard Deviation	.571	.700	.201	.362	.137
			Attitudes		
.00	4.6	−	6.7	0.0	−
.01 to .05	28.7	−	30.6	19.9	−
.06 to .10	21.2	−	12.0	15.2	−
.11 to .25	31.5	−	20.0	32.5	−
.26 to .50	10.3	−	18.7	23.2	−
.51 or more	3.7	−	12.0	9.3	−
Total	100.0	−	100.0	100.0	−
N	887	−	75	151	−
Mean Effect	.147	−	.219	.220	−
Standard Deviation	.203	−	.362	.205	−

Table B.3 Response Effect in Standard Deviation Units by Threat of Interview (Per Cent of Studies Showing Indicated Magnitude of Effects)

Response Effect in Standard Deviation Units	Threatening	Possibly Threatening	Non-Threatening
	Behavior		
—.51 or more negative	8.1	3.2	4.6
—.26 to —.50	10.5	7.0	6.0
—.11 to —.25	14.3	11.7	11.9
—.06 to —.10	7.8	7.3	9.6
.00 to —.05	20.4	16.9	19.6
.01 to .05	12.9	10.6	14.0
.06 to .10	6.8	8.6	10.0
.11 to .25	9.4	14.4	13.0
.26 to .50	5.3	12.3	6.8
.51 or more positive	4.5	8.0	4.5
Total	100.0	100.0	100.0
N	892	804	2,369
Mean Effect	—.028	.065	.009
Standard Deviation	.790	.331	.537
	Attitudes		
.00	2.8	2.7	4.6
.01 to .05	15.6	25.1	31.6
.06 to .10	17.0	21.3	20.7
.11 to .25	34.0	32.2	29.3
.26 to .50	27.7	12.3	8.3
.51 or more	2.8	6.9	5.6
Total	100.0	100.0	100.0
N	141	479	702
Mean Effect	.200	.170	.159
Standard Deviation	.215	.205	.259

Table B.4 Response Effect in Standard Deviation Units by Possibility of Socially Desirable Answer (Per Cent of Studies Showing Indicated Magnitude of Effects)

Response Effect in Standard Deviation Units	Strong Possibility	Some Possibility	Little Possibility
	Behavior		
−.51 or more negative	11.1	3.6	4.2
−.26 to −.50	3.4	9.2	7.2
−.11 to −.25	8.1	18.0	12.0
−.06 to −.10	3.4	9.2	9.4
.00 to −.05	9.8	19.0	20.4
.01 to .05	4.4	11.4	14.4
.06 to .10	2.7	8.4	9.8
.11 to .25	12.2	13.1	12.6
.26 to .50	24.3	4.5	6.4
.51 or more positive	20.6	3.6	3.6
Total	100.0	100.0	100.0
N	296	466	3,210
Mean Effect	.101	−.026	−.002
Standard Deviation	.790	.312	.481
	Attitudes		
.00	1.0	7.7	3.4
.01 to .05	11.5	29.8	29.3
.06 to .10	16.7	20.2	21.2
.11 to .25	46.9	25.0	29.7
.26 to .50	15.6	14.3	10.8
.51 or more	8.3	3.0	5.6
Total	100.0	100.0	100.0
N	94	168	1,035
Mean Effect	.221	.137	.165
Standard Deviation	.275	.152	.244

Table B.5 Response Effect in Standard Deviation Units by Saliency of Interview (Per Cent of Studies Showing Indicated Magnitude of Effects)

Response Effect in Standard Deviation Units	Salient	Possibly Salient	Not Salient
		Behavior	
−.51 or more negative	4.2	7.5	4.7
−.26 to −.50	7.3	7.0	7.2
−.11 to −.25	10.3	15.0	13.0
−.06 to −.10	9.3	8.9	8.2
.00 to −.05	20.6	18.1	18.5
.01 to .05	14.5	11.7	12.4
.06 to .10	8.9	8.8	9.2
.11 to .25	10.9	12.9	13.8
.26 to .50	7.9	6.0	8.1
.51 or more positive	6.1	4.1	4.9
Total	100.0	100.0	100.0
N	1,574	852	1,639
Mean Effect	.020	−.003	.012
Standard Deviation	.375	.768	.609
		Attitudes	
.00	2.6	2.9	5.0
.01 to .05	31.3	21.3	26.3
.06 to .10	20.8	21.3	20.0
.11 to .25	33.0	41.0	25.3
.26 to .50	10.4	11.1	13.3
.51 or more	1.9	2.4	10.1
Total	100.0	100.0	100.0
N	530	207	585
Mean Effect	.134	.150	.204
Standard Deviation	.148	.187	.303

Table B.6 Response Effect in Standard Deviation Units by Position of Question in Questionnaire (Per Cent of Studies Showing Indicated Magnitude of Effects)

Response Effect in Standard Deviation Units	Early	Middle	Late
	Behavior		
−.51 or more negative	5.7	1.9	8.8
−.26 to −.50	11.8	8.7	7.5
−.11 to −.25	13.5	14.9	11.3
−.06 to −.10	8.8	8.1	9.3
.00 to −.05	15.7	24.5	18.3
.01 to .05	12.5	13.3	11.3
.06 to .10	8.8	9.1	11.1
.11 to .25	13.5	14.9	10.9
.26 to .50	5.7	3.3	7.2
.51 or more positive	4.0	1.4	4.3
Total	100.0	100.0	100.0
N	594	518	442
Mean Effect	−.021	−.023	.060
Standard Deviation	.517	.206	.922
	Attitudes		
.00	6.4	4.5	2.8
.01 to .05	35.0	36.0	32.1
.06 to .10	18.9	25.8	26.4
.11 to .25	27.2	22.5	19.8
.26 to .50	10.6	10.1	12.3
.51 or more	1.9	1.1	6.6
Total	100.0	100.0	100.0
N	265	89	106
Mean Effect	.116	.112	.148
Standard Deviation	.128	.116	.165

Table B.7   Response Effect in Standard Deviation Units by Deliberate Bias or Deception in the Interview or Experiment (Per Cent of Studies Showing Indicated Magnitude of Effects)

Response Effect in Standard Deviation Units	Deliberate Bias	None
	Behavior	
−.51 or more negative	9.4	4.8
−.26 to −.50	8.2	7.2
−.11 to −.25	12.2	12.5
−.06 to −.10	6.7	9.0
.00 to −.05	10.9	19.9
.01 to .05	9.7	13.3
.06 to .10	5.0	9.4
.11 to .25	13.8	12.3
.26 to .50	13.8	6.8
.51 or more positive	10.3	4.8
Total	100.0	100.0
N	341	3,659
Mean Effect	.068	.005
Standard Deviation	.708	.562
	Attitudes	
.00	0.8	4.0
.01 to .05	12.4	29.4
.06 to .10	10.7	21.7
.11 to .25	24.0	31.0
.26 to .50	19.8	10.9
.51 or more	32.3	3.0
Total	100.0	100.0
N	121	1,164
Mean Effect	.457	.138
Standard Deviation	.507	.164

Bibliography

1. ACKERLEY, L. A. A comparison of attitude scales and the interview method. *Journal of Experimental Education,* 5 (1936), 137–46.
2. ADAIR, J. G. Demand characteristics or conformity? Suspiciousness of deception and experimenter bias in conformity research. Unpublished manuscript, University of Manitoba, 1968.
*3. ADAIR, J. G., and EPSTEIN, J. S. Verbal cues in the mediation of experimenter bias. *Psychological Reports,* 22 (1968), 1045–53.
*4. ADAMS, J. S. An experiment on question and response bias. *Public Opinion Quarterly,* 20 (1956), 593–98.
*5. ADLER, N. E. The influence of experimenter set and subject set on the experimenter expectancy effect. Unpublished B.A. thesis, Wellesley College, 1968.
6. ALDEN, P., and BENTON, A. L. Relationship of sex of examiner to incidence of Rorschach responses with sexual content. *Journal of Projective Techniques,* 15 (1951), 231–34.
7. ALLEN, C. N. Studies in sex differences. *Psychological Bulletin,* 24 (1927), 294–304.
8. ALLEN, C. N. Recent studies in sex differences. *Psychological Bulletin,* 27 (1930), 394–407.
*9. ALLEN, G. I., BRESLOW, L., WEISSMAN, A., and NISSELSON, H. Interviewing versus diary keeping in eliciting information in a morbidity survey. *American Journal of Public Health,* 44 (1954), 919–27.
10. ALLPORT, G. W., and KRAMER, B. M. Some roots of prejudice. *Journal of Psychology,* 22 (1946), 9–39.
11. ANDERSON, D. F., and ROSENTHAL, R. Some effects of interpersonal expectancy and social interaction on institutional-

NOTE: An asterisk preceding an entry indicates that the data in the item were coded and included in the subject index to the bibliography.

ized retarded children. *Proceedings of the American Psychological Association* (1968), 479–80.

12. ANDREWS, L. The interviewer problem in market research. *Journal of Marketing,* **13** (1949), 522–24.

*13. ANDRY, R. G. *Delinquency and parental pathology: A study in forensic and clinical psychology.* Springfield, Ill.: Thomas, 1960.

14. Application of survey techniques to the study of organizational structure and functioning. *Public Opinion Quarterly,* **21** (1957), 439–42.

15. ARONSON, E., TURNER, J. A., and CARLSMITH, J. M. Communicator credibility and communicator discrepancy as determinants of opinion change. *Journal of Abnormal and Social Psychology,* **67** (1963), 31–36.

16. ATHEY, K. R., COLEMAN, J. E., REITMAN, A. P., and TANG, J. Two experiments showing the effect of the interviewer's racial background on responses to questionnaires concerning racial issues. *Journal of Applied Psychology,* **44** (1960), 244–46.

17. BACK, K. W. Influence through social communication. *Journal of Abnormal and Social Psychology,* **46** (1951), 9–23.

18. BACK, K. W. Social research as a communications system. *Social Forces,* **41** (1962), 61–68.

19. BACK, K. W., FESTINGER, L., HYMOVITCH, B., KELLEY, H., SCHACHTER, S., and THIBAUT, J. The methodology of studying rumor transmission. *Human Relations,* **3** (1950), 307–12.

20. BACK, K. W., and GERGEN, K. J. "Apocalyptic and serial time orientations and the structure of opinions. *Public Opinion Quarterly,* **27** (1963), 427–42.

21. BACK, K. W., HILL, R., and STYCOS, J. M. Interviewer effect on scale reproducibility. *American Sociological Review,* **20** (1955), 443–46.

22. BACK, K. W., and STYCOS, J. M. *The survey under unusual conditions: The Jamaica human fertility investigation.* Monograph No. 1. Lexington, Ky.: Society for Applied Anthropology, University of Kentucky, 1959.

*23. BADER, L. Survey of the effectiveness of house-to-house canvassing. *Journal of Retailing,* **10** (1935), 111–18.

24. BAIER, D. E. Reply to Travers' "A critical review of the validity and rationale of the forced-choice ratings." *Psychological Bulletin,* **48** (1951), 421–34.

25. BAIN, R. Stability in questionnaire response. *American Journal of Sociology,* **37** (1931), 445–53.

26. BALDWIN, A. L., KALHORN, J., and BREESE, F. H. The appraisal of parent behavior. *Psychological Monographs: General and Applied,* **63**, No. 4 (1949), Whole No. 299.

27. BALLWEG, J. A. Husband-wife response similarities on evaluative and non-evaluative survey questions. *Public Opinion Quarterly,* **33** (1969), 249–54.

*28. BANCROFT, G. Consistency of information from records and interviews. *Journal of the American Statistical Association,* **35** (1940), 377–81.

29. BANCROFT, G., and WELCH, E. H. Recent experience with problems of labor force measurement. *Journal of the American Statistical Association,* **41** (1946), 303–12.

*30. BANDURA, A., and WALTERS, R. H. *Adolescent aggression: A study of the influence of child-training practices and family interrelationships.* New York: Ronald Press, 1959.

31. BARBER, T. X. Invalid arguments, postmortem analyses and the experimenter bias effect. *Journal of Consulting and Clinical Psychology,* **33** (1969), 11–14.

32. BARBER, T. X. Pitfalls in research: Nine investigator and experimenter effects. In R. TRAVERS (Ed.), *Handbook of research on teaching.* (2nd ed.) Chicago: Rand McNally, 1972.

33. BARBER, T. X., and CALVERLEY, D. S. Toward a theory of hypnotic behavior: Effects on suggestibility of defining the situation as hypnosis and defining response to suggestions as easy. *Journal of Abnormal and Social Psychology,* **68** (1964), 585–92.

*34. BARBER, T. X., FORGIONE, A., CHAVES, J. F., CALVERLEY, D. S., MCPEAKE, J. D., and BOWEN, B. Five attempts to replicate the experimenter bias effect. *Journal of Consulting and Clinical Psychology,* **33** (1969), 1–6.

35. BARBER, T. X., and SILVER, M. J. Fact, fiction, and the experimenter bias effect. *Psychological Bulletin Monograph Supplement,* **70** (December, 1968), 1–29. (a)

36. BARBER, T. X., and SILVER, M. J. Pitfalls in data analysis and interpretation: A reply to Rosenthal. *Psychological Bulletin Monograph Supplement,* **70** (December, 1968), 48–62. (b)

*37. BARKLEY, K. L. A consideration of the differences in readiness of recall of the same advertisements by men and women. *Journal of Applied Psychology,* **16** (1932), 308–14.

*38. BARLOW, R., MORGAN, J., and WIRICK, G. A study of validity in reporting medical care in Michigan. *Proceedings of the American Statistical Association,* Social Statistics Section (1960), 54–65.

*39. BARNARD, P. G. Interaction effects among certain experimenter and subject characteristics on a projective test. Unpublished Ph.D. dissertation, University of Washington, 1963.

40. BARNES, E. H. The relationship of biased test responses to psychopathology. Unpublished Ph.D. dissertation, Northwestern University, 1954.

*41. BARR, A. Differences between experienced interviewers. *Applied Statistics,* 6 (1957), 180–88.

42. BARRON, A. S. The effects of three styles of interviewing on the responses of women from two contrasting socio-economic groups. Unpublished Ph.D. dissertation, Columbia University, 1957.

43. BARTLETT, F. C. *Remembering: A study in experimental and social psychology.* Cambridge: University Press, 1932.

44. BARUCH, D. W., and WILCOX, J. A. A study of sex differences in preschool children's adjustment coexistent with interparental tensions. *Journal of Genetic Psychology,* 64 (1944), 281–303.

*45. BASSETT, S. J. Sex differences in history retention. *School and Society,* 29 (1929), 397–98.

46. BATTIN, T. C. "The use of the diary and survey method involving the questionnaire-interview technique to determine the impact of television on school children in regard to viewing habits and formal and informal education. Unpublished Ph.D. dissertation, University of Michigan, 1952.

47. BAUER, E. J. Response bias in a mail survey. *Public Opinion Quarterly,* 11 (1947), 594–600.

48. BAUGHMAN, E. E. Rorschach scores as a function of examiner difference. *Journal of Projective Techniques,* 15 (1951), 243–49.

49. BAYROFF, A. G., HAGGERTY, H. R., and RUNDQUIST, E. A. Validity of ratings as related to rating techniques and conditions. *Personnel Psychology,* 7 (1954), 93–113.

*50. BECKER, H. G. Experimenter expectancy, experience, and status as factors in observational data. Unpublished Master's thesis, University of Saskatchewan, 1968.

181

Bibliography

51. BECKER, H. S. A note on interviewing tactics. *Human Organization,* 12 (Winter, 1954), 31–32.
52. BECKER, H. S. Interviewing medical students. *American Journal of Sociology,* 62 (1956), 199–201.
53. BECKER, H. S., and GEER, B. Participant observation and interviewing: A comparison. *Human Organization,* 16 (Fall, 1957), 28–32.
54. BECKER, W. C., and KRUG, R. S. The parent attitude research instrument—A research review. *Child Development,* 36 (1965), 329–65.
55. BECKER, W. C., PETERSON, D. R., LURIA, Z., SHOEMAKER, D. J., and HELLMER, L. A. Relations of factors derived from parent-interview ratings to behavior problems in five-year-olds. *Child Development,* 33 (1962), 509–35.
56. BEEZ, W. V. Influence of biased psychological reports on teacher behavior and pupil performance. *Proceedings of the American Psychological Association* (1968), 605–6.
*57. BELL, C. G., and BUCHANAN, W. Reliable and unreliable respondents: Party registration and prestige pressure. *Western Political Quarterly,* 19 (1966), 37–43.
58. BELLAK, L. The concept of projection: An experimental investigation and study of the concept. *Psychiatry,* 7 (1944), 353–70.
*59. BELLOC, N. B. Validation of morbidity survey data by comparison with hospital records. *Journal of the American Statistical Association,* 49 (1954), 832–46.
*60. BELSON, W. A. *Studies in readership.* London: Business Publications, 1962.
61. BELSON, W. A. *The ability of respondents to recall their purchases of chocolate confectionery.* London: Survey Research Centre, London School of Economics and Political Science, 1966.
*62. BELSON, W. A. Tape recording: Its effect on accuracy of response in survey interviews. *Journal of Marketing Research,* 4 (1967), 253–60.
*63. BELSON, W. A., and DUNCAN, J. A. A comparison of the checklist and the open response questioning systems. *Applied Statistics,* 11 (1962), 120–32.
64. BENDICK, M. R., and KLOPFER, W. G. The effects of sensory deprivation and motor inhibition on Rorschach movement re-

sponses. *Journal of Projective Techniques and Personality Assessment,* **28** (1964), 261–64.

65. BENNETT, A. S. Toward a solution of the "cheater problem" among part-time research investigators." *Journal of Marketing,* **12** (1948), 470–74.

66. BENNETT, E. M., BLOOMQUIST, R. L., and GOLDSTEIN, A. C. Response stability in limited-response questioning. *Public Opinion Quarterly,* **18** (1954), 218–23.

67. BENNETT, J. W. The study of cultures: A survey of technique and methodology in field work. *American Sociological Review,* **13** (1948), 672–89.

*68. BENNEY, M., RIESMAN, D. and STAR, S. A. Age and sex in the interview. *American Journal of Sociology,* **62** (1956), 143–52.

*69. BENSON, L. E. Studies in secret-ballot technique. *Public Opinion Quarterly,* **5** (1941), 79–82.

70. BERG, I. A. The reliability of extreme position response sets in two tests. *Journal of Psychology,* **36** (1953), 3–9.

71. BERG, I. A. Response bias and personality: The deviation hypothesis. *Journal of Psychology,* **40** (1955), 61–72.

72. BERG, I. A., and COLLIER, J. S. Personality and group differences in extreme response sets. *Educational and Psychological Measurement,* **13** (1953), 164–69.

*73. BERG, I. A., and RAPAPORT, G. M. Response bias in an unstructured questionnaire. *Journal of Psychology,* **38** (1954), 475–81.

74. BERGER, D. Examiner influence on the Rorschach. *Journal of Clinical Psychology,* **10** (1954), 245–48.

75. BERGIN, A. E. The effect of dissonant persuasive communications upon changes in a self-referring attitude. *Journal of Personality,* **30** (1962), 423–38.

*76. BERNSTEIN, L. The examiner as an inhibiting factor in clinical testing. *Journal of Consulting Psychology,* **20** (1956), 287–90.

77. BERZINS, J. I., and SEIDMAN, E. Differential therapeutic responding of A and B quasi-therapists to schizoid and neurotic communications. Unpublished manuscript, University of Kentucky, 1968.

78. BEVIS, J. C. Interviewing with tape recorders. *Public Opinion Quarterly,* **13** (1949), 629–34.

79. BIDDLE, B. J. An application of social expectation theory to the

initial interview. Unpublished Ph.D. dissertation, University of Michigan, 1957.

80. BIERI, J. Parental identification, acceptance of authority, and within-sex differences in cognitive behavior. *Journal of Abnormal and Social Psychology*, **60** (1960), 76–79.

81. BILODEAU, E. A., and LEVY, C. M. Long-term memory as a function of retention time and other conditions of training and recall. *Psychological Review*, **71** (1964), 27–41.

*82. BINDER, A., MCCONNELL, D., and SJOHOLM, N. A. Verbal conditioning as a function of experimenter characteristics. *Journal of Abnormal and Social Psychology*, **55** (1957), 309–14.

*83. BINDMAN, A. M. Minority collective action against local discrimination: A study of the Negro community in Champaign-Urbana, Illinois. Unpublished Master's thesis, University of Illinois, 1961.

84. BINGHAM, W. V. Halo, invalid and valid. *Journal of Applied Psychology*, **23** (1939), 221–28.

85. BINGHAM, W. V., and MOORE, B. V. *How to interview.* (Revised ed.) New York: Harper, 1934. Pp. 180–216.

86. BIRD, C. The influence of the press upon the accuracy of report. *Journal of Abnormal and Social Psychology*, **22** (1927), 123–29.

87. BLANC, H. Multilingual interviewing in Israel. *American Journal of Sociology*, **62** (1956), 205–9.

88. BLANKENSHIP, A. B. Does the question form influence public opinion poll results? *Journal of Applied Psychology*, **24** (1940), 27–30. (a)

*89. BLANKENSHIP, A. B. The effect of the interviewer upon the response in a public opinion poll. *Journal of Consulting Psychology*, **4** (1940), 134–36. (b)

90. BLANKENSHIP, A. B. The influence of the question form upon the response in a public opinion poll. *Psychological Record*, **3** (1940), 345–424. (c)

91. BLANKENSHIP, A. B. *Consumer and opion research: The questionnaire technique.* New York: Harper, 1943.

92. BLANKENSHIP, A. B. A source of interviewer bias. *International Journal of Opinion and Attitude Research*, **3** (1949), 95–98.

93. BOLSTER, B. I., and SPRINGBETT, B. M. The reaction of interviewers to favorable and unfavorable information. *Journal of Applied Psychology*, **45** (1961), 97–103.

94. BONNEY, M. E. The constancy of sociometric scores and their relationship to teacher judgments of social success, and to personality self-ratings. *Sociometry,* 6 (1943), 409–24.

*95. BOOKER, H. S., and DAVID, S. T. Differences in results obtained by experienced and inexperienced interviewers. *Journal of the Royal Statistical Society, Series A,* 115 (1952), 232–57.

96. BOOTZIN, R. R. The experimenter: A credibility gap in psychology. Unpublished Ph.D. dissertation, Purdue University. 1969. (a)

97. BOOTZIN, R. R. Induced and stated expectancy in experimenter bias. *Proceedings of the American Psychological Association* (1969), 365–66. (b)

98. BOOTZIN, R. R. Expectancy and individual differences in experimenter bias. Unpublished manuscript, Northwestern University, n.d.

99. BORG, L. E. Interviewing school. *International Journal of Opinion and Attitude Research,* 2 (1948), 393–400.

*100. BORING, E. G. Capacity to report upon moving pictures as conditioned by sex and age: A contribution to the psychology of testimony. *Journal of the American Institute of Criminal Law and Criminology,* 6 (1916), 820–34.

*101. BORSKY, P. N., and FELDMAN, J. J. *A methodological study of accuracy in reporting medical costs.* NORC Report No. 80. Chicago: National Opinion Research Center, June, 1961.

102. BORUS, M. E. The economic effectiveness of retraining the unemployed: A study of the benefits and costs of retraining the unemployed based on the experience of workers in Connecticut. Unpublished Ph.D. dissertation, Yale University, 1964.

103. BORUS, M. E. Response error in survey reports of earnings information. *Journal of the American Statistical Association,* 61 (1966), 729–38.

104. BOX, K., and THOMAS, G. The wartime social survey. *Journal of the Royal Statistical Society,* 107 (1944), 151–77.

105. BOYD, H. W., JR., and WESTFALL, R. Interviewers as a source of error in surveys. *Journal of Marketing,* 19 (1955), 311–24.

106. BOYD, H. W., JR., and WESTFALL, R. Interviewer bias revisited. *Journal of Marketing Research,* 2 (1965), 58–63.

107. BOYNTON, P. L. Are girls superior to boys in visual memory? *Journal of Social Psychology,* 2 (1931), 496–500.

108. BRADBURN, N. M., and MASON, W. M. The effect of question

order on responses. *Journal of Marketing Research,* 1 (November, 1964), 57–61.

109. BRADLEY, J. Survey bias as a function of respondent-interviewer interaction. Unpublished Ph.D. dissertation, Pennsylvania State University, 1952.

110. BRADT, K. The usefulness of a postcard technique in a mail questionnaire study. *Public Opinion Quarterly,* 19 (1955), 218–22.

*111. BRANSON, R. E., and DILLIN, R. G., JR. *An analysis of response variations in telephone versus personal interviewing in consumer market surveys.* College Station, Tex.: Consumer Economics Section, Department of Agricultural Economics and Sociology, Texas A & M College System, n.d.

*112. BREKENFELD, H. Der Kommunikationsprozess beim Demoskopischen Interview in der Marktforschung und seine Beeinflussung durch situative Faktoren. Inaugural-Dissertation, Wirtschafts- und Sozialwissenschaftlichen Fakultät der Freien Universität Berlin, 1964.

113. BROADBENT, D. E. Word-frequency effect and response bias. *Psychological Review,* 74 (1967), 1–15.

114. BROGDEN, W. J. The experimenter as a factor in animal conditioning. *Psychological Reports,* 11 (1962), 239–42.

*115. BROIDA, A. L. Consumer surveys as a source of information for social accounting: The problems. In NATIONAL BUREAU OF ECONOMIC RESEARCH, *The flow-of-funds approach to social accounting: Appraisals, analysis, and applications.* Studies in Income and Wealth, Vol. 26. Princeton, N.J.: Princeton University Press, 1962. Pp. 335–81.

116. BROWN, J. M. Respondents rate public opinion interviewers. *Journal of Applied Psychology,* 39 (1955), 96–102.

117. BRUNER, J. S., and GOODMAN, C. Value and need as organizing factors in perception. *Journal of Abnormal and Social Psychology,* 42 (1947), 33–44.

*118. BRYAN, J. H., and LICHTENSTEIN, E. Effects of subject and experimenter attitudes in verbal conditioning. *Journal of Personality and Social Psychology,* 3 (1966), 182–89.

*119. BRYANT, E., GARDNER, I., JR., and GOLDMAN, M. Responses on racial attitudes as affected by interviewers of different ethnic groups. *Journal of Social Psychology,* 70 (1966), 95–100.

120. BUCHER, R., FRITZ, C. E., and QUARANTELLI, E. L. Tape

recorded interviews in social research. *American Sociological Review,* 21 (1956), 359–64. (a)

121. BUCHER, R., FRITZ, C. E., and QUARANTELLI, E. L. Tape recorded research: Some field and data processing problems. *Public Opinion Quarterly,* 20 (1956), 427–39. (b)

122. BURNHAM, J. R. Experimenter bias and lesion labeling. Unpublished manuscript, Purdue University, 1966.

*123. BURNHAM, J. R. Effects of experimenter's expectancies on children's ability to learn to swim. Unpublished Master's thesis, Purdue University, 1968.

124. BURTT, H. E., and GASKILL, H. V. Suggestibility and the form of the question. *Journal of Applied Psychology,* 16 (1932), 358–73.

125. BUSS, A. H., GERJOY, I. R., and ZUSSMAN, J. Verbal conditioning and extinction with verbal and nonverbal reinforcers. *Journal of Experimental Psychology,* 56 (1958), 139–45.

126. BYHAM, W. C. Accuracy of recall: Its correlates and predictors. Unpublished Ph.D. dissertation, Purdue University, 1963.

127. BYHAM, W. C., and PERLOFF, R. Recall of product purchase and use after six years. *Journal of Advertising Research,* 5 (September, 1965), 16–19.

128. CAFFYN, J. M. Psychological laboratory techniques in copy research. *Journal of Advertising Research,* 4 (December, 1964), 45–50.

*129. CAHALAN, D. Measuring newspaper readership by telephone: Two comparisons with face-to-face interviews. *Journal of Advertising Research,* 1 (December, 1960), 1–6.

*130. CAHALAN, D. Correlates of response accuracy in the Denver validity study. *Public Opinion Quarterly,* 32 (1968), 607–21.

131. CAHALAN, D. and MEIER, N. C. The validity of mail-ballot polls. *Psychological Record,* 3 (1939), 2–11.

132. CAHALAN, D., TAMULONIS, V., and VERNER, H. W. Interviewer bias involved in certain types of opinion survey questions. *International Journal of Opinion and Attitude Research,* 1 (March, 1947), 63–77.

133. CAHALAN, D., and TRAGER, F. N. Free answer stereotypes and anti-Semitism. *Public Opinion Quarterly,* 13 (1949), 93–104.

134. CAHEN, L. S. Experimental manipulation of bias in teachers'

scoring of subjective tests. Paper presented at the meetings of the American Psychological Association, New York, September, 1966.

135. CAMPBELL, A. Two problems in the use of the open question. *Journal of Abnormal and Social Psychology,* **40** (1945), 340–43.

136. CAMPELL, D. T. The use of interview surveys in federal administration. *Journal of Social Issues,* **2** (May, 1946), 14–22.

137. CAMPBELL, D. T., and FISKE, D. W. Convergent and discriminant validation by the multitrait-multimethod matrix. *Psychological Bulletin,* **56** (1959), 81–105.

*138. CAMPBELL, F. A., and FIDDLEMAN, P. B. The effect of examiner status upon Rorschach performance. *Journal of Projective Techniques,* **23** (1959), 303–6.

*139. CANADY, H. G. The effect of "rapport" on the I.Q.: A new approach to the problem of racial psychology. *Journal of Negro Education,* **5** (1936), 209–19.

140. CANNELL, C. F. A study of the effects of interviewers' expectations upon interviewing results. Unpublished Ph.D. dissertation, Ohio State University, 1953.

*141. CANNELL, C. F., and FOWLER, F. J. A comparison of a self-enumerative procedure and a personal interview: A validity study. *Public Opinion Quarterly,* **27** (1963), 250–64.

142. CANNELL, C. F., and FOWLER, F. J. A note on interviewer effect in self-enumerative procedures. *American Sociological Review,* **29** (1964), 270.

143. CANTRIL, H. Experiments in the wording of questions. *Public Opinion Quarterly,* **4** (1940), 330–32.

*144. CANTRIL, H. *Gauging public opinion.* Princeton, N.J.: Princeton University Press, 1944.

145. CAPLOW, T. The dynamics of information interviewing. *American Journal of Sociology,* **62** (1956), 165–71.

146. CARKHUFF, R. R., and PIERCE, R. Differential effects of therapist race and social class upon patient depth of self-exploration in the initial clinical interview. *Journal of Consulting Psychology,* **31** (1967), 632–34.

147. CARLSON, E. R., and CARLSON, R. Male and female subjects in personality research. *Journal of Abnormal and Social Psychology,* **61** (1960), 482–83.

148. CARLSON, J. A., and HERGENHAHN, B. R. Use of tape-recorded

instructions and a visual screen to reduce experimenter bias. Unpublished manuscript, Hamline University, 1968.

149. CARROLL, M. E., WHARTON, M. A., ANDERSON, B. L., and BROWN, E. C. Group method of food inventory vs. individual study method of weighted food intake. *Journal of the American Dietetic Association,* **28** (1952), 1146–50.

150. CARSON, R. C. A and B therapist "types": A possible critical variable in psychotherapy. *Journal of Nervous and Mental Disease,* **144** (1967), 47–54.

*151. CARTWRIGHT, A. The effect of obtaining information from different informants on a family morbidity inquiry. *Applied Statistics,* **6** (1957), 18–25.

*152. CARTWRIGHT, A. Memory errors in a morbidity survey. *Milbank Memorial Fund Quarterly,* **41** (1963), 5–24.

153. CATALDO, J. F., SILVERMAN, I., and BROWN, J. M. Demand characteristics associated with semantic differential ratings of nouns and verbs. *Educational and Psychological Measurement,* **27** (1967), 83–87.

154. CAVAN, R. S. The questionnaire in a sociological research project. *American Journal of Sociology,* **38** (1933), 721–27.

155. CAVANAGH, P., DRAKE, R. I., and TAYLOR, K. F. Youth employment service interviews: Part 2, Differences between interviews. *Occupational Psychology,* **36** (1962), 232–42.

156. CENTERS, R. Toward an articulation of two approaches to social class phenomena. *International Journal of Opinion and Attitude Research,* **4** (1950), 499–514, and **5** (1951), 159–78.

*157. CHAMBERLAIN, A. H. A memory test with school children. *Psychological Review,* **22** (1915), 71–76.

158. CHAMBERLAIN, K., and PYKE, M. *An experimental study of the accuracy of a method of surveys of individual diets, not directly based on weighing.* London: Ministry of Food, 1948.

159. CHAPMAN, L. J., and BOCK, R. D. Components of variance due to acquiescence and content in the F scale measure of authoritarianism. *Psychological Bulletin,* **55** (1958), 328–33.

160. CHURCH, H. N., CLAYTON, M. M., YOUNG, C. M., and FOSTER, W. D. Can different interviewers obtain comparable dietary survey data? *Journal of the American Dietetic Association,* **30** (1954), 777–79.

161. CIEUTAT, V. J. Sex differences and reinforcement in the conditioning and extinction of conversational behavior. *Psychological Reports,* **10** (1962), 467–74.

*162. CIEUTAT, V. J. Sex differences in verbal operant conditioning. *Psychological Reports,* 15 (1964), 259–75.

*163. CIEUTAT, V. J. Examiner differences with the Stanford-Binet IQ. *Perceptual and Motor Skills,* 20 (1965), 317–18.

*164. CIEUTAT, V. J., and FLICK, G. L. Examiner differences among Stanford-Binet items. *Psychological Reports,* 21 (1967), 613–22.

165. CLAIBORN, W. L. An investigation of the relationship between teacher expectancy, teacher behavior and pupil performance. Unpublished Ph.D. dissertation, Syracuse University, 1968.

*166. CLARK, A. L., and WALLIN, P. The accuracy of husbands' and wives' reports of the frequency of marital coitus. *Population Studies,* 18 (1964), 165–73.

167. CLARK, E. L. Value of student interviews. *Journal of Personnel Research,* 5 (1926), 204–7.

*168. CLARK, J. P., and TIFFT, L. L. Polygraph and interview validation of self-reported deviant behavior. *American Sociological Review,* 31 (1966), 516–23.

*169. CLARK, R. A. The projective measurement of experimentally induced levels of sexual motivation. *Journal of Experimental Psychology,* 44 (1952), 391–99.

170. CLARKSON, E. P. The problem of honesty. *International Journal of Opinion and Attitude Research,* 4 (1950), 84–90.

*171. CLAUSEN, A. R. Response validity: Vote report. *Public Opinion Quarterly,* 32 (1968), 588–606.

172. CLAUSEN, J. A., and FORD, R. N. Controlling bias in mail questionnaires. *Journal of the American Statistical Association,* 42 (1947), 497–511.

173. COBB, S., THOMPSON, D. J., ROSENBAUM, J., WARREN, J. E., and MERCHANT, W. R. On the measurement of prevalence of arthritis and rheumatism from interview data. *Journal of Chronic Diseases,* 3 (1956), 134–39.

174. COHEN, B. D., KALISH, H. I., THURSTON, J. R., and COHEN, E. Experimental manipulation of verbal behavior. *Journal of Experimental Psychology,* 47 (1954), 106–10.

*175. COHEN, S. E., and LIPSTEIN, B. Response errors in the collection of wage statistics by mail questionnaire. *Journal of the American Statistical Association,* 49 (1954), 240–50.

*176. COLE, D., and UTTING, J. E. G. Estimating expenditure, saving and income from household budgets. *Journal of the Royal Statistical Society, Series A.* 119 (1956), 371–87.

*177. COLOMBOTOS, J. Personal versus telephone interviews: Effect on responses. *Public Health Reports,* 84 (1969), 773–82.

*178. COLOMBOTOS, J., ELINSON, J., and LOEWENSTEIN, R. Effect of interviewer's sex on interview responses. *Public Health Reports,* 83 (1968), 685–90.

179. CONN, L. K., EDWARDS, C. N., ROSENTHAL, R., and CROWNE, D. Perception of emotion and response to teachers' expectancy by elementary school children. *Psychological Reports,* 22 (1968), 27–34.

180. CONNELLY, G. M. Now let's look at the real problem: Validity. *Public Opinion Quarterly,* 9 (1945), 51–60.

181. CONNELLY, G. M., and HARRIS, N. A symposium on interviewing problems. *International Journal of Opinion and Attitude Research,* 2 (1948), 69–84.

182. CONNORS, A. M. Two experimenter behaviors as mediators of experimenter expectancy. Unpublished A. B. thesis, Harvard University, 1968.

183. CONNORS, A. M., and HORST, L. The relationship between subjects' unbiased response tendencies and subsequent responses under two conditions of experimenter expectancy. Unpublished manuscript, Harvard University, 1966.

*184. CONRAD, H. S., and JONES, H. E. Psychological studies of motion pictures: V. Adolescent and adult sex differences in immediate and delayed recall. *Journal of Social Psychology,* 2 (1931), 433–56.

*185. COOPER, J., EISENBERG, L., ROBERT, J., and DOHRENWEND, B. S. The effect of experimenter expectancy and preparatory effort on belief in the probable occurrence of future events. *Journal of Social Psychology,* 71 (1967), 221–26.

*186. COPELAND, H. A. Studies in the reliability of personnel records. *Journal of Applied Psychology,* 22 (1938), 247–51.

187. CORDARO, L., and ISON, J. R. Observer bias in classical conditioning of the planarian. *Psychological Reports,* 13 (1963), 787–89.

188. CORNFIELD, J. On certain biases in samples of human populations. *Journal of the American Statistical Association,* 63 (1942), 63–68.

189. COUCH, A., and KENISTON, K. Yeasayers and naysayers: Agreeing response set as a personality variable. *Journal of Abnormal and Social Psychology,* 60 (1960), 151–74.

190. COVNER, B. J. Studies in phonographic recordings of verbal

material: IV. Written reports of interviews. *Journal of Applied Psychology,* 28 (1944), 89–98.

191. CRANDALL, V. J., and PRESTON, A. Patterns and levels of maternal behavior. *Child Development,* 26 (1955), 267–77.

192. CRESPI, L. P. The cheater problem in polling. *Public Opinion Quarterly,* 9 (1945), 431–45.

193. CRESPI, L. P. Further observations on the "cheater" problem. *Public Opinion Quarterly,* 10 (1946), 646–49.

194. CRESPI, L. P. The interview effect in polling. *Public Opinion Quarterly,* 12 (1948), 99–111.

*195. CRESPI, L. P. The influence of military government sponsorship in German opinion polling. *International Journal of Opinion and Attitude Research,* 4 (1950), 151–78.

196. CRISSY, W. J. E., and REGAN, J. J. Halo in the employment interview. *Journal of Applied Psychology,* 35 (1951), 338–41.

197. CRONBACH, L. J. Response sets and test validity. *Educational and Psychological Measurement,* 6 (1946), 475–94.

198. CROOG, S. H. Ethnic origins, educational level, and responses to a health questionnaire. *Human Organization,* 20 (1961), 65–69.

*199. CRUTCHFIELD, R. S., and GORDON, D. A. Variations in respondents' interpretations of an opinion-poll question. *International Journal of Opinion and Attitude Research,* 1 (September, 1947), 1–12.

200. CUBER, J. F., and GERBERICH, J. B. A note on consistency in questionnaire responses. *American Sociological Review,* 11 (1946), 13–15.

201. CURTIS, H. S., and WOLF, E. B. The influence of the sex of the examiner on the production of sex responses on the Rorschach. *American Psychologist,* 6 (1951), 345–46. (Abstract)

202. D'AMBROSIO, J. A. The effects of differential reinforcers and social class on performance. Unpublished Ph.D. dissertation, Indiana University, 1969.

*203. DAS, J. P. Prestige effects on body-sway suggestibility. *Journal of Abnormal and Social Psychology,* 61 (1960), 487–88.

*204. DAVID, M. The validity of income reported by a sample of families who received welfare assistance during 1959. *Journal of the American Statistical Association,* 57 (1962), 680–85.

*205. DAWIS, R. V., HAKES, D. T., ENGLAND, G. W., and LOFQUIST,

L. H. *Methodological problems in rehabilitation research.* Minnesota Studies in Vocational Rehabilitation, No. 5; Bulletin No. 25. Minneapolis: Industrial Relations Center, University of Minnesota, December, 1958.

206. DEAN, J. P., and WHYTE, W. F. How do you know if the informant is telling the truth? *Human Organization,* 17 (Summer, 1958), 34–38.

207. DEAN, L. R. Interaction, reported and observed: The case of one local union. *Human Organization,* 17 (Fall, 1958), 36–44.

208. DEASY, L. C. Socio-economic status and participation in the poliomyelitis vaccine trial. *American Sociological Review,* 21 (1956), 185–91.

209. DE JONGE, W. J., and STAPEL, J. De-exaggerating single-call interview data. *Admap,* 4 (1968), 150.

210. DEMING, W. E. On errors in surveys. *American Sociological Review,* 9 (1944), 359–69.

211. DENSEN, P. M., BALAMUTH, E., and DEARDORFF, N. R. Medical care plans as a source of morbidity data: The prevalence of illness and associated volume of service. *Milbank Memorial Fund Quarterly,* 38 (1960), 48–101.

212. DENTLER, R. A., and MONROE, L. J. Social correlates of early adolescent theft. *American Sociological Review,* 26 (1961), 733–43.

213. DENTON, J. C. The validation of interview-type data. *Personnel Psychology,* 17 (1964), 281–87.

214. DEPOID, P. Rapport sur le degre de precision des statistiques demographiques. *Bulletin of the International Statistical Institute,* 35, Pt. 3 (1957), 119–230.

215. DERATH, G., and CARP, F. M. The picture-choice test as an indirect measure of attitudes. *Journal of Applied Psychology,* 43 (1959), 12–15.

*216. DESABIE, J., and REMPP, J. M. Exemples d'une analyse méthodologique des résultats d'une enquête auprés des ménages. *Revue de Statistique Appliquée,* 16, No. 4 (1968), 5–34.

217. DEXTER, L. A. Role relationships and conceptions of neutrality in interviewing. *American Journal of Sociology,* 62 (1956), 153–57.

*218. DIETZE, A. G. Some sex differences in factual memory. *American Journal of Psychology,* 44 (1932), 319–21.

219. DINOFF, M. Subject awareness of examiner influence in a testing situation. *Journal of Consulting Psychology,* **24** (1960), 465.

220. DI VESTA, F. J., and BLAKE, K. The effects of instructional "sets" on learning and transfer. *American Journal of Psychology,* **72** (1959), 57–67.

221. DOHRENWEND, B. P. Social status and psychological disorder: An issue of substance and an issue of method. *American Sociological Review,* **31** (1966), 14–34.

*222. DOHRENWEND, B. S. An experimental study of directive interviewing. *Public Opinion Quarterly,* **34** (1970), 117–25.

*223. DOHRENWEND, B. S., COLOMBOTOS, J., and DOHRENWEND, B. P. Social distance and interviewer effects. *Public Opinion Quarterly,* **32** (1968), 410–22.

224. DOHRENWEND, B. S., and RICHARDSON, S. A. Directiveness and nondirectiveness in research interviewing: A reformulation of the problem. *Psychological Bulletin,* **60** (1963), 475–85.

225. DORN, H. F. Methods of measuring incidence and prevalence of disease. *American Journal of Public Health,* **41** (1951), 271–78.

226. DOWNES, J., and COLLINS, S. D. A study of illness among families in the Eastern Health District of Baltimore. *Milbank Memorial Fund Quarterly,* **18** (1940), 5–26.

*227. DOWNES, J., and MERTZ, J. C. Effect of frequency of family visiting upon reporting of minor illnesses. *Milbank Memorial Fund Quarterly,* **31** (1953), 371–90.

228. DRAKE, M. J., ROSLOW, S., and BENNETT, G. K. The relationship of self-rating and classmate rating on personality traits. *Journal of Experimental Education,* **7** (1939), 210–13.

*229. DRAYTON, L. E. Bias arising in wording consumer questionnaires. *Journal of Marketing,* **19** (1954), 140–45.

230. DREGER, R. M. Comparative psychological studies of Negroes and whites in the United States: A clarification. *Psychological Bulletin,* **60** (1963), 35–39.

231. DREGER, R. M., and MILLER, K. S. Comparative psychological studies of Negroes and whites in the United States. *Psychological Bulletin,* **57** (1960), 361–402.

*232. DUNNETTE, M. D. Accuracy of students' reported honor point averages. *Journal of Applied Psychology,* **36** (1952), 20–22.

233. DURANT, H. The "cheater" problem. *Public Opinion Quarterly,* **10** (1946), 288–91.

*234. DURBIN, J., and STUART, A. Differences in response rates of experienced and inexperienced interviewers. *Journal of the Royal Statistical Society, Series A,* 114 (1951), 163–95.

235. DURBIN, J. and STUART, A. Callbacks and clustering in sample surveys: An experimental study. *Journal of the Royal Statistical Society, Series A,* 117 (1954), 387–418.

236. ECKLER, A. R., and HURWITZ, W. N. Response variance and biases in censuses and surveys. *Bulletin of the International Statistical Institute,* 36, Pt. 2 (1958), 12–35.

237. ECKLER, A. R., and PRITZKER, L. Measuring the accuracy of enumerative surveys. *Bulletin of the International Statistical Institute,* 33, Pt. 4 (1951), 7–24.

238. EDELSTEIN, A. S., and LARSON, O. N. Communication, consensus and the community involvement of urban husbands and wives. *Acta Sociologica,* 5 (1961), 15–30.

239. EDGERTON, H. A., BRITT, S. H., and NORMAN, R. D. Objective differences among various types of respondents to a mailed questionnaire. *American Sociological Review,* 12 (1947), 435–44.

240. EDWARDS, A. L. The relationship between the judged desirability of a trait and the probability that the trait will be endorsed. *Journal of Applied Psychology,* 37 (1953), 90–93.

241. EHRENBERG, A. S. C. A study of some potential biases in the operation of a consumer panel. *Applied Statistics,* 9 (1960), 20–27.

242. EHRENBERG, A. S. C. A comparison of TV audience measures. *Journal of Advertising Research,* 4 (December, 1964), 11–16.

*243. EHRENBERG, A. S. C., and TWYMAN, W. A. On measuring television audiences. *Journal of the Royal Statistical Society, Series A,* 130 (1967), 1–48.

244. EHRLICH, H. J. Instrument error and the study of prejudice. *Social Forces,* 43 (1964), 197–206.

*245. EHRLICH, J. S., and RIESMAN, D. Age and authority in the interview. *Public Opinion Quarterly,* 25 (1961), 39–56.

*246. EICHORN, R. L., and MORRIS, W. H. M. Respondent errors in reporting cardiac conditions on questionnaires. *Proceedings of the Purdue Farm Cardiac Seminar,* Purdue University Agricultural Experiment Station, Lafayette, Ind. (1958), 46–49.

247. EKMAN, P. Body position, facial expression, and verbal behavior during interviews. *Journal of Abnormal and Social Psychology,* **68** (1964), 295–301.

248. EKMAN, P., and FRIESEN, W. V. Status and personality of the experimenter as a determinant of verbal conditioning. *American Psychologist,* **15** (1960), 430. (Abstract)

249. ELINSON, J., and HAINES, V. T. Role of anonymity in attitude surveys. *American Psychologist,* **5** (1950), 315. (Abstract)

250. ELINSON, J., and TRUSSEL, R. E. Some factors relating to degree of correspondence for diagnostic information as obtained by household interviews and clinical examinations. *American Journal of Public Health,* **47** (1957), 311–21.

251. ELLIS, A. The validity of personality questionnaires. *Psychological Bulletin,* **43** (1946), 385–440.

252. ELLIS, A. Comment on "The validity of personality questionnaires." *Psychological Bulletin,* **44** (1947), 80–82. (a)

253. ELLIS, A. A comparison of the use of direct and indirect phrasing in personality questionnaires. *Psychological Monographs,* **61**, No. 3 (1947), Whole No. 284. (b)

*254. ELLIS, A. Questionnaire versus interview methods in the study of human love relationships. *American Sociological Review,* **12** (1947), 541–53. (c)

255. ENGEL, J. F. Tape recorders in consumer research. *Journal of Marketing,* **26** (April, 1962), 73–74.

*256. ENTERLINE, P. E., and CAPT, K. G. A validation of information provided by household respondents in health surveys. *American Journal of Public Health,* **49** (1959), 205–12.

257. ERON, L. D., BANTA, T. J., WALDER, L. O., and LAULICHT, J. H. Comparison of data obtained from mothers and fathers on childrearing practices and their relation to child aggression. *Child Development,* **32** (1961), 457–72.

258. ERRITT, M. J., and NICHOLSON, J. L. The 1955 savings survey. *Bulletin of the Oxford University Institute of Statistics,* **20** (1958), 113–52.

259. EXLINE, R. V. Explorations in the process of person perception: Visual interaction in relation to competition, sex, and need for affiliation. *Journal of Personality,* **31** (1963), 1–20.

260. EXLINE, R. V., GRAY, D., and SCHUETTE, D. Visual behavior in a dyad as affected by interview content and sex of respondent. *Journal of Personality and Social Psychology,* **1** (1965), 201–9.

261. FELDMAN, J. J. The household interview survey as a technique for the collection of morbidity data. *Journal of Chronic Diseases,* 11 (1960), 535–57.

262. FELDMAN, J. J., HYMAN, H., and HART, C. W. A field study of interviewer effects on the quality of survey data. *Public Opinion Quarterly,* 15 (1951), 734–61.

263. FELDMAN, P. E. The personal element in psychiatric research. *American Journal of Psychiatry,* 113 (1956), 52–54.

264. FENSTERHEIM, H., and TRESSELT, M. E. The influence of value systems on the perception of people. *Journal of Abnormal and Social Psychology,* 48 (1953), 93–98.

265. FERBER, R. The problem of bias in mail returns: A solution. *Public Opinion Quarterly,* 12 (1948), 669–76.

266. FERBER, R. Observations on a consumer panel operation. *Journal of Marketing,* 17 (1953), 246–59.

*267. FERBER, R. On the reliability of purchase influence studies. *Journal of Marketing,* 19 (1955), 225–32. (a)

*268. FERBER, R. On the reliability of responses secured in sample surveys. *Journal of the American Statistical Association,* 50 (1955), 788–810. (b)

*269. FERBER, R. Does a panel operation increase the reliability of survey data: The case of consumer savings. *Proceedings of of the American Statistical Association,* Social Statistics Section (1964), 210–16.

*270. FERBER, R. *The reliability of consumer reports of financial assets and debts.* Studies in Consumer Savings, No. 6. Urbana, Ill.: Bureau of Economic and Business Research, University of Illinois, 1966.

*271. FERBER, R., FORSYTHE, J., GUTHRIE, H. W., and MAYNES, E. S. Validation of a national survey of consumer financial characteristics: Savings accounts. *Review of Economics and Statistics,* 51 (1969), 436–44. (a)

*272. FERBER, R., FORSYTHE, J., GUTHRIE, H. W., and MAYNES, E. S. Validation of consumer financial characteristics: Common stock. *Journal of the American Statistical Association,* 64 (1969), 415–32. (b)

273. FERBER, R., and WALES, H. G. Detection and correction of interviewer bias. *Public Opinion Quarterly,* 16 (1952), 107–27.

*274. FERGUSON, D. C., and BUSS, A. H. Operant conditioning of hostile verbs in relation to experimenter and subject characteristics. *Journal of Consulting Psychology,* **24** (1960), 324–27.

275. FERRISS, A. L. A note on stimulating response to questionnaires. *American Sociological Review,* **16** (1951), 247–49.

276. FINGER, F. W. Sex beliefs and practices among male college students. *Journal of Abnormal and Social Psychology,* **42** (1947), 57–67.

277. FISCHER, R. P. Signed versus unsigned questionnaires. *Journal of Applied Psychology,* **30** (1946), 220–25.

278. FISCHER, R. P., and ANDREWS, A. L. A study of the effect of conformity to social expectancy on evaluative attitudes. *Educational and Psychological Measurement,* **7** (1947), 331–35.

279. FISHER, G. A discriminant analysis of reporting errors in health interviews. *Applied Statistics,* **11** (1962), 148–63.

*280. FISCHER, H. Interviewer bias in the recording operation. *International Journal of Opinion and Attitude Research,* **4** (1950), 391–411.

281. FISK, G. Methods of handling certain field research problems. *Journal of Marketing,* **12** (1948), 382–84.

282. FLORES, A. M. The theory of duplicated samples and its use in Mexico. *Bulletin of the International Statistical Institute,* **36**, Pt. 3 (1958), 120–26.

283. FLOWERS, C. E. Effects of an arbitrary accelerated group placement on the tested academic achievement of educationally disadvantaged students. Unpublished Ph.D. dissertation, Columbia University, 1966.

284. FODE, K. L. The effect of non-visual and non-verbal interaction on experimenter bias. Unpublished Master's thesis, University of North Dakota, 1960.

*285. FODE, K. L. The effects of experimenters' anxiety, and subjects' anxiety, social desirability and sex, on experimenter outcome-bias. Unpublished Ph.D. dissertation, University of North Dakota, 1967.

286. FORD, R. N., and ZEISEL, H. Bias in mail surveys cannot be controlled by one mailing. *Public Opinion Quarterly,* **13** (1949), 495–501.

287. FORLANO, G., and AXELROD, H. C. The effect of repeated praise or blame on the performance of introverts and extroverts. *Journal of Educational Psychology,* **28** (1937), 92–100.

288. FORRESTER, B. J., and KLAUS, R. A. The effect of race of the

examiner on intelligence test scores of Negro kindergarten children. *Peabody Papers in Human Development,* **2,** No. 7 (1964), 1–7.

289. FOSTER, W. S. Experiments on rod-divining. *Journal of Applied Psychology,* **7** (1923), 303–11.

290. FOWLER, F. J., JR. Education, interaction, and interview performance. Unpublished Ph.D. dissertation, University of Michigan, 1966.

291. FRANZEN, R., and WILLIAMS, R. A method for measuring error due to variance among interviewers. *Public Opinion Quarterly,* **20** (1956), 587–92.

*292. FREEMAN, H. A note on the prediction of who votes. *Public Opinion Quarterly,* **17** (1953), 288–92.

293. FRICKE, B. G. Response set as a suppressor variable in the OAIS and MMPI. *Journal of Consulting Psychology,* **20** (1956), 161–69.

294. FRIEDMAN, N. *The social nature of psychological research: The psychological experiment as a social interaction.* New York: Basic Books, 1967.

295. FRIEDMAN, N., KURLAND, D., and ROSENTHAL, R. Experimenter behavior as an unintended determinant of experimental results. *Journal of Projective Techniques and Personality Assessment,* **29** (1965), 479–90.

*296. FRIEDMAN, P. A second experiment on interviewer bias. *Sociometry,* **5** (1942), 378–81.

297. FRIEND, I., and SCHOR, S. Who saves? *Review of Economics and Statistics,* **41,** No. 2, Pt. 2 (1959), 213–48.

298. FRY, H. G., and MCNAIR, S. Data gathering by long distance telephone. *Public Health Reports,* **73** (1958), 831–35.

*299. GALES, K., and KENDALL, M. G. An inquiry concerning interviewer variability. *Journal of the Royal Statistical Society, Series A,* **120** (1957), 121–38.

*300. GALL, M., and MENDELSOHN, G. A. Effects of facilitating techniques and subject-experimenter interaction on creative problem solving. *Journal of Personality and Social Psychology,* **5** (1967), 211–16.

301. GALLUP, G. Question wording in public opinion polls. *Sociometry,* **4** (1941), 259–68.

*302. GATES, G. S., and RISSLAND, L. Q. The effect of encouragement and of discouragement upon performance. *Journal of Educational Psychology,* **14** (1923), 21–26.

303. GETTER, H., MULRY, R. C., HOLLAND, C., and WALKER, P. Experimenter bias and the WAIS. Unpublished data, University of Connecticut, 1967.

304. GETZELS, J. W. The question-answer process. *Public Opinion Quarterly,* **18** (1954), 80–91.

305. GEWIRTZ, J. L. Three determinants of attention-seeking in young children. *Monographs of the Society for Research in Child Development,* **19**, No. 2 (1954), Serial No. 59.

306. GEWIRTZ, J. L., and BAER, D. M. The effect of brief social deprivation on behaviors for a social reinforcer. *Journal of Abnormal and Social Psychology,* **56** (1958), 49–56.

*307. GHOSH, A. A note on the accuracy of family budget data with reference to the period of recall. *Calcutta Statistical Association Bulletin,* **5** (1953), 16–23.

308. GIBBY, R. G. Examiner influence on the Rorschach inquiry. *Journal of Consulting Psychology,* **16** (1952), 449–55.

309. GIBBY, R. G., MILLER, D. R., and WALKER, E. L. The examiner's influence on the Rorschach protocol. *Journal of Consulting Psychology,* **17** (1953), 425–28.

*310. GILCHRIST, E. P. The extent to which praise and reproof affect a pupil's work. *School and Society,* **4** (1916), 872–74.

*311. GIRARD, A. The first opinion research in Uruguay and Chile. *Public Opinion Quarterly,* **22** (1958), 251–60.

312. GLASER, W. A. International mail surveys of informants. *Human Organization,* **25** (1966), 78–86.

*313. GLIXMAN, A. F. Psychology of the scientist: XXII. Effects of examiner, examiner-sex, and subject-sex upon categorizing behavior. *Perceptual and Motor Skills,* **24** (1967), 107–17.

*314. GLUCKSBERG, S., and LINCE, D. L. *The influence of military rank of experimenter on the conditioning of a verbal response.* U.S. Army Technical Memorandum 10–62. Aberdeen Proving Ground, Md.: U.S. Army Ordinance Human Engineering Laboratories, 1962.

*315. GODDARD, K. E., BRODER, G., and WENAR, C. Reliability of pediatric histories: A preliminary study. *Pediatrics,* **28** (1961), 1011–18.

316. GOLDBERG, D., SHARP, H., and FREEMAN, R. The stability and reliability of expected family size data. *Milbank Memorial Fund Quarterly,* **37** (1959), 369–85.

317. GOLDBLATT, R. A., and SCHACKNER, R. A. Categorizing emotion depicted in facial expressions and reaction to the experimental situation as a function of experimenter "friendliness." Paper presented at the meetings of the Eastern Psychological Association, Washington, D. C., April, 1968.

318. GOLDMAN-EISLER, F. Individual differences between interviewers and their effect on interviewees' conversational behavior. *Journal of Mental Science,* 98 (1952), 660–71.

*319. GOLDRING, P. The initial interview with Negro adolescents. Unpublished Ph.D. dissertation, University of Rochester, 1968.

320. GOODENOUGH, F. L. *Anger in young children.* Minneapolis: University of Minnesota Press, 1931.

321. GOODRICH, D. W., and BOOMER, D. S. Experimental assessment of modes of conflict resolution. *Family Process,* 2 (1963), 15–24.

322. GOODSON, C., and BERDY, D. Memory in advertising. *Admap,* 3 (1967), 261.

323. GORDEN, R. L. Dimensions of the depth interview. *American Journal of Sociology,* 62 (1956), 158–64.

*324. GORDON, L. V., and DUREA, M. A. The effect of discouragement on the revised Stanford-Binet scale. *Journal of Genetic Psychology,* 73 (1948), 201–7.

*325. GRAY, P. G. The memory factor in social surveys. *Journal of the American Statistical Association,* 50 (1955), 344–63.

326. GRAY, P. G. A sample survey with both a postal and an interview stage. *Applied Statistics,* 6 (1957), 139–53.

327. GRAY, P. G., and CORLETT, T. Sampling for The Social Survey. *Journal of the Royal Statistical Society, Series A,* 113 (1950), 150–99.

*328. GREENSPOON, J. The reinforcing effect of two spoken sounds on the frequency of two responses. *American Journal of Psychology,* 68 (1955), 409–16.

329. GRIFFITH, R. M. Rorschach water percepts: A study in conflicting results. *American Psychologist,* 16 (1961), 307–11.

330. GROSS, N., and MASON, W. S. Some methodological problems of eight-hour interviews. *American Journal of Sociology,* 59 (1953), 197–204.

331. GUEST, L. A study of interviewer competence. *International Journal of Opinion and Attitude Research,* 1 (December, 1947), 17–30.

332. GUEST, L. A new training method for opinion interviewers. *Public Opinion Quarterly,* 18 (1954), 287–99.

333. GUEST, L., and NUCKOLS, R. A laboratory experiment in recording public opinion interviewing. *International Journal of Opinion and Attitude Research*, 4 (1950), 336–52.

334. GUSTAFSON, L. A., and ORNE, M. T. Effects of perceived role and role success on the detection of deception. *Journal of Applied Psychology*, 49 (1965), 412–17.

335. GUTHRIE, H. W. Some methodological issues in validation studies. *Proceedings of the American Statistical Association, Social Statistics Section* (1965), 193–96.

326. HAASE, W. Rorschach diagnosis, socio-economic class, and examiner bias. Unpublished Ph.D. dissertation, New York University, 1956.

*337. HABER, L. D. Evaluating response error in the reporting of the income of the aged: Benefit income. *Proceedings of the American Statistical Association, Social Statistics Section* (1966), 412–19.

*338. HABERMAN, P. W., and ELINSON, J. Family income reported in surveys: Husbands versus wives. *Journal of Marketing Research*, 4 (1967), 191–94.

*339. HAEDRICH, G. *Der Interviewer-Einfluss in der Marktforschung.* Wiesbaden: T. Gabler, 1964.

*340. HAGBURG, E. C. Validity of questionnaire data: Reported and observed attendance in an adult education program. *Public Opinion Quarterly*, 32 (1968), 453–56.

341. HAGGARD, E. A., BREKSTAD, A., and SKARD, A. G. On the reliability of the anamnestic interview. *Journal of Abnormal and Social Psychology*, 61 (1960), 311–18.

342. HAGGERTY, R. J. Family diagnosis: Research methods and their reliability for studies of the medical-social unit, the family. *American Journal of Public Health*, 55 (1965), 1521–33.

343. HAMILTON, C. H. Bias and error in multiple-choice tests. *Psychometrika*, 15 (1950), 151–68.

344. HANSEN, M. H., and HURWITZ, W. N. The problem of nonresponse in sample surveys. *Journal of the American Statistical Association*, 41 (1946), 517–29.

345. HANSEN, M. H., HURWITZ, W. N., and BERSHAD, M. A. Measurement errors in censuses and surveys. *Bulletin of the International Statistical Institute*, 38, Pt. 2 (1960), 359–74.

346. HANSEN, M. H., HURWITZ, W. N., MARKS, E. S., and MAULDIN, W. P. Response errors in surveys. *Journal of the American Statistical Association*, 46 (1951), 147–90.

347. HANSEN, M. H., and STEINBERG, J. Control of errors in surveys. *Biometrics,* 12 (1956), 462–74.

*348. HANSON, R. H., and MARKS, E. S. Influence of the interviewer on the accuracy of survey results. *Journal of the American Statistical Association,* 53 (1958), 635–55.

*349. HARDIN, E., and HERSHEY, G. L. Accuracy of employee reports on changes in pay. *Journal of Applied Psychology,* 44 (1960), 269–75.

350. HARDT, R. H., and BODINE, G. E. *Development of self-report instruments in delinquency research: A conference report.* Syracuse, N.Y.: Youth Development Center, Syracuse University, 1965.

351. HARDT, R. H., and PETERSON, S. J. How valid are self-report measures of delinquency. Paper presented at the meetings of the Eastern Sociological Society, Philadelphia, April, 1966.

*352. HARE, A. P. Interview responses: Personality or conformity? *Public Opinion Quarterly,* 24 (1960), 679–85.

353. HART, C. W. Bias in interviewing in studies of opinions, attitudes, and consumer wants. *Proceedings of the American Philosophical Society,* 92 (1948), 399–404.

354. HART, C. W. Interviewer bias. In AMERICAN SOCIETY FOR TESTING MATERIALS, *Symposium on Measurement of Consumer Wants.* Special Technical Publication No. 117. Philadelphia: American Society for Testing Materials, 1952. Pp. 38–45.

355. HARVEY, S. M. A preliminary investigation of the interview. *British Journal of Psychology,* 28 (1938), 263–87.

356. HAUCK, M., and STEINKAMP, S. *Survey reliability and interviewer competence.* Studies in Consumer Savings, No. 4. Urbana, Ill.: Bureau of Business and Economic Research. University of Illinois, 1965.

357. HAZARD, G. C., JR. Reflections on four studies of the legal profession. *Social Problems,* 13, Supplement (Summer, 1965). 46–54.

358. HEFNER, L. T. Reliability of mothers' reports on child development. Unpublished Ph.D. dissertation, University of Michigan, 1963.

359. HEISERMAN, M. S. The relationship between teacher expectations and pupil occupational aspirations. Unpublished Master's thesis, Iowa State University, 1967.

360. HELLER, K., MYERS, R. A., and VIKAN-KLINE, L. Interviewer behavior as a function of standardized client roles. *Journal of Consulting Psychology.* 27 (1963), 117–22.

361. HENEMAN, H. G., JR., and PATERSON, D. G. Refusal rates and interviewer quality. *International Journal of Opinion and Attitude Research,* 3 (1949), 392–98.

*362. HETHERINGTON, M., and ROSS, L. E. Effect of sex of subject, sex of experimenter and reinforcement condition on serial verbal learning. *Journal of Experimental Psychology,* 65 (1963), 572–75.

*363. HILDUM, D. C., and BROWN, R. W. Verbal reinforcement and interviewer bias. *Journal of Abnormal and Social Psychology,* 53 (1956), 108–11.

364. HILGARD, E. R., and PAYNE, S. L. Those not at home: Riddle for pollsters. *Public Opinion Quarterly,* 8 (1944), 254–61.

*365. HILL, K. T., and STEVENSON, H. W. The effects of social reinforcement vs. nonreinforcement and sex of E on the performance of adolescent girls. *Journal of Personality,* 33 (1965), 30–36.

366. HILL, R. J., and HALL, N. E. A note on rapport and the quality of interview data. *Southwestern Social Science Quarterly,* 44 (1963), 247–55.

*367. HOCHSTIM, J. R. Comparison of three information-gathering strategies in a population study of sociomedical variables. *Proceedings of the American Statistical Association,* Social Statistics Section (1962), 154–59.

*368. HOCHSTIM, J. R. Evaluation of three approaches to information collection in an epidemiological study of cervical cytology. Human Population Laboratory, California State Department of Public Health, 1963. (a)

*369. HOCHSTIM, J. R. Validation of patients' responses to two questions in an epidemiological study on cervical cytology. Human Population Laboratory, California State Department of Public Health, 1963. (b)

*370. HOCHSTIM, J. R. A critical comparison of three strategies of collecting data from households. *Journal of the American Statistical Association,* 62 (1967), 976–89.

371. HOCHSTIM, J. R., and SMITH, D. M. K. Area sampling or quota control?—Three sampling experiments. *Public Opinion Quarterly,* 12 (1948), 73–80.

*372. HOFFER, C. R. Medical needs of the rural population in Michigan. *Rural Sociology,* 12 (1947), 162–68.

*373. HOFFER, C. R., and SCHULER, E. A. Determination of unmet need for medical attention among Michigan farm families.

Journal of the Michigan State Medical Society, **46** (1947), 443–46.

374. HOFFMAN, M. L. Power assertion by the parent and its impact on the child. *Child Development,* **31** (1960), 129–43.

*375. HORN, C. H., JR. The field-dependent person's response to experimenter effects. Unpublished Master's thesis, George Washington University, 1968.

*376. HORN, W. Reliability survey: A survey on the reliability of response to an interview survey. *Het PTT-bedrijf,* **10** (October, 1960), 105–56.

377. HORST, L. Research in the effect of the experimenter's expectancies—A laboratory model of social influence. Unpublished manuscript, Harvard University, 1966.

378. HORVITZ, D. G. Sampling and field procedures of the Pittsburgh morbidity survey. *Public Health Reports,* **67** (1952), 1003–12.

*379. HORVITZ, D. G. Problems in designing interview surveys to measure population growth. *Proceedings of the American Statistical Association,* Social Statistics Section (1966), 245–49.

380. HOVLAND, C. I., and WONDERLIC, E. F. Prediction of industrial success from a standardized interview. *Journal of Applied Psychology,* **23** (1939), 537–46.

*381. HUENEMANN, R. L., and TURNER, D. Methods of dietary investigation. *Journal of the American Dietetic Association,* **18** (1942), 562–68.

382. HUMM, D. G., and HUMM, K. A. Validity of the Humm-Wadsworth temperament scale—With consideration of the effects of subjects' response bias. *Journal of Psychology,* **18** (1944), 55–64.

383. HURWITZ, S., and JENKINS, V. The effects of experimenter expectancy on performance of simple learning tasks. Unpublished manuscript, Harvard University, 1966.

384. HUTCHISON, G. B., SHAPIRO, S., and DENSEN, P. M. Evaluation of a mailed health questionnaire. *American Journal of Public Health,* **52** (1962), 1894–1917.

385. HUTH, H. V. The effect of a deliberative interviewing technique on a public opinion survey. Unpublished Master's thesis, University of Denver, 1949.

*386. HYMAN, H. H. Do they tell the truth? *Public Opinion Quarterly,* **8** (1944), 557–59.

387. HYMAN, H. H. Inconsistencies as a problem in attitude measurement. *Journal of Social Issues*, **5**, No. 3 (1949), 38–42.
388. HYMAN, H. H. Problems in the collection of opinion-research data. *American Journal of Sociology*, **55** (1950), 362–70.
*389. HYMAN, H. H. *Interviewing in social research*. Chicago: University of Chicago Press, 1954.
390. HYMAN, H. H., and SHEATSLEY, P. B. The Kinsey report and survey methodology. *International Journal of Opinion and Attitude Research*, **2** (1948), 183–95.

391. INDIA. OFFICE OF THE REGISTRAR GENERAL. *Sample verification of the 1951 census count*. Census of India Paper No. 1. New Delhi, 1953.
392. INGRAHAM, L. H., and HARRINGTON, G. M. Psychology of the scientist: XVI. Experience of E as a variable in reducing experimenter bias. *Psychological Reports*, **19** (1966), 455–61.
*393. INSTITUT NATIONAL DE LA STATISTIQUE ET DES ÉTUDES ÉCONOMIQUES DIRECTION GÉNÉRALE. Enquête-pilote 1965–1966 sur les soins médicaux: Note complementaire sur la qualité des résultats de l'enquête. Paris, September 25, 1968. (Dittoed.)
*394. ITO, R. An analysis of response errors: A case study. *Journal of Business*, **36** (1963), 440–47.

395. JACKSON, E. H. Duration of disabling acute illness among employed males and females—Eastern Health District of Baltimore, 1938–43. *Milbank Memorial Fund Quarterly*, **29** (1951), 294–330.
396. JACKSON, J. The relative effectiveness of paper-pencil test, interview, and ratings as techniques for personality evaluation. *Journal of Social Psychology*, **23** (1946), 35–54.
*397. JACKSON, R. M., and ROTHNEY, J. W. M. A comparative study of the mailed questionnaire and the interview in follow-up studies. *Personnel and Guidance Journal*, **39** (1961), 569–71.
398. JAEGER, C. M., and PENNOCK, J. L. An analysis of consistency of response in household surveys. *Journal of the American Statistical Association*, **56** (1961), 320–27.
399. JAHODA, M., DEUTSCH, M., and COOK, S. W. *Research methods in social relations*. New York: Dryden Press, 1951. Pp. 151–208.
*400. JENKINS, J. G., and CORBIN, H. H., JR. Dependability of psy-

chological brand barometers: II. The problem of validity. *Journal of Applied Psychology,* 22 (1938), 252–60.

401. JENKINS, V. The unspoken word: A study in non-verbal communication. Unpublished A. B. thesis, Harvard University, 1966.

*402. JOHNSON, W. J. Subject performance as affected by experimenter expectancy, sex of experimenter and verbal reinforcing. Unpublished Master's thesis, Mount Allison University, 1967.

*403. JONES, H. E. Psychological studies of motion pictures: II. Observation and recall as a function of age. *University of California Publications in Psychology,* 3 (1928), 225–43.

404. JOURARD, S. M. Project replication: Experimenter-subject acquaintance and outcome in psychological research. Unpublished manuscript, University of Florida, 1968.

405. JOYCE, T. A new technique for studying reading behavior. *Admap,* 3 (1967), 235.

406. JUNG, A. F. Interviewer differences among automobile purchasers. *Applied Statistics,* 10 (1961), 93–97.

*407. KAHN, R. L. A comparison of two methods of collecting data for social research: The fixed-alternative questionnaire and the open-ended interview. Unpublished Ph.D. dissertation, University of Michigan, 1952.

408. KAHN, R. L., and CANNELL, C. F. *The dynamics of interviewing: Theory, technique and cases.* New York: Wiley, 1957.

409. KANFER, F. H. Verbal conditioning: Reinforcement schedules and experimenter influence. *Psychological Reports,* 4 (1958), 443–52.

410. KANFER, F. H., and KARAS, S. C. Prior experimenter-subject interaction and verbal conditioning. *Psychological Reports,* 5 (1959), 345–53.

411. KARCHER, E. K., and KING, S. H. Effect of number and order of ratings on reliability and validity. *American Psychologist,* 5 (1950), 333. (Abstract)

412. KATONA, G., and LANSING, J. B. The wealth of the wealthy. *Review of Economics and Statistics,* 46 (1964), 1–13.

*413. KATZ, D. Do interviewers bias poll results? *Public Opinion Quarterly,* 6 (1942), 248–68.

414. KATZ, D. The interpretation of survey findings. *Journal of Social Issues,* 2 (May, 1946), 33–44.

415. KATZ, D., and BRALY, K. Racial stereotypes of one hundred

college students. *Journal of Abnormal and Social Psychology,* 28 (1933), 280–90.

416. KATZ, I. Review of evidence relative to effects of desegregation on the intellectual performance of Negroes. *American Psychologist,* 19 (1964), 381–99.

417. KATZ, I., and BENJAMIN, L. Effects of white authoritarianism in biracial work groups. *Journal of Abnormal and Social Psychology,* 61 (1960), 448–56.

*418. KATZ, I., and GREENBAUM, C. Effects of anxiety, threat, and racial environment on task performance of Negro college students. *Journal of Abnormal and Social Psychology,* 66 (1963), 562–67.

*419. KATZ, I., ROBERTS, S. O., and ROBINSON, J. M. Effects of task difficulty, race of administrator, and instructions on digit-symbol performance of Negroes. *Journal of Personality and Social Psychology,* 2 (1965), 53–59.

*420. KATZ, I., ROBINSON, J. M., EPPS, E. G., and WALY, P. The influence of race of the experimenter and instructions upon the expression of hostility by Negro boys. *Journal of Social Issues,* 20, No. 2 (1964), 54–59.

421. KEATING, E., PATERSON, D. G., and STONE, C. H. Validity of work histories obtained by interview. *Journal of Applied Psychology,* 34 (1950), 6–11.

*422. KELLEY, H. H. Salience of membership and resistance to change of group-anchored attitudes. *Human Relations,* 8 (1955), 275–89.

423. KELLEY, H. H., and RING, K. Some effects of "suspicious" versus "trusting" training schedules. *Journal of Abnormal and Social Psychology,* 63 (1961), 294–301.

424. KEMPER, R. A. Secret ballots, open ballots, and personal interviews in opinion polling. Unpublished Ph.D. dissertation, Teachers College, Columbia University, 1950.

425. KEMPER, R. A., and THORNDIKE, R. L. Interview vs. secret ballot in the survey administration of a personality inventory. *American Psychologist,* 6 (1951), 362. (Abstract)

426. KEMSLEY, W. F. F. Interviewer variability and a budget survey. *Applied Statistics,* 9 (1960), 122–28.

427. KEMSLEY, W. F. F. The household expenditure enquiry of the Ministry of Labour: Variability in the 1953–54 enquiry. *Applied Statistics,* 10 (1961), 117–35.

428. KEMSLEY, W. F. F. Some technical aspects of a postal survey

into professional earnings. *Applied Statistics,* **11** (1962), 93–105.

*429. KEMSLEY, W. F. F. Interviewer variability in expenditure surveys. *Journal of the Royal Statistical Society, Series A,* **128** (1965), 118–39.

*430. KEMSLEY, W. F. F., and NICHOLSON, J. L. Some experiments in methods of conducting family expenditure surveys. *Journal of the Royal Statistical Society, Series A,* **123** (1960), 307–28.

431. KENKEL, W. F. Influence differentiation in family decision making. *Sociology and Social Research,* **42** (1957), 18–25.

432. KENKEL, W. F., and HOFFMAN, D. K. Real and conceived roles in family decision making. *Marriage and Family Living,* **18** (1956), 311–16.

433. KENNEDY, J. J., COOK, P. A., and BREWER, R. R. An examination of the effects of three selected experimenter variables in verbal conditioning research. Unpublished manuscript, University of Tennessee, 1968.

434. KENNEDY, J. J., EDWARDS, B. C., and WINSTEAD, J. C. The effects of experimenter outcome expectancy in a verbal conditioning situation: A failure to detect the "Rosenthal Effect." Unpublished manuscript, University of Tennessee, 1968.

*435. KENNEDY, J. L., and UPHOFF, H. F. Experiments on the nature of extra-sensory perception: III. The recording error criticism of extra-change scores. *Journal of Parapsychology,* **3** (1939), 226–45.

436. KENNEDY, M. E. Administration and methods of enumeration of the sickness survey in Alberta. *Canadian Journal of Public Health,* **44** (1953), 177–79.

*437. KENNEDY, W. A., TURNER, A. J., and LINDNER, R. Effectiveness of praise and blame as a function of intelligence. *Perceptual and Motor Skills,* **15** (1962), 143–49.

438. KENNEDY, W. A., VAN DE RIET, V., and WHITE, J. C., JR. A normative sample of intelligence and achievement of Negro elementary school children in the Southeastern United States. *Monographs of the Society for Research in Child Development,* **28**, No. 6 (1963), Serial No. 90.

*439. KENNEDY, W. A., and VEGA, M. Negro children's performance on a discrimination task as a function of examiner race and verbal incentive. *Journal of Personality and Social Psychology,* 2 (1965), 839–43.

440. KILLIAN, L. M., and GRIGG, C. M. Rank orders of discrimination of Negroes and whites in a southern city. *Social Forces,* 39 (1961), 235–39.

441. KINCAID, H. V. and BRIGHT, M. The tandem interview: A trial of the two-interviewer team. *Public Opinion Quarterly,* 21 (1957), 304–12.

442. KING, M. B., JR. The reliability of the idea-centered question in interview schedules. *American Sociological Review,* 9 (1944), 57–64.

*443. KINSEY, A. C., POMEROY, W. B., and MARTIN, C. E. *Sexual behavior in the human male.* Philadelphia: Saunders, 1948.

444. KINTZ, B. L., DELPRATO, D. J., METTEE, C. E., PERSONS, C. E., and SCHAPPE, R. H. The experimenter effect. *Psychological Bulletin,* 63 (1965), 223–32.

*445. KIRKPATRICK, E. A. An experimental study of memory. *Psychological Review,* 1 (1894), 602–9.

446. KISH, L. Studies of interviewer variance for attitudinal variables. *Journal of the American Statistical Association,* 57 (1962), 92–115.

*447. KISH, L., and LANSING, J. B. Response errors in estimating the value of homes. *Journal of the American Statistical Association,* 49 (1954), 520–38.

448. KISH, L., and SLATER, C. W. Two studies of interviewer variance of socio-psychological variables. *Proceedings of the American Statistical Association,* Social Statistics Section (1960), 66–70.

449. KLEIN, G. S., SCHLESINGER, H. J., and MEISTER, D. E. The effect of personal values on perception: An experimental critique. *Psychological Review,* 58 (1951), 96–112.

450. KLINGER, E. Modeling effects on achievement imagery. *Journal of Personality and Social Psychology,* 7 (1967), 49–62.

*451. KNUDSEN, D. D., POPE, H., and IRISH, D. P. Response differences to questions on sexual standards: An interview-questionnaire comparison. *Public Opinion Quarterly,* 31 (1967), 290–97.

*452. KOHN, M. L., and CARROLL, E. E. Social class and the allocation of parental responsibilities. *Sociometry,* 23 (1960), 372–92.

453. KOUNIN, J., POLANSKY, N., BIDDLE, B., COBURN, H., and

FENN, A. Experimental studies of clients' reactions to initial interviews. *Human Relations,* 9 (1956), 265–93.

454. KRASNER, L. Studies of the conditioning of verbal behavior. *Psychological Bulletin,* 55 (1958), 148–70.

455. KRAUS, A. S. The use of hospital data in studying the association between a characteristic and a disease. *Public Health Reports,* 69 (1954), 1211–14.

456. KROGER, R. O. Effects of role demands and test-cue properties upon personality test performance. *Journal of Consulting Psychology,* 31 (1967), 304–12.

*457. KRUEGER, D. E. Measurement of prevalence of chronic disease by household interviews and clinical evaluations. *American Journal of Public Health,* 47 (1957), 953–60.

458. KRUEGER, W. C. F. Students' honesty in correcting grading errors. *Journal of Applied Psychology,* 31 (1947), 533–35.

459. KURLANDER, A. B., HILL, E. H., and ENTERLINE, P. E. An evaluation of some commonly used screening tests for heart disease and hypertension. *Journal of Chronic Diseases,* 2 (1955), 427–39.

460. LAHIRI, D. B. Recent developments in the use of techniques for assessment of errors in nation-wide surveys in India. *Bulletin of the International Statistical Institute,* 36, Pt. 2 (1958), 71–93.

461. LANSING, J. B., and EAPEN, A. T. Dealing with missing information in surveys. *Journal of Marketing,* 24 (October, 1959), 21–28.

*462. LANSING, J. B., GINSBURG, G. P., and BRAATEN, K. *An investigation of response error.* Studies in Consumer Savings, No. 2. Urbana, Ill.: Bureau of Economic and Business Research, University of Illinois, 1961.

*463. LARRABEE, L. L., and KLEINSASSER, L. D. The effect of experimenter bias on WISC performance. Unpublished manuscript, Psychological Associates, St. Louis, 1967.

*464. LARSEN, O. N. The comparative validity of telephone and face-to-face interviews in the measurement of message diffusion from leaflets. *American Sociological Review,* 17 (1952), 471–76.

465. LARSON, R. F.,and CATTON, W. R., JR. Can the mail-back bias contribute to a study's validity? *American Sociological Review,* 24 (1959), 243–45.

466. LASZLO, J. P., and ROSENTHAL, R. Subject dogmatism, experimenter status, and experimenter expectancy effects. Unpublished manuscript, Harvard University, 1967.
467. LAZARSFELD, P. F. The change of opinion during a political discussion. *Journal of Applied Psychology,* **23** (1939), 131–47.
468. LAZARSFELD, P. F. The controversy over detailed interviews— An offer for negotiation. *Public Opinion Quarterly,* **8** (1944), 38–60.
469. LAZARUS, R. S., DEESE, J., and OSLER, S. F. The effects of psychological stress upon performance. *Psychological Bulletin,* **49** (1952), 293–317.
*470. LAZARUS, R. S., and ERIKSEN, C. W. Effects of failure stress upon skilled performance. *Journal of Experimental Psychology,* **43** (1952), 100–105.
*471. LENSKI, G. E., and LEGGETT, J. C. Caste, class and deference in the research interview. *American Journal of Sociology,* **65** (1960), 463–67.
472. LENTZ, T. F. Acquiescence as a factor in the measurement of personality. *Psychological Bulletin,* **35** (1938), 659. (Abstract)
473. LEVIN, S. M. The effects of awareness on verbal conditioning. *Journal of Experimental Psychology,* **61** (1961), 67–75.
*474. LEVINE, D. B., and MILLER, H. P. *Response variation encountered with different questionnaire forms: An experimental study of selected techniques used in agricultural marketing research.* Marketing Research Report No. 163. Washington, D. C.: Agricultural Marketing Service, U.S. Department of Agriculture, April, 1957.
475. LEVINGER, G. Task and social behavior in marriage. *Sociometry,* **27** (1964), 433–48.
*476. LEVINGER, G. Systematic distortion in spouses' reports of preferred and actual sexual behavior. *Sociometry,* **29** (1966), 291–99.
477. LEVITT, E. E., and BRADY, J. P. Expectation and performance in hypnotic phenomena. *Journal of Abnormal and Social Psychology,* **69** (1964), 572–74.
478. LEVY, L. H., and ORR, T. B. The social psychology of Rorschach validity research. *Journal of Abnormal and Social Psychology,* **58** (1959), 79–83.
479. LEVY, M. R. Examiner bias on the Rorschach test as a function

of patients' socioeconomic status. Unpublished Ph.D. dissertation, Ohio University, 1968.

480. LEWIS, C., and BIBER, B. Reactions of Negro children toward Negro and white teachers. *Journal of Experimental Education,* **20** (1951), 97–104.

*481. LEWIS, H. E. A comparison of consumer responses to weekly and monthly purchase panels. *Journal of Marketing,* **12** (1948), 449–54.

482. L'HARDY, P. Les caisses d'épargne et leur public. *Études et Conjoncture,* **24** (March, 1969), 111–31.

483. LIENAU, C. C. Selection, training and performance of the National Health Survey field staff. *American Journal of Hygiene,* **34,** Sec. A (1941), 110–32.

*484. LILIENFELD, A. M., and GRAHAM, S. Validity of determining circumcision status by questionnaire as related to epidemiological studies of cancer of the cervix. *Journal of the National Cancer Institute,* **21** (1958), 713–20.

*485. LINDZEY, G. A note on interviewer bias. *Journal of Applied Psychology,* **35** (1951), 182–84.

486. LINZ, H. C., and FREIBERG, A. D. The problem of validity vs. reliability in public opinion polls. *Public Opinion Quarterly,* **6** (1942), 87–98.

487. LIPSETT, L. The personal investigation in the selection of employees. *Personnel Administration,* **9** (September, 1946), 23–28.

488. LITWAK, E. A classification of biased questions. *American Journal of Sociology,* **62** (1956), 182–86.

*489. LOCKE, H. J. *Predicting adjustment in marriage: A comparison of a divorced and a happily married group.* New York: Holt, 1951.

*490. LOEWENSTEIN, R. *Two approaches to health interview surveys.* New York: School of Public Health and Administrative Medicine, Columbia University, 1969.

491. LONGWORTH, D. S. Use of a mail questionnaire. *American Sociological Review,* **18** (1953), 310–13.

492. LORANGER, A. W., PROUT, C. T., and WHITE, M. A. The placebo effect in psychiatric drug research. *Journal of the American Medical Association,* **176** (1961), 920–25.

493. LORD, E. Experimentally induced variations in Rorschach performance. *Psychological Monographs: General and Applied,* **64,** No. 10 (1950), Whole No. 316.

*494. LOUTTIT, C. M. Racial comparisons of ability in immediate recall of logical and nonsense material. *Journal of Social Psychology,* **2** (1931), 205–14.

495. LOVINGER, P., and DOBIE, S. Race, religion and social class in the initial interview: A study of the psychiatrist's attitudes. Cited in V. D. SANUA, Sociocultural aspects of psychotherapy and treatment: A review of the literature. In L. E. ABT and B. F. REISS (Eds.), *Progress in clinical psychology.* Vol. 7. New York: Grune & Stratton, 1966. Pp. 151–90.

496. LUCAS, D. B., and BRITT, S. H. Measurement of advertising audiences. *Harvard Business Review,* **28** (September, 1950), 90–101.

*497. LUFT, J. Interaction and projection. *Journal of Projective Techniques,* **17** (1953), 489–92.

498. MACFARLANE, J. W. Studies in child guidance: I. Methodology of data collection and organization. *Monographs of the Society for Research in Child Development,* **3**, No. 6 (1938), Serial No. 19.

499. MADOW, W. G. On some aspects of response error measurement. *Proceedings of the American Statistical Association,* Social Statistics Section (1965), 182–92.

500. MAGID, F. N., FOTION, N. G., and GOLD, D. A mail-questionnaire adjunct to the interview. *Public Opinion Quarterly,* **26** (1962), 111–14.

501. MAHALANOBIS, P. C. On large-scale sample surveys. *Philosophical Transactions of the Royal Society of London, Series B,* **231** (1946), 329–451. (a)

502. MAHALANOBIS, P. C. Recent experiments in statistical sampling in the Indian Statistical Institute. *Journal of the Royal Statistical Society,* **109** (1946), 326–70. (b)

503. MAHALANOBIS, P. C., and DAS GUPTA, A. The use of sample surveys in demographic studies in India. *U.N. World Population Conference, Rome, 1954.* Pp. 363–84.

*504. MAHALANOBIS, P. C., and LAHIRI, D. B. Analysis of errors in censuses and surveys with special reference to experience in India. *Bulletin of the International Statistical Institute,* **38**, Pt. 2 (1961), 401–33.

*505. MAHALANOBIS, P. C., and SEN, S. B. On some aspects of the Indian National Sample Survey. *Bulletin of the International Statistical Institute,* **34**, Pt. 2 (1954), 5–14.

506. MALLER, J. B. The effect of signing one's name. *School and Society,* 31 (1930), 882–84.

*507. MANDEL, B. J., WOLKSTEIN, I., and DELANEY, M. Coordination of old-age and survivors insurance wage records and the post-enumeration survey. In NATIONAL BUREAU of ECONOMIC RESEARCH, *An appraisal of the 1950 Census income data.* Studies in Income and Wealth, Vol. 23. Princeton, N.J.: Princeton University Press, 1958. Pp. 169–78.

*508. MANDLER, G., and KAPLAN, W. K. Subjective evaluation and reinforcing effect of a verbal stimulus. *Science,* 124 (1956), 582–83.

*509. MANDLER, G., and SARASON, S. B. A study of anxiety and learning. *Journal of Abnormal and Social Psychology,* 47 (1952), 166–73.

510. MARCIA, J. E. Hypothesis-making, need for social approval, and their effects on unconscious experimenter bias. Unpublished Master's thesis, Ohio State University, 1961.

511. MARINE, E. L. *The effect of familiarity with the examiner upon Stanford-Binet test performance.* Contributions to Education, No. 381. New York: Teachers College, Columbia University, 1929.

512. MARION, A. J. The influence of experimenter status upon verbal conditioning. Unpublished Ph.D. dissertation, University of California, Los Angeles, 1956.

513. MARKS, E. S., and MAULDIN, W. P. Response errors in census research. *Journal of the American Statistical Association,* 45 (1950), 424–38.

514. MARQUIS, K. H., and CANNELL, C. F. *A study of interviewer-respondent interaction in the urban employment survey.* Ann Arbor: Survey Research Center, University of Michigan, 1969.

515. MARSH, C. J. The influence of supplementary verbal directions upon results obtained with questionnaires. *Journal of Social Psychology,* 21 (1945), 275–80.

516. MARWIT, S. J. An investigation of the communication of tester-bias by means of modeling. Unpublished Ph.D. dissertation, State University of New York at Buffalo, 1969.

*517. MARWIT, S. J., and MARCIA, J. E. Tester bias and response to projective instruments. *Journal of Consulting Psychology,* 31 (1967), 253-58.

518. MARYLAND, UNIVERSITY OF. BUREAU OF BUSINESS AND ECO-

NOMIC RESEARCH. *Measuring newspaper readership: Critique and experiment.* Studies in Business and Economics, Vol. 4, No. 3. College Park, Md.: Bureau of Business and Economic Research, College of Business and Public Administration, University of Maryland, 1950.

519. MASLING, J. The effects of warm and cold interaction on the administration and scoring of an intelligence test. *Journal of Consulting Psychology,* 23 (1959), 336–41.

520. MASLING, J. The influence of situational and interpersonal variables in projective testing. *Psychological Bulletin,* 57 (1960), 65–85.

*521. MASLING, J. Differential indoctrination of examiners and Rorschach responses. *Journal of Consulting Psychology,* 29 (1965), 198–201.

522. MASLING, J. Role-related behavior of the subject and psychologist and its effects upon psychological data. *Nebraska Symposium on Motivation,* 14 (1966), 67–103.

523. MASUYAMA, M., and SENGUPTA, J. M. On a bias in a crop-cutting experiment (Application of integral geometry to areal sampling problems—Part V). *Sankhya,* 15 (1955), 373–76.

524. MATARAZZO, J. D. The interview. In B. B. WOLMAN (Ed.), *Handbook of clinical psychology.* New York: McGraw-Hill, 1965. Pp. 403–50.

525. MATARAZZO, J. D., SASLOW, G., and PAREIS, E. N. Verbal conditioning of two response classes: Some methodological considerations. *Journal of Abnormal and Social Psychology,* 61 (1960), 190–206.

526. MAULDIN, W. P., and MARKS, E. S. Problems of response in enumerative surveys. *American Sociological Review,* 15 (1950), 649–57.

527. MAUSNER, B. Studies in social interaction: I. A conceptual scheme. *Journal of Social Psychology,* 41 (1955), 259–70.

528. MAYER, C. S. The interviewer and his environment. *Journal of Marketing Research,* 1 (November, 1964), 24–31.

*529. MAYNES, E. S. The anatomy of response errors: Consumer saving. *Journal of Marketing Research,* 2 (1965), 378–87.

530. MAZUMDER, M. Vital rates. The National Sample Survey, No. 54. The Cabinet Secretariat, Government of India. 1962.

531. McCORD, H. Discovering the "confused" respondent: A possible projective method. *Public Opinion Quarterly,* 15 (1951), 363–66.

*532. McCord, J., and McCord, W. Cultural stereotypes and the validity of interviews for research in child development. *Child Development,* 32 (1961), 171–85.

533. McDonagh, E. C., and Rosenblum, A. L. A comparison of mailed questionnaires and subsequent structured interviews. *Public Opinion Quarterly,* 29 (1965), 131–36.

*534. McFall, R. M. Unintentional communication: The effect of congruence and incongruence between subject and experimenter constructions. Unpublished Ph.D. dissertation, Ohio State University, 1965.

*535. McGeoch, J. A. The influence of sex and age upon the ability to report. *American Journal of Psychology,* 40 (1928), 458–66.

536. McGinnies, E. Personal values as determinants of word association. *Journal of Abnormal and Social Psychology,* 45 (1950), 28–36.

537. McGraw, M. B., and Molloy, L. B. The pediatric anamnesis: Inaccuracies in eliciting developmental data. *Child Development,* 12 (1941), 255–65.

538. McGuigan, F. J. The experimenter: A neglected stimulus object. *Psychological Bulletin,* 60 (1963), 421–28.

539. McMurry, R. N. Validating the patterned interview. *Personnel,* 23 (1947), 263–72.

540. McQuitty, L. L. Conditions affecting the validity of personality inventories: I. *Journal of Social Psychology,* 15 (1942), 33–39.

541. Mechanic, D., and Newton, M. Some problems in the analysis of morbidity data. *Journal of Chronic Diseases,* 18 (1965), 569–80.

542. Meichenbaum, D. H., Bowers, K. S., and Ross, R. R. A behavioral analysis of teacher expectancy effect. Unpublished manuscript, University of Waterloo, 1968.

*543. Meltzer, H. Sex differences in forgetting pleasant and unpleasant experiences. *Journal of Abnormal and Social Psychology,* 25 (1931), 450–64.

544. Menefee, S. C. The effect of stereotyped words on political judgments. *American Sociological Review,* 1 (1936), 614–21.

545. Mercado, S. J., Guerrero, R. D., and Gardner, R. W. Cognitive control in children of Mexico and the United States. *Journal of Social Psychology,* 59 (1963), 199–208.

*546. MEREDITH, A., MATTHEWS, A., ZICKEFOOSE, M., WEAGLEY, E., WAYAVE, M., and BROWN, E. G. How well do school children recall what they have eaten? *Journal of the American Dietietic Association,* 27 (1951), 749–51.

547. MERTON, R. K. Fact and factitiousness in ethnic opinionnaires. *American Sociological Review,* 5 (1940), 13–28.

548. MERTON, R. K. Selected problems of field work in the planned community. *American Sociological Review,* 12 (1947), 304–12.

549. MERTON, R. K., and KENDALL, P. L. The focused interview. *American Journal of Sociology,* 51 (1946), 541–57.

*550. METZ, J. F., JR. Accuracy of response obtained in a milk consumption study. Methods of Research in Marketing. Paper No. 5. Ithaca, N.Y.: Cornell University Agricultural Experiment Station, July, 1956.

*551. METZNER, C. A. Three tests for errors of report in a sample interview survey. *International Journal of Opinion and Attitude Research,* 3 (1949), 547–54.

*552. METZNER, H., and MANN, F. A limited comparison of two methods of data collection: The fixed alternative questionnaire and the open-ended interview. *American Sociological Review,* 17 (1952), 486–91.

553. METZNER, H., and MANN, F. Effects of grouping related questions in questionnaires. *Public Opinion Quarterly,* 17 (1953), 136–41.

554. MEYER, M. L., and PARTIPILO, M. A. Examiner personality as an influence on the Rorschach test. *Psychological Reports,* 9 (1961), 221–22.

555. MEYROWITZ, A., and FISKE, M. The relative preference of low income groups for small stations. *Journal of Applied Psychology,* 23 (1939), 158–62.

*556. MILAM, J. R. Examiner influences on thematic apperception test stories. *Journal of Projective Techniques,* 18 (1954), 221–26.

557. MILLER, F. B. "Resistentialism" in applied social research. *Human Organization,* 12 (Winter, 1954), 5–8.

*558. MILLER, H. P., and PALEY, L. R. Income reported in the 1950 Census and on income tax returns. In NATIONAL BUREAU OF ECONOMIC RESEARCH, *An appraisal of the 1950 Census income data.* Studies in Income and Wealth, Vol. 23. Princeton, N.J.: Princeton University Press, 1958. Pp. 179–201.

559. MILLER, M. The Waukegan study of voter turnout prediction. *Public Opinion Quarterly,* 16 (1952), 381–98.

560. MILLS, J., and ARONSON, E. Opinion change as a function of the communicator's attractiveness and desire to influence. *Journal of Personality and Social Psychology,* 1 (1965), 173–77.

561. MINARD, J. G. The measurement and conditioning of "perceptual defense" and response suppression. Unpublished Ph.D. dissertation, University of Colorado, 1964.

562. MINOR, M. W. Experimenter expectancy effect as a function of evaluation apprehension. Unpublished Ph.D. dissertation, University of Chicago, 1967.

563. MINTZ, E. E. Personal problems and diagnostic errors of clinical psychologists. *Journal of Projective Techniques,* 21 (1957), 123–28.

*564. MÖBIUS, G. *Zur Genauigkeit standardisierter Verbraucherbefragungen.* Weisbaden: T. Gabler, 1966.

*565. MONNEY, H. W. *Methodology in two California health surveys: San Jose (1952) and statewide (1954–55).* Public Health Monograph No. 70. Washington, D. C.: Government Printing Office, 1962.

*566. MOONEY, H. W., POLLACK, B. R., and CORSA, L., JR. Use of telephone interviewing to study human reproduction. *Public Health Reports,* 83 (1968), 1049–60.

567. MOORE, E. H. The factor of sex in testimonial accuracy. *Journal of Social Psychology,* 6 (1935), 485–90.

568. MORRISON, D. E., and HENKEL, R. E. Significance tests reconsidered. *American Sociologist,* 4 (1969), 131–40.

569. MOSEL, J. N., and COZAN, L. W. The accuracy of application blank work histories. *Journal of Applied Psychology,* 36 (1952), 365–69.

570. MOSER, C. A. Interview bias. *International Statistical Institute Revue,* 19 (1951), 28–40.

571. MOSER, C. A. *Survey methods in social investigation.* London: W. Heinemann, 1958.

*572. MUDD, E. H., STEIN, M., and MITCHELL, H. E. Paired reports of sexual behavior of husbands and wives in conflicted marriages. *Comprehensive Psychiatry,* 2 (1961), 149–56.

573. MÜLLER, W., and TIMAEUS, E. Conformity behavior and experimenter bias. Unpublished manuscript, University of Cologne, 1967.

574. MULRY, R. C. The effects of the experimenter's perception of

his own performance on subject performance in a pursuit rotor task. Unpublished Master's thesis, University of North Dakota, 1962.

*575. MURRAY, J., BLAKE, E. C., DICKINS, D., and MOSER, A. M. *Collection methods in dietary surveys: A comparison of the food list and record in two farming areas in the South.* Southern Cooperative Series Bulletin 23, April, 1952.

576. MUSSEN, P. H. *Handbook of research methods in child development.* New York: Wiley, 1960.

*577. MYERS, G. C. A comparative study of recognition and recall. *Psychological Review,* 21 (1914), 442–56. (a)

*578. MYERS, G. C. Recall in relation to retention. *Journal of Educational Psychology,* 5 (1914), 119–30. (b)

579. MYERS, R. J. Errors and bias in the reporting of ages in Census data. *Transactions of the Actuarial Society of America,* 41 (1940), 395–415.

580. MYERS, R. J. Underenumeration in the Census as indicated by Selective Service data. *American Sociological Review,* 13 (1948), 320–25.

*581. NAKAMURA, C. Y. Salience of norms and order of questionnaire items: Their effect on responses to the items. *Journal of Abnormal and Social Psychology,* 59 (1959), 139–42.

582. NAMIAS, J. A rapid method to detect differences in interviewer performance. *Journal of Marketing,* 26 (April, 1962), 68–72.

*583. NEELY, T. E. A study of error in the interview. Ph.D. dissertation, Columbia University, 1937.

584. NETER, J. Measurement errors in reports of consumer expenditures. *Journal of Marketing Research,* 7 (1970), 11–25.

585. NETER, J., MAYNES, E. S., and RAMANATHAN, R. The effect of mismatching on the measurement of response errors. *Proceedings of the American Statistical Association,* Social Statistics Section (1964), 2–8.

*586. NETER, J., and WAKSBERG, J. Measurement of nonsampling errors in a survey of homeowners' expenditures for alterations and repairs. *Proceedings of the American Statistical Association,* Social Statistics Section (1961), 201–10.

*587. NETER, J., and WAKSBERG, J. Effects of interviewing designated respondents in a household survey of home owners'

220

Response Effects in Surveys

expenditures on alterations and repairs. *Applied Statistics,* **12** (1963), 46–60.

*588. NETER, J., and WAKSBERG, J. A study of response errors in expenditures data from household interviews. *Journal of the American Statistical Association,* **59** (1964), 18–55.

589. NETER, J., and WAKSBERG, J. *Response errors in collection of expenditures data by household interviews: An experimental study.* Bureau of the Census Technical Paper No. 11. Washington, D.C.: Government Printing Office, 1965.

590. NEW, P. K. The personal identification of the interviewer. *American Journal of Sociology,* **62** (1956), 213–14.

591. NICHOLS, M. Data desirability and experimenter expectancy as unintended determinants of experimental results. Unpublished data, Harvard University, 1967.

*592. NISSELSON, H., and WOOLSEY, T. D. Some problems of the household interview design for the National Health Survey. *Journal of the American Statistical Association,* **54** (1959), 69–87.

593. NOELLE, E. *Über den methodischen Fortschritt in der Umfrageforschung.* Allensbacher Schriften Nr. 7. Allensbach: Verlag für Demoskopie, 1962.

594. NOELLE, E. *Umfragen in der Massengesellschaft: Einführung in die Methoden der Demoskopie.* Munich: Rowohlt Deutsche Enzyklopädie, 1963.

595. NYE, F. I., and SHORT, J. F., JR. Scaling delinquent behavior. *American Sociological Review,* **22** (1957), 326–31.

596. OAKES, R. H. Differences in responsiveness in telephone versus personal interviews. *Journal of Marketing,* **19** (1954), 169.

*597. OGAWA, J., and OAKES, W. F. Sex of experimenter and manifest anxiety as related to verbal conditioning. *Journal of Personality,* **33** (1965), 553–69.

*598. OLSON, W. C. The waiver of signature in personal reports. *Journal of Applied Psychology,* **20** (1936), 442–50.

*599. ONO, M., PATTERSON, G. F., and WEITZMAN, M. S. The quality of reporting social security numbers in two surveys. *Proceedings of the American Statistical Association,* Social Statistics Section (1968), 197–205.

600. ORMONT, L. R. Tendency to differentiate in perceiving others as related to anxiety and adjustment. Unpublished Ph.D. dissertation, Columbia University, 1960.

601. O'ROURKE, J. F. Field and laboratory: The decision-making behavior of family groups in two experimental conditions. *Sociometry,* **26** (1963), 422–35.
602. OVERALL, B., and ARONSON, H. Expectations of psychotherapy in patients of lower socioeconomic class. *American Journal of Orthopsychiatry,* **33** (1963), 421–30.

603. PAGE, M. M., and LUMIA, A. R. Cooperation with demand characteristics and the bimodel distribution of verbal conditioning data. *Psychonomic Science,* **12** (1968), 243–44.
604. PAL, G. The influence of reproducing process in memorization. *Indian Journal of Psychology,* **1** (1926), 39–44.
605. PALMER, G. L. The reliability of response in labor market inquiries. Technical Paper No. 22. In *Report to federal statistical agencies.* No. 49. Washington, D. C.: Division of Statistical Standards, Bureau of the Budget, July 31, 1942.
606. PALMER, G. L. Factors in the variability of response in enumerative studies. *Journal of the American Statistical Association,* **38** (1943), 143–52.
*607. PARRY, H. J., and CROSSLEY, H. M. Validity of responses to survey questions. *Public Opinion Quarterly,* **14** (1950), 61–80.
608. PARTEN, M. B. *Surveys, polls, and samples: Practical procedures.* New York: Harper, 1950.
*609. PATEL, A. S. *Interviewer bias: An experimental study of some of its sources.* Baroda, India: Department of Psychology, M.S. University of Baroda, March, 1964.
610. PATERSON, D. G., and THORNBURG, P. M. High school scholarship standing of freshmen engineering students. *Journal of Engineering Education,* **17** (1927), 808–11.
611. PAYNE, D. E., and MUSSEN, P. H. Parent-child relations and father identification among adolescent boys. *Journal of Abnormal and Social Psychology,* **52** (1956), 358–62.
612. PAYNE, S. L. Interviewer memory faults. *Public Opinion Quarterly,* **13** (1949), 684–85.
613. PEART, A. F. W. Canada's sickness survey: Review of methods. *Canadian Journal of Public Health,* **43** (1952), 401–14.
*614. PEEL, W. C., JR. The influence of the examiner's expectancy and level of anxiety on the subject's responses to the Holtzman inkblots. Unpublished Master's thesis, Memphis State University, 1967.

*615. PERSINGER, G. W. The effect of acquaintanceship on the media-
       tion of experimenter bias. Unpublished Master's thesis, Uni-
       versity of North Dakota, 1962.

*616. PETTIGREW, T. F. *A profile of the Negro American.* Princeton,
       N.J.: Van Nostrand, 1964.

*617. PFLUGRATH, J. Examiner influence in a group testing situation
       with particular reference to examiner bias. Unpublished Mas-
       ter's thesis, University of North Dakota, 1962.

*618. PHILLIPS, D. L., and CLANCY, K. J. Response biases in field
       studies of mental illness. *American Sociological Review,* 35
       (1970), 503–15.

 619. PHILLIPS, D. L., and SEGAL, B. E. Sexual status and psychiatric
       symptoms. *American Sociological Review,* 34 (1969), 58–72.

 620. PITT, C. C. V. An experimental study of the effects of teachers'
       knowledge or incorrect knowledge of pupil IQ's on teachers'
       attitudes and practices and pupils' attitudes and achievement.
       Unpublished Ph.D. dissertation, Columbia University, 1956.

 621. POLITZ, A., and SIMMONS, W. An attempt to get the "not at
       homes" into the sample without callbacks. *Journal of the
       American Statistical Association,* 44 (1949), 9–31.

 622. POMEROY, W. B. The reluctant respondent. *Public Opinion
       Quarterly,* 27 (1963), 287–93.

 623. POSER, E. G. The effect of therapists' training on group thera-
       peutic outcome. *Journal of Consulting Psychology,* 30 (1966),
       283–89.

*624. POTI, S. J., CHAKRABORTI, B., and MALAKER, C. R. Reliability
       of data relating to contraceptive practices. In C. V. KISER
       (Ed.), *Research in family planning.* Princeton, N.J.: Prince-
       ton University Press, 1962. Pp. 51–65.

 625. POTI, S. J., MALAKER, C. R., and CHAKRABORTI, B. An enquiry
       into the prevalence of contraceptive practices in Calcutta
       City (1956–57). *Proceedings of the Sixth International Con-
       ference on Planned Parenthood.* New Delhi, 1959.

 626. POWELL, B. A., and PRITZKER, L. Effects of variation in field
       personnel on Census results. *Demography,* 2 (1965), 8–32.

*627. PRAIS, S. J. Some problems in the measurement of price changes
       with special reference to the cost of living. *Journal of the
       Royal Statistical Society, Series A,* 121 (1958), 312–23.

 628. PRAIS, S. J., and HOUTHAKKER, H. S. *The analysis of family
       budgets.* Cambridge: University Press, 1955.

*629. PRICE, D. O., and SEARLES, R. Some effects of interviewer-respondent interaction on responses in a survey situation. *Proceedings of the American Statistical Association,* Social Statistics Section (1961), 211–21.

630. PROJECTOR, D. S., and WEISS, G. S. *Survey of financial characteristics of consumers.* Washington, D.C.: Board of Governors of the Federal Reserve System, 1966.

631. PUTNEY, R. W. Validity of the placement interview. *Personnel Journal,* **26** (1947), 144–45.

*632. PYLE, W. H. The relation of sex differences to the kind of material used. *Journal of Educational Psychology,* **16** (1925), 261–64.

*633. PYLES, M. K., STOLZ, H. R., and MACFARLANE, J. W. The accuracy of mothers' reports on birth and developmental data. *Child Development,* **6** (1935), 165–76.

*634. QUACKENBUSH, G. G., and SHAFFER, J. D. *Collecting food purchase data by consumer panel: A methodological report on the M. S. U. Consumer Panel, 1951–58.* Technical Bulletin 279. East Lansing, Mich.: Agricultural Experiment Station, Michigan State University, August, 1960.

635. QUAY, H. The effect of verbal reinforcement on the recall of early memories. *Journal of Abnormal and Social Psychology,* **59** (1959), 254–57.

636. QUINN, S. B., and BELSON, W. A. *Thought processes and accuracy in the recall of purchases: Petrol buying.* London: Survey Research Centre, London School of Economics and Political Science, 1970.

*637. RADKE, M. J. *The relation of parental authority to children's behavior and attitudes.* Minneapolis: University of Minnesota Press, 1946.

*638. RAFFETTO, A. M. Experimenter effects on subjects' reported hallucinatory experiences under visual and auditory deprivation. Unpublished Master's thesis, San Francisco State College, 1967.

*639. RANKIN, R. E., and CAMPBELL, D. T. Galvanic skin response to Negro and white experimenters. *Journal of Abnormal and Social Psychology,* **51** (1955), 30–33.

640. RASKIN, E., and COOK, S. W. A further investigation of the measurement of an attitude toward fascism. *Journal of Social Psychology,* **9** (1938), 201–6.

*641. REAGAN, B. B. *Condensed vs. detailed schedule for collection of family expenditure data.* Washington, D.C.: Agricultural Research Service, U.S. Department of Agriculture, March, 1954.

*642. REAGAN, B. B., and GROSSMAN, E. *Rural levels of living in Lee and Jones Counties, Mississippi, 1945, and a comparison of two methods of data collection.* Agriculture Information Bulletin 41. Washington, D.C.: Bureau of Human Nutrition and Home Economics, U.S. Department of Agriculture, 1951.

*643. REECE, M. M., and WHITMAN, R. N. Expressive movements, warmth and verbal reinforcement. *Journal of Abnormal and Social Psychology,* 64 (1962), 234–36.

644. REISZ, A. B. A budget survey in the urban areas of Greece. In INTERNATIONAL LABOUR OFFICE, *Family living studies: A symposium.* Studies and Reports, New Series, No. 63. Geneva: International Labour Office, 1961. Pp. 67–86.

645. REUSS, C. F. Differences between persons responding and not responding to a mailed questionnaire. *American Sociological Review,* 8 (1943), 433–38.

646. RHINE, J. B., SHEFFIELD, F. D., and KAUFMAN, R. S. A PK experiment at Yale starts a controversy. *Journal of the American Society for Psychical Research,* 46 (1952), 111–17.

647. RICE, S. A. Contagious bias in the interview: A methodological note. *American Journal of Sociology,* 35 (1929), 420–23.

648. RICHARDSON, M. W. Note on Travers' critical review of the forced-choice technique. *Psychological Bulletin,* 48 (1951), 435–37.

649. RICHARDSON, S. A. A study of selected personality characteristics of social science field workers. Unpublished Ph.D. dissertation, Cornell University, 1954.

650. RICHARDSON, S. A. The use of leading questions in non-schedule interviews. *Human Organization,* 19 (1960), 86–89.

*651. RICHARDSON, S. A., DOHRENWEND, B. S., and KLEIN, D. *Interviewing: Its forms and functions.* New York: Basic Books, 1965.

652. RIDDLE, G. W. N. Validity of readership studies. *Journal of Marketing,* 18 (1953), 26–32.

653. RIECKEN, H. W. The unidentified interviewer. *American Journal of Sociology,* 62 (1956), 210–12.

654. RIESMAN, D., and BENNEY, M. The sociology of the interview.

In D. Riesman, *Abundance for what? And other essays.* Garden City, N.Y.: Doubleday, 1964. Pp. 517–39.

655. Riley, M. W., Cohn, R., Toby, J., and Riley, J. W., Jr. Interpersonal orientations in small groups: A consideration of the questionnaire approach. *American Sociological Review,* 19 (1954), 715–24.

656. Robbins, D. The measurement of voluntary health insurance coverage in the United States. *American Journal of Public Health,* 49 (1959), 875–80.

*657. Robbins, L. C. Parental recall of aspects of child development and of child-rearing practices. Unpublished Ph.D. dissertatation, New York University, 1961.

658. Robbins, L. C. The accuracy of parental recall of aspects of child development and of child rearing practices. *Journal of Abnormal and Social Psychology,* 66 (1963), 261–70.

659. Robertson, A. E., and Stromberg, E. L. The agreement between associates' ratings and self-ratings of personality. *School and Society,* 50 (1939), 126–27.

*660. Robinson, D., and Rohde, S. Two experiments with an anti-Semitism poll. *Journal of Abnormal and Social Psychology,* 41 (1946), 136–44.

661. Robinson, J. T., and Cohen, L. D. Individual bias in psychological reports. *Journal of Clinical Psychology,* 10 (1954), 333–36.

662. Roede, H. *Befrager und Befragte: Probleme der Durchführung des soziologischen Interviews.* Berlin: Deutscher Verlag der Wissenschaften, 1968.

663. Rogers, E. M., and Beal, G. M. Projective techniques in interviewing farmers. *Journal of Marketing,* 23 (1958), 177–79.

664. Rose, A. M. A research note on experimentation in interviewing. *American Journal of Sociology,* 51 (1945), 143–44.

665. Rose, A. M. Reliability of answers to factual questions. *Ohio Valley Sociologist,* 31 (June, 1966), 14–18.

666. Rosenberg, M. J. When dissonance fails: On eliminating evaluation apprehension from attitude measurement. *Journal of Personality and Social Psychology,* 1 (1965), 28–42.

*667. Rosenberg, M. J. The conditions and consequences of evaluation apprehension. In R. Rosenthal and R. L. Rosnow (Eds.), *Artifact in behavioral research.* New York: Academic Press, 1969. Pp. 279–349.

668. Rosenhan, D., and Greenwald, J. A. The effects of age, sex,

and socioeconomic class on responsiveness to two classes of verbal reinforcement. *Journal of Personality,* **33** (1965), 108–21.

669. ROSENTHAL, R. Experimenter modeling effects as determinants of subject's responses. *Journal of Projective Techniques and Personality Assessment,* **27** (1963), 467–71. (a)

670. ROSENTHAL, R. On the social psychology of the psychological experiment: The experimenter's hypothesis as unintended determinant of experimental results. *American Scientist,* **51** (1963), 268–83. (b)

671. ROSENTHAL, R. Experimenter outcome-orientation and the results of the psychological experiment. *Psychological Bulletin,* **61** (1964), 405–12.

*672. ROSENTHAL, R. *Experimenter effects in behavioral research.* New York: Appleton-Century-Crofts, 1966.

673. ROSENTHAL, R. Covert communication in the psychological experiment. *Psychological Bulletin,* **67** (1967), 356–67. (a)

674. ROSENTHAL, R. Psychology of the scientist: XXIII. Experimenter expectancy, experimenter experience, and Pascal's wager. *Psychological Reports,* **20** (1967), 619–22. (b)

675. ROSENTHAL, R. Psychology of the scientist: XXVI. Experimenter expectancy, one tale of Pascal, and the distribution of three tails. *Psychological Reports,* **21** (1967), 517–20. (c)

676. ROSENTHAL, R. Experimenter expectancy and the reassuring nature of the null hypothesis decision procedure. *Psychological Bulletin Monograph Supplement,* **70** (December, 1968), 30–47.

677. ROSENTHAL, R. On not so replicated experiments and not so null results. *Journal of Consulting and Clinical Psychology,* **33** (1969), 7–10. (a)

678. ROSENTHAL, R. Teacher expectation and pupil learning. Paper prepared for a conference, The Unstudied Curriculum, Washington, D.C., January, 1969. (b)

679. ROSENTHAL, R., and FODE, K. L. Psychology of the scientist: V. Three experiments in experimenter bias. *Psychological Reports,* **12** (1963), 491–511.

680. ROSENTHAL, R., FODE, K. L., FRIEDMAN, C. J., and VIKAN, L. L. Subjects' perception of their experimenter under conditions of experimenter bias. *Perceptual and Motor Skills,* **11** (1960), 325–31.

681. ROSENTHAL, R., and HALAS, E. S. Experimenter effect in the

study of invertebrate behavior. *Psychological Reports,* 11 (1962), 251–56.

682. ROSENTHAL, R., and JACOBSON, L. *Pygmalion in the classroom: Teacher expectation and pupils' intellectual development.* New York: Holt, Rinehart and Winston, 1968.

*683. ROSENTHAL, R., KOHN, P., GREENFIELD, P. M., and CAROTA, N. Data desirability, experimenter expectancy, and the results of psychological research. *Journal of Personality and Social Psychology,* 3 (1966), 20–27.

*684. ROSENTHAL, R., and PERSINGER, G. W. Subjects' prior experimental experience and experimenters' outcome consciousness as modifiers of experimenter expectancy effects. Unpublished manuscript, Harvard University, 1968.

685. ROSENTHAL, R., PERSINGER, G. W., and FODE, K. L. Experimenter bias, anxiety, and social desirability. *Perceptual and Motor Skills,* 15 (1962), 73–74.

*686. ROSENTHAL, R., PERSINGER, G. W., VIKAN-KLINE, L., and FODE, K. L. The effect of early data returns on data subsequently obtained by outcome-biased experimenters. *Sociometry,* 26 (1963), 487–98.

687. ROSENTHAL, R., and ROSNOW, R. L. (Eds.). *Artifact in behavioral research.* New York: Academic Press, 1969.

688. ROSLOW, S., and BLANKENSHIP, A. B. Phrasing the question in consumer research. *Journal of Applied Psychology,* 23 (1939), 612–22.

*689. ROSLOW, S., WULFECK, W. H., and CORBY, P. G. Consumer and opinion research: Experimental studies on the form of the question. *Journal of Applied Psychology,* 24 (1940), 334–46.

690. RUCH, F. L. Effects of repeated interviewing on the respondent's answers. *Journal of Consulting Psychology,* 5 (1941), 179–82.

691. RUGG, D. Experiments in wording questions: II. *Public Opinion Quarterly,* 5 (1941), 91–92.

*692. RUTTER, M., and BROWN, G. W. The reliability and validity of measures of family life and relationships in families containing a psychiatric patient. *Social Psychiatry,* 1 (1966), 38–53.

693. SACKS, E. L. Intelligence scores as a function of experimentally established social relationships between child and examiner. *Journal of Abnormal and Social Psychology,* 47 (1952), 354–58.

694. SAGEN, O. K., DUNHAM, R. E., and SIMMONS, W. R. Health

statistics from record sources and household interviews compared. *Proceedings of the American Statistical Association, Social Statistics Section* (1959), 6–14.

695. SALZINGER, K. Experimental manipulation of verbal behavior: A review. *Journal of General Psychology,* **61** (1959), 65–94.

696. SALZINGER, K., and PISONI, S. Reinforcement of affect responses of schizophrenics during the clinical interview. *Journal of Abnormal and Social Psychology,* **57** (1958), 84–90.

697. SALZINGER, K., and PISONI, S. Reinforcement of verbal affect responses of normal subjects during the interview. *Journal of Abnormal and Social Psychology,* **60** (1960), 127–30.

698. SANDAGE, C. H. Do research panels wear out? *Journal of Marketing,* **20** (1956), 397–401.

699. SANDERS, R., and CLEVELAND, S. E. The relationship between certain examiner personality variables and subjects' Rorschach scores. *Journal of Projective Techniques,* **17** (1953), 34–50.

*700. SARASON, I. G. Effect of anxiety, motivational instructions, and failure on serial learning. *Journal of Experimental Psychology,* **51** (1956), 253–60. (a)

701. SARASON, I. G. The relationship of anxiety and "lack of defensiveness" to intellectual performance. *Journal of Consulting Psychology,* **20** (1956), 220–22. (b)

*702. SARASON, I. G. The effect of anxiety and two kinds of failure on serial learning. *Journal of Personality,* **25** (1957), 383–92. (a)

*703. SARASON, I. G. Effect of anxiety and two kinds of motivating instructions on verbal learning. *Journal of Abnormal and Social Psychology,* **54** (1957), 166–71. (b)

704. SARASON, I. G. Effects on verbal learning of anxiety, reassurance, and meaningfulness of material. *Journal of Experimental Psychology,* **56** (1958), 472–77.

*705. SARASON, I. G. Relationships of measures of anxiety and experimental instructions to word association test performance. *Journal of Abnormal and Social Psychology,* **59** (1959), 37–42.

*706. SARASON, I. G. Individual differences, situational variables, and personality research. *Journal of Abnormal and Social Psychology,* **65** (1962), 376–80.

*707. SARASON, I. G., and MINARD, J. Interrelationships among subject, experimenter and situational variables. *Journal of Abnormal and Social Psychology,* **67** (1963), 87–91.

*708. SARASON, I. G., and PALOLA, E. G. The relationship of test and general anxiety, difficulty of task, and experimental instructions to performance. *Journal of Experimental Psychology*, **59** (1960), 185–91.

709. SARASON, S. B., DAVIDSON, K. S., LIGHTHALL, F. F., WAITE, R. R., and RUEBUSH, B. K. *Anxiety in elementary school children: A report of research.* New York: Wiley, 1960.

710. SATTLER, J. M., HILLIX, W. A., and NEHER, L. A. The halo effect in examiner scoring of intelligence test responses. Unpublished manuscript, San Diego State College, 1967.

711. SATTLER, J. M., and THEYE, F. Procedural, situational, and interpersonal variables in individual intelligence testing. *Psychological Bulletin*, **68** (1967), 347–60.

712. SAYRE, J. A comparison of three indices of attitude toward radio advertising. *Journal of Applied Psychology*, **23** (1939), 23–33.

713. SCHACHTEL, E. G. Subjective definitions of the Rorschach test situation and their effect on test performance: Contributions to an understanding of Rorschach's test, III. *Psychiatry, 8* (1945), 419–48.

714. SCHEUCH, E. K. Das Interview in der Sozialforschung. In R. KÖNIG (Ed.), *Handbuch der empirischen Sozialforschung.* Vol. 1. Stuttgart: F. Enke, 1967. Pp. 136–96.

715. SCHILLER, P. H. A Hungarian survey on sympathetic attitudes. *International Journal of Opinion and Attitude Research, 1* (September, 1947), 85–92.

*716. SCHMIDT, H. O. The effects of praise and blame as incentives to learning. *Psychological Monographs, 53*, No. 3 (1941), Whole No. 240.

*717. SCHMIEDESKAMP, J. W. Reinterviews by telephone. *Journal of Marketing, 26* (January, 1962), 28–34.

718. SCHREIBER, K. Interviewer-Einflüss. Unpublished manuscript, Berlin, n.d.

*719. SCHULER, E. A., MAYO, S. C., and MAKOVER, H. B. Measuring unmet needs for medical care: An experiment in method. *Rural Sociology, 11* (1946), 152–58.

720. SCHULZ, W. *Kausalität und Experiment in den Socialwissenschaften: Methodologie und Forschungstechnik.* Mainz: Hase und Koehler, 1970.

*721. SCHUMAN, H., and CONVERSE, J. M. The effects of black and white interviewers on black responses in 1968. *Public Opinion Quarterly,* 35 (1971), 44–68.

*722. SCOTT, C. *The postal services and the general public.* SS 286B. n.p.: The Social Survey, Central Office of Information, 1959.

723. SCOTT, C. Research on mail surveys. *Journal of the Royal Statistical Society, Series A,* 124 (1961), 143–95.

724. SCHWARTZ, M. M., COHEN, B. D., and PAVLIK, W. B. The effects of subject-and-experimenter-induced defensive response sets on picture-frustration test reactions. *Journal of Projective Techniques and Personality Assessment,* 28 (1964), 341–45.

725. SEARS, R. R., MACCOBY, E. E., and LEVIN, H. *Patterns of child rearing.* Evanston, Ill.: Row, Peterson, 1957.

726. SEELEMAN, V. The influence of attitude upon the remembering of pictorial material. *Archives of Psychology,* No. 258 (September, 1940).

727. SENG, Y. P. Errors in age reporting in statistically underdeveloped countries (with special reference to the Chinese population of Singapore). *Population Studies,* 13 (1959), 164–82.

728. SERRANO, R. G. The radio in Cuba. *International Journal of Opinion and Attitude Research,* 1 (June, 1947), 62–70.

729. SEWELL, W. H. Field techniques in social psychological study in a rural community. *American Sociological Review,* 14 (1949), 718–26.

730. SGAN, M. L. Social reinforcement, socioeconomic status, and susceptibility to experimenter influence. *Journal of Personality and Social Psychology,* 5 (1967), 202–10.

731. SHAFFER, J. D. The reporting period for a consumer purchase panel. *Journal of Marketing,* 19 (1955), 252–57.

*732. SHAMES, M. L., and ADAIR, J. G. Experimenter-bias as a function of the type and structure of the task. Paper presented at the meetings of the Canadian Psychological Association, Ottawa, May, 1967.

733. SHAPIRO, A. K. A contribution to a history of the placebo effect. *Behavioral Science,* 5 (1960), 109–35.

*734. SHAPIRO, J. L. The effects of sex, instructional set, and the problem of awareness in a verbal conditioning paradigm. Unpublished Master's thesis, Northwestern University, 1967.

735. SHAPIRO, S., and EBERHART, J. C. Interviewer differences in an intensive interview survey. *International Journal of Opinion and Attitude Research,* 1 (June, 1947), 1–17.

736. SHARP, H. The mail questionnaire as a supplement to the per-

sonal interview. *American Sociological Review,* **20** (1956), 718.

737. SHARP, H., and MOTT, P. Consumer decisions in the metropolitan family. *Journal of Marketing,* **21** (1956), 149–56.

738. SHAVER, J. P. Experimenter bias and the training of observers. *Proceedings of the Utah Academy of Sciences, Arts, and Letters,* **43**, Pt. I (1966), 143–52.

739. SHEATSLEY, P. B. Some uses of interviewer-report forms. *Public Opinion Quarterly,* **11** (1947), 601–11.

*740. SHEATSLEY, P. B. The influence of sub-questions on interviewer performance. *Public Opinion Quarterly,* **13** (1949), 310–13.

741. SHEATSLEY, P. B. An analysis of interviewer characteristics and their relationship to performance. *International Journal of Opinion and Attitude Research,* **4** (1950), 473–98, and **5** (1951), 79–94 and 191–220.

742. SHEATSLEY, P. B. The art of interviewing and a guide to interviewer selection and training. In M. JAHODA, M. DEUTSCH, and S. W. COOK, *Research methods in social relations.* New York: Dryden Press, 1951. Pp. 463–92.

743. SHERIF, M. The problem of inconsistency in intergroup relations. *Journal of Social Issues,* **5**, No. 3 (1949), 32–37.

744. SHUEY, A. M. *The testing of Negro intelligence.* (2nd ed.) New York: Social Science Press, 1966.

745. SILVERMAN, I. The effects of experimenter outcome expectancy on latency of word association. *Journal of Clinical Psychology,* **24** (1968), 60–63. (a)

746. SILVERMAN, I. Role-related behavior of subjects in laboratory studies of attitude change. *Journal of Personality and Social Psychology,* **8** (1968), 343–48. (b)

747. SILVERMAN, I., and REGULA, C. R. Evaluation apprehension, demand characteristics, and the effects of distraction on persuasibility. *Journal of Social Psychology,* **75** (1968), 273–81.

748. SIRKEN, M. G., MAYNES, E. S., and FRECHTLING, J. A. The survey of consumer finances and the Census quality check. In NATIONAL BUREAU OF ECONOMIC RESEARCH, *An appraisal of the 1950 Census income data.* Studies in Income and Wealth, Vol. 23. Princeton, N.J.: Princeton University Press, 1958. Pp. 127–68.

749. SKELLY, F. R. Interviewer-appearance stereotypes as a possible source of bias. *Journal of Marketing,* **19** (1954), 74–75.

750. SLOCUM, W., EMPEY, L. T., and SWANSON, H. S. Increasing re-

sponse to questionnaires and structured interviews. *American Sociological Review,* **21** (1956), 221–25.

751. SMILTENS, G. J. A study of experimenter expectancy effects with two expectancies being manipulated. Unpublished A.B. thesis, Harvard University, 1966.

*752. SMITH, F. F. The direct validation of questionnaire data. *Educational Administration and Supervision,* **21** (1935), 561–75.

*753. SMITH, H. L., and HYMAN, H. The biasing effect of interviewer expectations on survey results. *Public Opinion Quarterly,* **14** (1950), 491–506.

754. SMITH, H. T. A comparison of interview and observation measures of mother behavior. *Journal of Abnormal and Social Psychology,* **57** (1958), 278–82.

*755. SMITH, H. W., and MAY, W. T. Individual differences among inexperienced psychological examiners. *Psychological Reports,* **20** (1967), 759–62.

*756. SMITH, H. W., MAY, W. T., and LEBOVITZ, L. Testing experience and Stanford-Binet scores. *Journal of Educational Measurement,* **3** (1966), 229–33.

757. SMITH, M. B. Personal values as determinants of a political attitude. *Journal of Psychology,* **28** (1949), 477–86.

758. SOBOL, M. G. Panel mortality and panel bias. *Journal of the American Statistical Association,* **54** (1959), 52–68.

759. SOM, R. K. On recall lapse in demographic studies. In INTERNATIONAL UNION FOR THE SCIENTIFIC STUDY OF POPULATION, *International Population Conference, Vienna, 1959.* Pp. 50–61.

760. SOM, R. K., and DAS, N. C. On recall lapse in infant death reporting. *Sankhya,* **21** (1959), 205–8.

761. SPENCE, J. T., and SEGNER, L. L. Verbal versus nonverbal reinforcement combinations in the discrimination learning of middle- and lower-class children. *Child Development,* **38** (1967), 29–38.

762. SPIELBERGER, C. D. The role of awareness in verbal conditioning. In C. W. ERIKSEN (Ed.), *Behavior and awareness: A symposium of research and interpretation.* Durham, N.C.: Duke University Press, 1962. Pp. 73–101.

*763. SPILLMAN, W. J. *Validity of the survey method of research.* Bulletin No. 529. Washington, D.C.: U.S. Department of Agriculture, April, 1917.

764. SPIRES, A. M. Subject-experimenter interaction in verbal condi-

tioning. Unpublished Ph.D. dissertation, New York University, 1960.

765. STANTON, F. Notes on the validity of mail questionnaire returns. *Journal of Applied Psychology, 23* (1939), 95–104.

*766. STANTON, F., and BAKER, K. H. Interviewer-bias and the recall of incompletely learned materials. *Sociometry, 5* (1942), 123–34.

767. STANTON, H., BACK, K. W., and LITWAK, E. Role-playing in survey research. *American Journal of Sociology, 62* (1956), 172–76.

768. STEMBER, H. Which respondents are reliable? *International Journal of Opinion and Attitude Research, 5* (1951), 475–79.

*769. STEMBER, H., and HYMAN, H. How interviewer effects operate through question form. *International Journal of Opinion and Attitude Research, 3* (1949), 493–512. (a)

*770. STEMBER, H., and HYMAN, H. Interviewer effects in the classification of responses. *Public Opinion Quarterly, 13* (1949), 669–82. (b)

*771. STEVENSON, H. W. Social reinforcement with children as a function of CA, sex of E, and sex of S. *Journal of Abnormal and Social Psychology, 63* (1961), 147–54.

*772. STEVENSON, H. W., and ALLEN, S. Adult performance as a function of sex of experimenter and sex of subject. *Journal of Abnormal and Social Psychology, 68* (1964), 214–16.

*773. STEVENSON, H. W., KEEN, R., and KNIGHTS, R. M. Parents and and strangers as reinforcing agents for children's performance. *Journal of Abnormal and Social Psychology, 67* (1963), 183–86.

*774. STEVENSON, H. W., and KNIGHTS, R. M. Social reinforcement with normal and retarded children as a function of pretraining, sex of E, and sex of S. *American Journal of Mental Deficiency, 66* (1962), 866–71.

775. STOCK, J. S. Lecture before Attitude and Opinion Research Seminar of the Chicago Chapter, American Marketing Association, October 20, 1954.

776. STOCK, J. S., and HOCHSTIM, J. R. A method of measuring interviewer variability. *Public Opinion Quarterly, 15* (1951), 322–34.

777. STOCKS, P. *Sickness in the population of England and Wales in 1944–1947.* General Register Office, Studies on Medical and

Population Subjects, No. 2. London: H. M. Stationery Office, 1949.

*778. STOKE, S. M., and LEHMAN, H. C. The influence of self-interest upon questionnaire replies. *School and Society,* 32 (1930), 435–38.

779. STOUFFER, S. A., GUTTMAN, L., SUCHMAN, E. A., LAZARSFELD, P. F., STAR, S., and CLAUSEN, J. A. *Measurement and prediction.* Studies in Social Psychology in World War II, Vol. IV. Princeton, N.J.: Princeton University Press, 1950. Pp. 720–21.

780. STRANG, R. The interview. *Review of Educational Research,* 9 (1939), 498–501 and 607–8.

781. STRAUSS, M. E. Examiner expectancy: Effects on Rorschach experience balance. *Journal of Consulting and Clinical Psychology,* 32 (1968), 125–29.

782. STREIB, G. F. The use of survey methods among the Navaho. *American Anthropologist,* 54 (1952), 30–40.

783. STRODTBECK, F. L. The family as a three-person group. *American Sociological Review,* 19 (1954), 23–29.

*784. STRONG, E. K., JR. The effect of length of series upon recognition memory. *Psychological Review,* 19 (1912), 447–62.

785. STROSCHEIN, F. *Die Befragungstaktik in der Marktforschung.* Weisbaden: T. Gabler, 1965.

786. STUDENSKI, P. How polls can mislead. *Harper's Magazine,* December, 1939, pp. 80–83.

787. SUCHMAN, E. A. An analysis of "bias" in survey research. *Public Opinion Quarterly,* 26 (1962), 102–11.

788. SUCHMAN, E. A., and GUTTMAN, L. A solution to the problem of question "bias." *Public Opinion Quarterly,* 11 (1947), 445–55.

789. SUCHMAN, E. A., and MCCANDLESS, B. Who answers questionnaires? *Journal of Applied Psychology,* 24 (1940), 758–69.

*790. SUCHMAN, E. A., PHILLIPS, B. S., and STREIB, G. F. An analysis of the validity of health questionnaires. *Social Forces,* 36 (1958), 223–32.

*791. SUDMAN, S. On the accuracy of recording of consumer panels. *Journal of Marketing Research,* 1 (May, 1964), 14–20, and 1 (August, 1964), 69–83.

792. SUDMAN, S., GREELEY, A. M., and PINTO, L. The effectiveness of self-administered questionnaires. *Journal of Marketing Research,* 2 (1965), 293–97.

793. SUGISAKI, Y., and BROWN, W. The correlation between the sex of observers and the sex of pictures recognized. *Journal of Experimental Psychology,* 1 (1916), 351–54.

*794. SUMMERS, G. F., and HAMMONDS, A. D. Effect of racial characteristics of investigator on self-enumerated responses to a Negro prejudice scale. *Social Forces,* 44 (1966), 515–18.

795. Survey on problems of interviewer cheating. *International Journal of Opinion and Attitude Research,* 1 (September, 1947), 93–106.

796. SWEDEN. NATIONAL CENTRAL BUREAU OF STATISTICS. *Theory and method of party sympathy surveys.* Research Report No. 1. (Summary in English) Stockholm: National Central Bureau of Statistics, 1970. Pp. 18–19.

797. SWEDEN. NATIONAL CENTRAL BUREAU OF STATISTICS. *Evaluation of education data in the Census of Population and Housing, 1970.* Stockholm: National Central Bureau of Statistics, 1972.

798. SYDENSTRICKER, E. A study of illness in a general population group. *Public Health Reports,* 41 (1926), 2069–88.

799. TAFFEL, C. Anxiety and conditioning of verbal behavior. *Journal of Abnormal and Social Psychology,* 51 (1955), 496–501.

*800. TAIETZ, P. Conflicting group norms and the "third" person in the interview. *American Journal of Sociology,* 68 (1962), 97–104.

801. TAYLOR, G. The effect of hospital staff expectations upon patients' disposition. Unpublished manuscript, Harvard University, 1966.

802. TAYLOR, J. A., and SPENCE, K. W. The relationship of anxiety to level of performance in serial learning. *Journal of Experimental Psychology,* 44 (1952), 61–64.

*803. TERMAN, L. M. *Psychological factors in marital happiness.* New York: McGraw-Hill, 1938.

804. THOMAS, A., BIRCH, H. G., CHESS, S., and ROBBINS, L. C. Individuality in responses of children to similar environmental situations. *American Journal of Psychiatry,* 117 (1961), 798–803.

805. THOMAS, A., CHESS, S., BIRCH, H., and HERTZIG, M. E. A longitudinal study of primary reaction patterns in children. *Comprehensive Psychiatry,* 1 (1960), 103–12.

*806. THOMPSON, D. J., and TAUBER, J. Household survey, individual

236

Response Effects in Surveys

interview, and clinical examination to determine prevalence of heart disease. *American Journal of Public Health,* **47** (1957), 1131–40.

*807. THORNDIKE, R. L., HAGEN, E., and KEMPER, R. A. Normative data obtained in the house-to-house administration of a psychosomatic inventory. *Journal of Consulting Psychology,* **16** (1952), 257–60.

*808. THUMIN, F. J. Watch for those unseen variables. *Journal of Marketing,* **26** (July, 1962), 58–60.

809. TIBER, N., and KENNEDY, W. A. The effects of incentives on the intelligence test performance of different social groups. *Journal of Consulting Psychology,* **28** (1964), 187.

810. TITTLE, C. R., and HILL, R. J. The accuracy of self-reported data and prediction of political activity. *Public Opinion Quarterly,* **31** (1967), 103–6.

811. TOOPS, H. A. Validating the questionnaire method. *Journal of Personnel Research,* **2** (1923), 153–69.

812. TRACHTMAN, J. P. Socio-economic class bias in Rorschach diagnosis: Contributing psychosocial attributes of the clinician. Unpublished Ph.D. dissertation, New York University, 1968.

813. TRAVERS, R. M. W. A critical review of the validity and rationale of the forced-choice technique. *Psychological Bulletin,* **48** (1951), 62–70.

*814. TRENT, R. D. The color of the investigator as a variable in experimental research with Negro subjects. *Journal of Social Psychology,* **40** (1954), 281–87.

815. TROFFER, S. A., and TART, C. T. Experimenter bias in hypnotist performance. *Science,* **145** (1964), 1330–31.

816. TRULSON, M. F., and MCCANN, M. B. Comparison of dietary survey methods. *Journal of the American Dietetic Association,* **35** (1959), 672–76.

*817. TRUSSELL, R. E., ELINSON. J., and LEVIN, M. L. Comparisons of various methods of estimating the prevalence of chronic disease in a community—The Hunterdon County study. *American Journal of Public Health,* **46** (1956), 173–82.

818. TURNER, A. J. Discrimination reaction time as a function of anxiety and task difficulty. Unpublished Ph.D. dissertation, Florida State University, 1962.

819. TURNER, G. C., and COLEMAN, J. C. Examiner influence on thematic apperception test responses. *Journal of Projective Techniques,* **26** (1962), 478–86.

820. TURNER, R. Inter-week variations in expenditure recorded during a two-week survey of family expenditure. *Applied Statistics,* **10** (1961), 136–46.

*821. UDOW, A. B. The "interviewer-effect" in public opinion and market research surveys. *Archives of Psychology,* No. 277 (November, 1942).

822. U.S. BUREAU OF THE CENSUS. *The Current Population Survey reinterview program—Some notes and discussion.* Technical Paper No. 6. Washington, D.C.: Government Printing Office, 1963. (a)

823. U.S. BUREAU OF THE CENSUS. *The Current Population Survey— A report on methodology.* Technical Paper No. 7. Washington, D.C.: Government Printing Office, 1963. (b)

824. U.S. BUREAU OF THE CENSUS. *Evaluation and research program of the U.S. Censuses of Population and Housing, 1960: Accuracy of data on population characteristics as measured by reinterviews.* Series ER60, No. 4. Washington, D.C.: Government Printing Office, 1964. (a)

825. U.S. BUREAU OF THE CENSUS. *Evaluation and research program of the U.S. Censuses of Population and Housing, 1960: Record check studies of population coverage.* Series ER60, No. 2. Washington, D.C.: Government Printing Office, 1964. (b)

826. U.S. BUREAU OF THE CENSUS. *Household survey of victims of crime: First and second pretest results.* Washington, D.C.: Government Printing Office, 1970.

*827. U.S. NATIONAL CENTER FOR HEALTH STATISTICS. *Measurement of personal health expenditures.* Vital and Health Statistics, Series 2, No. 2. Washington, D.C.: Government Printing Office, 1963.

828. U.S. NATIONAL CENTER FOR HEALTH STATISTICS. *Comparison of hospitalization reporting in three survey procedures.* Vital and Health Statistics, Series 2, No. 8. Washington, D.C.: Government Printing Office, 1965. (a)

*829. U.S. NATIONAL CENTER FOR HEALTH STATISTICS. *Health interview responses compared with medical records.* Vital and Health Statistics, Series 2, No. 7. Washington, D.C.: Government Printing Office, 1965. (b)

*830. U.S. NATIONAL CENTER FOR HEALTH STATISTICS. *Reporting of hospitalization in the Health Interview Survey.* Vital and Health Statistics, Series 2, No. 6. Washington, D.C.: Government Printing Office, 1965. (c)

*831. U.S. NATIONAL CENTER FOR HEALTH STATISTICS. *Interview response on health insurance compared with insurance records: United States—1960.* Vital and Health Statistics, Series 2, No. 18. Washington, D.C.: Government Printing Office, 1966.

*832. U.S. NATIONAL CENTER FOR HEALTH STATISTICS. *Interview data on chronic conditions compared with information derived from medical records.* Vital and Health Statistics, Series 2, No. 23. Washington, D.C.: Government Printing Office, 1967.

833. U.S. NATIONAL CENTER FOR HEALTH STATISTICS. *Comparability of age on the death certificate and matching Census record: United States—May–August 1960.* Vital and Health Statistics, Series 2, No. 29. Washington, D.C.: Government Printing Office, 1968. (a)

834. U.S. NATIONAL CENTER FOR HEALTH STATISTICS. *The influence of interviewer and respondent psychological and behavioral variables on the reporting in household interviews.* Vital and Health Statistics, Series 2, No. 26. Washington, D.C.: Government Printing Office, 1968. (b)

835. U.S. NATIONAL CENTER FOR HEALTH STATISTICS. *Comparability of marital status, race, nativity, and country of origin on the death certificate and matching Census record: United States—May–August 1960.* Vital and Health Statistics, Series 2, No. 34. Washington, D.C.: Government Printing Office, 1969. (a)

836. U.S. NATIONAL CENTER FOR HEALTH STATISTICS. *Comparison of the classification of place of residence on death certificates and matching Census records: United States—May–August 1960.* Vital and Health Statistics, Series 2, No. 30. Washington, D.C.: Government Printing Office, 1969. (b)

*837. U.S. NATIONAL CENTER FOR HEALTH STATISTICS. *Effect of some experimental interviewing techniques on reporting in the Health Interview Survey.* Vital and Health Statistics, Series 2, No. 41. Washington, D.C.: Government Printing Office, 1971.

838. UNO, Y., FRAGER, R. D., and ROSENTHAL, R. Interpersonal expectancy effects among Japanese experimenters. Unpublished data, Harvard University, 1968.

839. VAN ARSDOL, M. D., and JAHN, J. A. Time and population sam-

pling applied to the estimation of expenditures of university students. *American Sociological Review,* 17 (1952), 738–46.

*840. VAN DEN BERG, A. S., and MAYER, J. Comparison of one-day food record and research dietary history on a group of obese pregnant women. *Journal of the American Dietetic Association,* 30 (1954), 1239–44.

841. VAN KOOLWIJK, J. Fragebogenprofile. *Kölner Zeitschrift für Soziologie und SozialPsychologie,* 20 (1968), 780–91.

842. VAN KOOLWIJK, J. Unangenehme Fragen. Paradigma für die Reaktionen des Befragten im Interview. *Kölner Zeitschrift für Soziologie und SozialPsychologie,* 21 (1969), 864–75.

*843. VAUGHAN, G. M. The effect of the ethnic grouping of the experimenter upon children's responses to tests of an ethnic nature. *British Journal of Social and Clinical Psychology,* 2 (1963), 66–70.

844. VAUGHN, C. L., and REYNOLDS, W. A. Reliability of personal interview data. *Journal of Applied Psychology,* 35 (1951), 61–63.

845. VENKATESAN, M. Laboratory experiments in marketing: The experimenter effect. *Journal of Marketing Research,* 4 (1967), 142–46.

846. VERPLANCK, W. S. The control of the content of conversation: Reinforcement of statements of opinion. *Journal of Abnormal and Social Psychology,* 51 (1955), 668–76. (a)

847. VERPLANCK, W. S. The operant, from rat to man: An introduction of some recent experiments on human behavior. *Transactions of the New York Academy of Science, Series 2,* 17 (1955), 594–601. (b)

848. VIDICH, A., and BENSMAN, J. The validity of field data. *Human Organization,* 13 (Spring, 1954), 20–27. (Also in R. N. ADAMS and J. J. PREISS [Eds.], *Human organization research.* Homewood, Ill.: Dorsey Press, 1960. Pp. 188–204.)

*849. VIKAN-KLINE, L. The effect of an experimenter's perceived status on the mediation of experimenter bias. Unpublished Master's thesis, University of North Dakota, 1962.

850. VOGT, E. Z. Interviewing water-dowsers. *American Journal of Sociology,* 62 (1956), 198.

851. VONDRACEK, F. W. The manipulation of self-disclosure in an experimental interview situation. Unpublished Ph.D. dissertation, Pennsylvania State University, 1968.

852. VON HOFFMAN, N., and CASSIDY, S. W. Interviewing Negro

Pentecostals. *American Journal of Sociology,* 62 (1956), 195–97.

853. VON HOFSTEN, E. A budget survey in Sweden. In INTERNATIONAL LABOUR OFFICE. *Family living studies: A symposium.* Studies and Reports, New Series, No. 63. Geneva: International Labour Office, 1961. Pp. 15–35.

854. WADSWORTH, R. N. The experience of a user of a consumer panel. *Applied Statistics,* 1 (1952), 169–78.

855. WAISANEN, F. B. A note on the response to a mailed questionnaire. *Public Opinion Quarterly,* 18 (1954), 210–12.

856. WAKSBERG, J., and PEARL, R. B. The Current Population Survey: A case history in panel operations. Unpublished manuscript, U.S. Bureau of the Census, Washington, D.C., n.d.

*857. WALKER, K. P. Examining personal information items of a questionnaire study. *Journal of Educational Research,* 31 (1937), 281–82.

*858. WALKER, R. E., DAVIS, W. E., and FIRETTO, A. An experimenter variable: The psychologist-clergyman. *Psychological Reports,* 22 (1968), 709–14.

859. WALKER, R. E., and FIRETTO, A. The clergyman as a variable in psychological testing. *Journal for the Scientific Study of Religion,* 4 (1965), 234–36.

860. WALLERSTEIN, J. S., and WYLE, C. J. Our law-abiding law-breakers. *Probation,* 25 (1947), 107–12, 118.

*861. WALLIN, P., and CLARK, A. Cultural norms and husbands' and wives' reports of their marital partners' preferred frequency of coitus relative to their own. *Sociometry,* 21 (1958), 247–54. (a)

862. WALLIN, P., and CLARK, A. Marital satisfaction and husbands' and wives' perception of similarity in their preferred frequency of coitus. *Journal of Abnormal and Social Psychology,* 57 (1958), 370–73. (b)

*863. WALSH, W. B. Validity of self-report. *Journal of Counseling Psychology,* 14 (1967), 18–23.

*864. WALTERS, C., PARSONS, O. A., and SHURLEY, J. T. Male-female differences in underwater sensory isolation. *British Journal of Psychiatry,* 109 (1964), 290–95.

*865. WALTERS, C., SHURLEY, J. T., and PARSONS, O. A. Differences in male and female responses to underwater sensory deprivation: An exploratory study. *Journal of Nervous and Mental Disease,* 135 (1962), 302–10.

866. WALTERS, J. Relationship between reliability of responses in family life research and method of data collection. *Marriage and Family Living,* 22 (1960), 232–37.

867. WARE, J. R., KOWAL, B., and BAKER, R. A., JR. The role of experimenter attitude and contingent reinforcement in a vigilance task. Unpublished manuscript, U.S. Army Armor Human Research Unit, Fort Knox, Ky., 1963.

868. WARTENBERG-EKREN, U. The effect of experimenter knowledge of a subject's scholastic standing on the performance of a reasoning task. Unpublished Master's thesis, Marquette University, 1962.

869. WAX, M., and SHAPIRO, L. J. Repeated interviewing. *American Journal of Sociology,* 62 (1956), 215–17.

870. WAXLER, N. E., and MISHLER, E. G. Scoring and reliability problems in interaction process analysis: A methodological note. *Sociometry,* 29 (1966), 28–40.

871. WECHSLER, J. Interviews and interviewers. *Public Opinion Quarterly,* 4 (1940), 258–60.

*872. WEDELL, C., and SMITH, K. U. Consistency of interview methods in appraisal of attitudes. *Journal of Applied Psychology,* 35 (1951), 392–96.

*873. WEISS, C. Validity of welfare mothers' interview responses. *Public Opinion Quarterly,* 32 (1968), 622–33.

874. WEISS, D. J., and DAWIS, R. V. An objective validation of factual interview data. *Journal of Applied Psychology,* 44 (1960), 381–85.

*875. WEISS, D. J., DAWIS, R. V., ENGLAND, G. W., and LOFQUIST, L. H. *Validity of work histories obtained by interview.* Minnesota Studies in Vocational Rehabilitation, No. 12; Bulletin No. 34. Minneapolis: Industrial Relations Center, University of Minnesota, September, 1961.

876. WEISS, L. R. Experimenter bias as a function of stimulus ambiguity. Unpublished manuscript, State University of New York at Buffalo, 1967.

*877. WELLS, W. D. The influence of yeasaying response style. *Journal of Advertising Research,* 1 (June, 1961), 1–12.

*878. WELLS, W. D. How chronic overclaimers distort survey findings. *Journal of Advertising Research,* 3 (June, 1963), 8–18.

*879. WELLS, W. D., and DAMES, J. Hidden errors in survey data. *Journal of Marketing,* 26 (October, 1962), 50–54.

880. WENAR, C. The reliability of developmental histories: Summary

and evaluation of evidence. *Psychosomatic Medicine,* 25 (1963), 505–9.

881. WENAR, C., and COULTER, J. B. A reliability study of developmental histories. *Child Development,* 33 (1962), 453–62.

882. WENK, E. A. Notes on some motivational aspects of test performance of white and Negro CYA inmates. Unpublished manuscript, Deuel Vocational Institution, Tracy, Cal., 1966.

*883. WESSLER, R. L. The experimenter effect in a task-ability problem experiment. Unpublished Ph.D. dissertation, Washington University, 1966.

*884. WESSLER, R. L. Experimenter expectancy effects in psychomotor performance. *Perceptual and Motor Skills,* 26 (1968), 911–17.

*885. WESSLER, R. L., and STRAUSS, M. E. Experimenter expectancy: A failure to replicate. *Psychological Reports,* 22 (1968), 687–88.

886. WESTEFELD, A. A problem of interpretation in survey results. *Journal of Marketing,* 17 (1953), 295–97.

887. WHEELER, R. W. A study of the relationship between selected interviewer variables and the interpretation of interview information. Unpublished Ph.D. dissertation, University of Houston, 1969.

*888. WHELPTON, P. K., and KISER, C. V. Social and psychological factors affecting fertility: III. The completeness and accuracy of the household survey of Indianapolis. *Milbank Memorial Fund Quarterly,* 23 (1945), 254–96.

889. WHITE, C. R. The effect of induced subject expectations on the experimenter bias situation. Unpublished Ph.D. dissertation, University of North Dakota, 1962.

890. WHITE, M. Experience with probability sampling in private agencies. *Public Opinion Quarterly,* 12 (1948), 799–800.

891. WHITEHORN, J. C., and BETZ, B. J. A study of psychotherapeutic relationships between physicians and schizophrenic patients. *American Journal of Psychiatry,* 111 (1954), 321–31.

892. WHITING, J. W. M., and CHILD, I. L. *Child training and personality: A cross-cultural study.* New Haven, Conn.: Yale University Press, 1953.

893. WHITTAKER, J. O. Parameters of social influence in the autokinetic situation. *Sociometry,* 27 (1964), 88–95.

894. WHYTE, W. F. Interviewing for organizational research. *Human Organization,* 12 (Summer, 1953), 15–22.

*895. WICKES, T. A., JR. Examiner influence in a testing situation. *Journal of Consulting Psychology,* 20 (1956), 23–26.

896. WIGGINS, J. S., and RUMRILL, C. Social desirability in the MMPI and Welsh's factor scales A and R. *Journal of Consulting Psychology,* 23 (1959), 100–106.

897. WILKENING, E. A., and MORRISON, D. E. A comparison of husband and wife responses concerning who makes farm and home decisions. *Marriage and Family Living,* 25 (1963), 349–51.

898. WILLCUTT, H. C., and KENNEDY, W. A. Relation of intelligence to effectiveness of praise and reproof as reinforcers for fourth-graders. *Perceptual and Motor Skills,* 17 (1963), 695–97.

*899. WILLIAMS, F., and CANTRIL, H. The use of interviewer rapport as a method of detecting differences between "public" and "private" opinion. *Journal of Social Psychology,* 22 (1945), 171–75.

*900. WILLIAMS, J. A., JR. Interviewer-respondent interaction. *Sociometry,* 27 (1964), 338–52.

*901. WILLIAMS, J. A., JR. Interviewer role performance: A further note on bias in the information interview. *Public Opinion Quarterly,* 32 (1968), 287–94.

*902. WILLIAMS, M. The measurement of memory in clinical practice. *British Journal of Social and Clinical Psychology,* 7 (1968), 19–34.

*903. WINKEL, G. H. The effect of an experimenter variable, subject variables and situational variables on a serial learning task. Unpublished Master's thesis, University of Washington, 1963.

*904. WINKEL, G. H., and SARASON, I. G. Subject, experimenter, and situational variables in research on anxiety. *Journal of Abnormal and Social Psychology,* 68 (1964), 601–8.

905. WINOKUR, G., and GASTON, W. R. Sex, anger, and anxiety: Intrapersonal interaction in married couples. *Diseases of the Nervous System,* 22 (1961), 256–60.

906. WITHEY, S. B. Consistency of immediate and delay report of financial data. Unpublished Ph.D. dissertation, University of Michigan, 1952.

907. WITHEY, S. B. Reliability of recall of income. *Public Opinion Quarterly,* 18 (1954), 197–204.

*908. WOLGAST, E. H. Do husbands or wives make the purchasing decisions? *Journal of Marketing,* 23 (1958), 151–58.

909. WOMACK, W. M., and WAGNER, N. N. Negro interviewers and

white patients: The question of confidentiality and trust. *Archives of General Psychiatry,* 16 (1967), 685–92.

*910. WOOLSEY, T. D. Results of the sick-leave memory test of October 1952. National Center for Health Statistics, Washington, D.C., 1953. (Dittoed.)

911. WOOLSEY, T. D., LAWRENCE, P. S., and BALAMUTH, E. An evaluation of chronic disease prevalence data from the Health Interview Survey. *American Journal of Public Health,* 52 (1962), 1631–37.

*912. WYATT, D. F., and CAMPBELL, D. T. A study of interviewer bias as related to interviewers' expectations and own opinions. *International Journal of Opinion and Attitude Research,* 4 (1950), 77–83.

*913. WYLIE, A. T. To what extent may we rely upon the answers to a school questionnaire. *Journal of Educational Method,* 6 (1927), 252–57.

*914. WYNDER, E. L., and LICKLIDER, S. D. The question of circumcision. *Cancer,* 13 (1960), 442–45.

915. WYSOCKI, B. A. Assessment of intelligence level by the Rorschach test as compared with objective tests. *Journal of Educational Psychology,* 48 (1957), 113–17.

916. YAGODA, G., and WOLFSON, W. Examiner influence on projective test responses. *Journal of Clinical Psychology,* 20 (1964), 389.

917. YAMAMURA, D. S., and ZALD, M. N. A note on the usefulness and validity of the Herbst Family Questionnaire. *Human Relations,* 9 (1956), 217–21.

918. YANG, H. P. *Fact-finding with rural people: A guide to effective social survey.* FAO Agricultural Development Paper No. 52. Rome: Food and Agriculture Organization of the United Nations, 1955.

919. YARROW, M. R. Problems of methods in parent-child research. *Child Development,* 34 (1963), 215–26.

920. YARROW, M. R., CAMPBELL, J. D., and BURTON, R. V. Reliability of maternal retrospection: A preliminary report. *Family Process,* 3 (1964), 207–18.

921. YAUKEY, D. W. *Fertility differences in a modernizing country: A survey of Lebanese couples.* Princeton, N.J.: Princeton University Press, 1961.

*922. YAUKEY, D. W., ROBERTS, B. J., and GRIFFITHS, W. Husbands' vs. wives' responses to a fertility survey. *Population Studies,* **19** (1965), 29–43.

*923. YOUNG, B. A. The effects of sex, assigned therapist or peer role, topic intimacy, and expectations of partner compatibility on dyadic communication patterns. Unpublished Ph.D. dissertation, University of Southern California, 1969.

924. YOUNG, C. M., CHALMERS, F. W., CHURCH, H. N., CLAYTON, M. M., TUCKER, R. E., WERTZ, A. W., and FOSTER, W. D. A comparison of dietary study methods: I. Dietary history vs. seven-day-record. *Journal of the American Dietetic Association,* **28** (1952), 124–28.

925. YOUNG, C. M., *et al. Cooperative nutritional status studies in the Northeast region: III. Dietary methodological studies.* Bulletin No. 469. Amherst, Mass.: University of Massachusetts Agricultural Experiment Station, August, 1952.

926. YOUNG, F. W., and YOUNG, R. C. Key informant reliability in rural Mexican villages. *Human Organization,* **20** (1961), 141–48.

927. YOUNG, P. V. *Interviewing in social casework: A sociological analysis.* New York: McGraw-Hill, 1935.

928. ZANDER, A., and HAVELIN, A. Social comparison and interpersonal attraction. *Human Relations,* **13** (1960), 21–32.

929. ZARKOVICH, S. S. Agricultural statistics and multisubject household surveys. *Monthly Bulletin of Agricultural Economics and Statistics,* **11** (May, 1962), 1–5.

930. ZARKOVICH, S. S. *Sampling methods and censuses.* Rome: Food and Agriculture Organization of the United Nations, 1965.

*931. ZARKOVICH, S. S. *Quality of statistical data.* Rome: Food and Agriculture Organization of the United Nations, 1966.

*932. ZEGERS, R. A. Expectancy and the effects of confirmation and disconfirmation. *Journal of Personality and Social Psychology,* **9** (1968), 67–71.

933. ZELLER, A. F. An experimental analogue of repression: III. The effect of induced failures and success on memory measured by recall. *Journal of Experimental Psychology,* **42** (1951), 32–38.

*934. ZOBLE, E. J. Interaction of subject and experimenter expectancy effects in a tone length discrimination task. Unpublished A.B. thesis, Franklin and Marshall College, 1968.

935. ZUKEL, W. J., *et al.* A short-term community study of the epidemiology of coronary heart disease. Paper presented at the meetings of the American Public Health Association, St. Louis, 1958.

Subject Index
to Bibliography

Conditions of interview. See Interview, conditions of

Data, type of: *ability,* 5, 45, 100, 123, 138, 139, 157, 163, 164, 184, 186, 218, 222, 285, 300, 302, 310, 314, 319, 362, 365, 375, 402, 403, 418, 419, 420, 437, 439, 445, 463, 485, 494, 509, 517, 534, 535, 577, 578, 597, 599, 609, 614, 615, 629, 632, 667, 700, 702, 703, 705, 716, 732, 734, 750, 752, 755, 756, 771, 774, 778, 784, 849, 883, 884, 885, 902, 903, 913, 914, 934; *attitudes,* 3, 4, 23, 34, 37, 39, 41, 50, 68, 73, 83, 89, 95, 111, 112, 119, 144, 151, 152, 177, 195, 199, 222, 245, 254, 280, 296, 299, 311, 338, 339, 352, 363, 373, 389, 407, 413, 422, 451, 457, 476, 497, 521, 551, 552, 556, 564, 572, 581, 616, 629, 637, 638, 660, 665, 672, 684, 692, 717, 721, 732, 753, 769, 794, 800, 821, 843, 858, 861, 872, 878, 895, 899, 900, 901, 912; *behavior,* 9, 13, 23, 28, 30, 38, 57, 59, 60, 62, 63, 69, 82, 83, 101, 111, 112, 118, 129, 130, 141, 151, 152, 162, 166, 168, 171, 175, 176, 177, 203, 205, 216, 222, 227, 229, 232, 234, 243, 246, 256, 267, 268, 271, 272, 274, 292, 299, 307, 313, 315, 324, 325, 328, 337, 339, 340, 348, 367, 368, 369, 370, 372, 379, 381, 386, 389, 393, 397, 400, 429, 430, 435, 443, 447, 452, 464, 470, 474, 476, 481, 484, 490, 503, 508, 529, 532, 543, 546, 550, 564, 565, 566, 572, 575, 583, 586, 587, 588, 592, 607, 624, 627, 629, 633, 634, 637, 638, 639, 641, 643, 651, 657, 672, 683, 686, 689, 706, 707, 708, 717, 719, 722, 766, 770, 772, 773, 774, 791, 803, 806, 808, 814, 817, 827, 829, 830, 832, 837, 840, 857, 863, 864, 865, 873, 875, 877, 878, 879, 888, 900, 904, 910, 922, 923, 931, 932; *expectations,* 83, 89, 112, 177, 185, 268, 311, 339, 471, 717, 740; *financial,* 83, 111, 112, 115, 204, 234, 269, 270, 338, 349, 376, 389, 394, 462, 507, 529, 558, 607, 641, 642, 717, 763, 831, 873, 908; *personality,* 76, 169, 178, 223, 256, 489, 598, 617, 618, 790, 807

Interview, conditions of: *in home, no one else present,* 13, 30, 62, 83, 112, 151, 152, 223, 443, 451, 452, 462, 489, 529, 532, 583, 624, 657, 692, 719, 800, 807, 827, 873, 922; *in home, some distractions,* 111, 112, 505, 607, 624, 642, 878, 879; *in home, other adults present,* 60, 62, 111, 112, 267, 268, 490, 637, 800, 827; *outside home, no one else present,* 5, 13, 34, 39, 50, 76, 82, 112, 118, 119, 139, 163, 164, 177, 185, 203, 245, 274, 285, 296, 300, 302, 314, 319, 324, 328,

NOTE: References are to entry number in bibliography.

325, 338, 339, 348, 349, 367, 372, 376, 379, 386, 389, 394, 397, 407, 413, 419, 420, 422, 443, 457, 462, 471, 476, 489, 504, 507, 532, 543, 552, 556, 558, 564, 565, 572, 581, 583, 586, 587, 588, 592, 607, 629, 632, 700, 703, 705, 717, 719, 763, 770, 772, 773, 778, 803, 806, 807, 817, 821, 827, 829, 930, 832, 837, 843, 857, 861, 863, 873, 875, 888, 899, 900, 901, 903, 908, 913, 922; *possibly salient,* 4, 9, 13, 28, 37, 38, 45, 59, 63, 73, 83, 89, 100, 115, 123, 141, 144, 151, 152, 157, 168, 177, 184, 186, 195, 204, 205, 218, 227, 234, 246, 256, 268, 280, 299, 310, 315, 338, 339, 340, 367, 368, 369, 370, 373, 386, 393, 422, 429, 430, 437, 447, 452, 457, 464, 481, 484, 494, 529, 550, 556, 564, 565, 566, 586, 587, 588, 592, 599, 607, 624, 629, 632, 633, 641, 660, 702, 703, 708, 753, 769, 790, 794, 806, 808, 829, 830, 831, 832, 840, 863, 872, 875, 900, 901, 903, 908, 912, 914, 922; *not salient,* 3, 5, 9, 23, 34, 37, 38, 39, 41, 50, 57, 60, 62, 76, 82, 83, 111, 118, 129, 138, 139, 141, 144, 162, 163, 164, 166, 169, 177, 184, 185, 186, 203, 205, 216, 222, 227, 229, 243, 245, 254, 256, 267, 274, 285, 296, 300, 302, 313, 314, 315, 319, 324, 328, 337, 338, 339, 352, 362, 363, 365, 375, 381, 400, 402, 403, 413, 418, 419, 420, 422, 429, 430, 435, 439, 445, 451, 457, 463, 470, 474, 481, 485, 490, 497, 505, 508, 509, 517, 521, 529, 534, 535, 546, 550, 551, 565, 566, 575, 577, 578, 586, 587, 588, 592, 597, 598, 607, 609, 614, 615, 616, 617, 618, 627, 629, 633, 634, 637, 638, 639, 641, 642, 643, 657, 667, 672, 683, 684, 686, 689, 692, 700, 702, 703, 705, 706, 707, 708, 716, 721, 722, 732, 734, 740, 750, 752, 755, 756, 766, 771, 774, 784, 791, 814, 821, 829, 830, 831, 849, 858, 863, 864, 865, 875, 877, 878, 879, 883, 884, 885, 895, 900,

901, 902, 903, 904, 910, 923, 931, 932, 934

Socially desirable answer: *not possible,* 3, 5, 9, 13, 23, 30, 34, 37, 38, 39, 41, 45, 50, 57, 59, 60, 62, 69, 76, 82, 83, 89, 95, 100, 101, 111, 112, 115, 118, 119, 123, 129, 138, 139, 141, 144, 151, 152, 157, 162, 163, 164, 166, 175, 176, 177, 184, 185, 186, 195, 199, 203, 205, 216, 218, 222, 227, 229, 232, 234, 243, 245, 246, 254, 256, 267, 268, 269, 271, 272, 274, 280, 285, 296, 299, 300, 302, 307, 310, 311, 313, 314, 315, 319, 324, 325, 328, 337, 338, 339, 348, 349, 362, 363, 365, 367, 368, 369, 370, 373, 375, 379, 381, 386, 389, 393, 397, 400, 402, 407, 413, 418, 419, 420, 429, 430, 435, 437, 439, 443, 445, 447, 455, 457, 462, 463, 470, 471, 474, 476, 481, 484, 485, 489, 490, 494, 497, 504, 505, 507, 508, 509, 517, 521, 529, 532, 534, 535, 543, 546, 550, 551, 556, 558, 564, 565, 566, 575, 577, 578, 581, 583, 586, 587, 588, 592, 597, 598, 599, 607, 609, 614, 615, 617, 629, 632, 633, 634, 637, 638, 639, 641, 642, 643, 651, 657, 660, 667, 672, 683, 684, 686, 689, 692, 700, 703, 705, 706, 707, 708, 716, 717, 719, 721, 722, 732, 734, 740, 750, 752, 753, 755, 756, 763, 769, 770, 771, 774, 778, 784, 790, 791, 803, 806, 807, 808, 814, 817, 821, 827, 829, 830, 832, 837, 840, 843, 849, 857, 858, 863, 865, 872, 875, 877, 878, 879, 883, 884, 885, 888, 895, 899, 900, 901, 902, 903, 904, 908, 912, 913, 914, 922, 923, 931, 932, 934; *some possibility,* 28, 30, 38, 63, 68, 73, 83, 111, 112, 141, 151, 152, 169, 177, 205, 254, 256, 268, 270, 315, 339, 340, 352, 368, 369, 370, 376, 389, 394, 422, 457, 476, 489, 529, 532, 552, 564, 572, 581, 607, 618, 629, 633, 637, 641, 642, 708, 821, 829, 830, 831, 861, 875, 878, 901; *strong possibility,* 30, 130, 168, 171, 178,

ABOUT NORC

The National Opinion Research Center is a non-profit social research institute, founded in 1941 and affiliated with the University of Chicago since 1947.

Since 1941 NORC has conducted over one thousand surveys on a wide variety of practical and theoretical social science topics.

Recent research includes studies of ethnic groups, race relations, occupational prestige and social stratification, public political participation and attitudes, the components of happiness, educational needs, and career choice.

For more information about NORC, write:

The Librarian
National Opinion Research Center
6030 South Ellis Avenue
Chicago, Illinois 60637